Berlin 1945

1   Aerial photograph of the bombed-out Mitte district in 1945.
To the left is Charlottenstraße, to the right Markgrafenstraße. The Gendarmenmarkt is visible on the upper edge of the picture.

Berlin 1945

A Documentation

Edited by Reinhard Rürup

Translated from the German edition
by Pamela E. Selwyn

Verlag Willmuth Arenhövel

Organiser:
Stiftung Topographie des Terrors
Internationales Dokumentations- und Begegnungszentrum,
Berlin

Direction:
Prof Reinhard Rürup

Academic Collaborators:
Frank Dingel
Marcus Funck
Andreas Hallen
Dr Siegfried Heimann
Klaus Hesse
Andreas Sander

Additional Research:
Thomas Friedrich
Dr Ekhard Haack
Ulrich Haupt
Katja Lucke
Eva Reusch

Interns:
Rolf Schmolling
Norbert Schulz
Philipp Springer

Public Relations and Organisation:
Dr Andreas Nachama

Editors:
Prof Reinhard Rürup
Marcus Funck
Andreas Sander

The exhibition was funded by the
Stiftung Deutsche Klassenlotterie Berlin.

Preparation for Production:
Alfons Arenhövel, Hannah Arenhövel

Cover Design:
Margret Schmitt

Production:
Reiter-Druck

Typesetting:
Mega-Satz-Service

Bookbinding:
Stein + Lehmann GmbH

All in Berlin

Published by
Verlag Willmuth Arenhövel · Berlin
All rights reserved
ISBN 3-922912-33-8
(German edition: ISBN 3-922912-32-X)

Berlin 1945
A Documentation

Former Staatliche Kunsthalle
Budapester Str. 42, 10787 Berlin
(near the Memorial Church)
10 April to 13 August 1995.

The documentation was prepared for the fiftieth
anniversary of 8 May 1945.

Exhibition design and production:
Margret Schmitt

Mounting of the Exhibition:
Museumstechnik GmbH

Photo reproduction:
Hans-Dietrich Beyer
Margret Nissen
Wolfgang Schackla
et al.

Preparation of the Exhibition Panels:
Studio für Großfotos Wolfgang Schackla
Fotosatz Univers

We thank the archives, photo archives and other collections
whose materials we were able to use for the documentation for
their kind support.
We are particularly indebted to:
Ian Blackwell (Northhampton), Reinhold Bauer (Koblenz),
Yevgeny Khaldeiij (Moscow), Prof Dr Laurenz Demps (Berlin),
Dr Klaus Drobisch (Berlin), Bettina Erlenkamp (Dresden),
Monika Göttlicher (Dahlwitz-Hoppegarten), Ute Grallert
(Berlin), Dr Ruth Gross (Berlin), Jürgen Grothe (Berlin), Gesa
Heinrich (Berlin), Dr Rainer Hofmann (Koblenz), Dr Peter Jahn
(Berlin), Dr Wilhelm van Kampen (Berlin), Dr Paul Kemp
(London), Elke Kilian (Dresden), Heidrun Klein (Berlin), Brigitte
Kuhl (Koblenz), Detlef Mädje (Heidelberg), Bernhard Maegele
(Munich), Wolf-Dieter Mattausch (Berlin), Leon Meyer (London),
Alexander Nikonov (Moscow), Claudia Promnitz (Berlin),
Regina Rousaway (Berlin), Gabriele Steinmayer (Munich),
Ingrid Streckbein (Berlin), Dr Peter Vier (Berlin), Erika Weber
(Berlin), Barbara Welker (Berlin), Gert J Wlasich (Berlin).

The cover arrangement makes use of a photograph
from the Bilderdienst Süddeutscher Verlag.
On the image the sovjet lyric poet Jevgenij A. Dolmatovski
as photographed Jevgenij Chaldeij in Berlin, 2 May 1945.

Table of Contents

2 Students of the Berlin University Unter den Linden waiting for their immatriculation, 1945

Introduction

When Bertolt Brecht returned to Berlin in 1948 from exile in the United States he tersely described his impression of the city, in a reference to the Potsdam Conference, as *"Berlin. The rubble heap near Potsdam"*.

Only one and a half decades earlier, Berlin had been one of the great metropolises of Europe and of the world, an extraordinarily vital and fascinating city in spite of all the crises it had experienced. The Berlin of the Weimar Republic was an impressive centre of industry, of commerce and banking, of science and technology, of the artistic avant garde and of the new mass culture. A willingness to innovate and increased urbanity helped the city to compensate for the loss of political power resulting from the defeat of 1918. At the same time, however, the political and social conflicts arising from the early twentieth-century crisis of civil society assumed a particularly radical form here. Only by recalling this Berlin, which Heinrich Mann was not alone in regarding as the embodiment of the future of a truly democratic Germany, can one begin to understand what it meant for Berliners, and others, to experience the city as a "rubble heap".

In reality, to be sure, Berlin's fall had already occurred in 1933 when the National Socialists assumed power and erected their dictatorial regime of domestic and foreign aggression. The inner destruction of the city began with the political and racist persecutions, with the ostracism of prominent scholars and artists, the nazification of cultural life. Many of Berlin's authors were among the "burnt writers", and almost all of the visual artists and musicians upon whom Berlin's reputation as an international city of the arts rested were forbidden to exhibit or perform their works, and often to work at all. Everything that had established the city's intellectual and artistic aura was destroyed within a very short space of time. The external destruction began soon afterwards, with those in power lighting the first match themselves in November 1938. The Second World War, unleashed from Berlin, brought death and destruction to large sections of Europe, particularly Poland and the Soviet Union, before striking back at the German Reich and its capital. When Germany surrendered in May 1945 Berlin could claim the sad distinction of being the European city hit by the greatest number of bombs and shells. The city had been reduced to rubble: it was, as a study determined, "the largest continuous ruin in Germany and Europe".

The sight of the devastated city also shocked members of the victorious powers, who spoke of a "second Carthage", and often compared what they saw from the air to the ruins of classical antiquity. Johannes R. Becher, who returned to Berlin in June 1945 from exile in Moscow, noted his impressions in a personal letter: *"The impression is difficult to describe. The drive through the ruins is distressing. From an airplane everything looks like junk, but driving through the city streets the façades on the verge of collapse, the mountains of debris and rubble heaps rise ghostly for kilometres to one's right and left. [...]"* The less destroyed areas on the city's outskirts gave the impression of oases in a desert of debris. *"You need to sit among the ruins for a long time, to let them get to you, and experience the pain and the judgment fully"*, said Alfred Döblin, reflecting upon his relationship to the destroyed city in a 1948 discussion.

"Judgment" was a word often used in 1945, although the Berliners had not been more National Socialist than other Germans and, until 1933, had even given the NSDAP far fewer votes than the national average. But Berlin had harboured the headquarters of power and terror; it was here that those responsible for the war crimes and genocide sat behind their desks. Even if by the end of the war most of them had long since left the city, the destruction of Berlin was constantly referred to as just punishment for the crimes perpetrated by the "Third Reich".

Even those who had come to regard National Socialism with a critical eye, and who longed for the war to end, feared the defeat and the Red Army's vengeance. The final weeks of the war and first weeks of the occupation were indeed terrible, marked by looting, rape and other acts of violence. Aside from foreign prisoners of war and forced labourers, only a small number of dedicated opponents of Hitler felt an immediate sense of liberation. For most people it was possible only after quite some time had passed, if at all, to recognise that the defeat they had experienced as a personal and national catastrophe represented an unexpected opportunity, even for those who had not wanted to be liberated.

For most Berliners, the greatest surprise of 1945 was that life continued at all after the capitulation. The Red Army not only assumed authority in the city, but tried from the beginning to ensure that the population received at least basic provisions. They instituted a strict occupation regime, dismissing and arresting National Socialist functionaries, and taking drastic measures against suspected "Werewolf" actions by former members of the "Hitler Youth", but also immediately installed provisional administrations on the district and municipal level, and backed the rebuilding of the police force and judicial system. The Soviet City Commandant initiated clearing work, supported repairs to water, gas and electric power lines and helped in the resumption of rail and bus service in parts of the city. When the Western Allies took over their sectors in July, these policies were continued as a matter of course. The Allies also agreed unanimously that the beginnings of economic reconstruction were to be accompanied by the dismantlement of industrial plant for reparations purposes.

Life in the ruins was characterised by an unimagined capacity for improvisation, for creative adaptation to the prevailing scarcity. 1945 was the hour of women fighting for the survival of their families. People concentrated on the immediate, lived from one day to the next, moved in small, circumscribed spaces. The Norwegian Theo Findahl had already noted during the final phase of the air war that, in the attempt *"to make the ruins as livable as possible"*, something *"strange"* had occurred: *"before our eyes a small town began to grow up on the remnants of the metropolis"*. Everyday existence in the post-war period did indeed take on something of the character of small-town life, and not only the family but also house communities and neighbourhoods assumed new significance.

At the beginning of November the American correspondent William L. Shirer wrote of the "conquering people" of the "master race", "whom you now see poking about in the ruins, broken, dazed, shivering, hungry human beings without will or purpose or direction, reduced like animals to foraging for food and seeking shelter in order to cling to life for another day". Prospects for the future were highly uncertain; only in a very limited sense might one speak of a mood of new beginnings. Although the first political parties were already permitted in mid-June, democratic modes of thought and action developed only very slowly. Even with the best of intentions, the absolute authority of the occupation forces was not the most fertile soil for the growth of democracy, and attempts to grapple critically with the Nazi period initially met with little response among a population that had been more numbed than converted.

Only a few days and weeks after the surrender Berlin's cultural life was revived with the vigorous support of Soviet cultural officers. It was a significant achievement that concerts, plays and even ballet evenings took place at all. Attempts at reorienting the contents of culture were, in contrast, comparatively modest. Beginning in the summer, the "Cultural Federation for a Democratic Renewal of Germany" [*Kulturbund für eine demokratischen Erneuerung Deutschlands*] began devising guidelines for the role of culture in building a democratic society, but practice tended to take up where cultural production had left off in 1933. Clearly, more distance was necessary in order to make the drastic experiences of the present fruitful for artistic production.

Although some conflicts of interest among the occupying powers had already appeared in 1945, relations were not yet those of a "Cold War". Beginning in the latter half of 1945, however, the other political parties came to regard the KPD's obvious power politics with increasing suspicion. From the autumn, resistance to the "Unity Party" demanded by the KPD grew quickly, particularly among the Social Democrats.

The exhibition seeks to recall the history of Berlin in 1945 – before and after 2 May – as concretely and from as many perspectives as possible. In the face of the generally unsatisfactory state of research, it attempts to bring together the fragmentary evidence without papering over the ambiguities and contradictions inherent in the events. It recounts and analyses the history gathered from more than 50 German, Russian and English archives and collections. Alongside the official documents, diaries and autobiographical works from 1945 have been accorded a special role. It is no accident that in many cases the written testimonies of women – both well-known and unknown – are in the foreground.

The exhibition has been prepared for the fiftieth anniversary of the 8th of May 1945. Using the example of Berlin, it recalls the war, National Socialist tyranny and the first tentative efforts at making a life without the double threat of war and terror. It documents the experiences of an unusual period of crisis and hardship, and demonstrates not least how arduous were the beginnings of a post-fascist democratic society whose success was uncertain.

We thank the *Stiftung Deutsche Klassenlotterie Berlin* for making the exhibition financially possible. Particular thanks are due to Prof Ulrich Eckhardt and the *Berliner Festspielen* for years of collaboration and reliable support. Finally, we would like to thank Margret Schmitt for designing the exhibition and Dr Willmuth Arenhövel for supervising the publication of this volume.

A catalogue reproducing the entire exhibition would have been too costly, and too voluminous, so that the present work, which lists all the objects in the exhibition, could reproduce only a selection of the photos and documents.

3   American B-17 bomber on a bombing mission over Berlin, 1945.
Over the right wing Tempelhof Airfield is visible, and in the upper area of the picture the Landwehrkanal with the Urbanhafen and Belle-Alliance-Platz (today: Mehringplatz).

1. The War and the Destruction of Berlin

1.1. The Air-raids

On 1 September 1939 the first air alert ("flyers alert") took place in Berlin. It was based on an error; three German planes had been mistaken for Polish aircraft. The first bombing raids began a year later: on the night of 25 August 1940, after the German bombings of Warsaw, Rotterdam, Marseille and London, the first bombs fell on Berlin. The first phase of the air war lasted until the autumn of 1941. After that there were practically no more air-raids until January 1943. During the whole of 1942 there were only nine alerts in Berlin.

Berlin was, to be sure, not the only target of the British and, after March 1944, the American strategic air war, but it was the most significant one. It was the capital of the "Third Reich", the headquarters of terrorism not just for Germany but also for the occupied territories of Europe, the seat of the military leadership and one of the most important industrial and armaments centres of the German Reich.

On 2 March 1943, the city experienced the most severe air-raid up to that point (over 700 dead and 65,000 made homeless). The "Battle of Berlin" began on 18 November 1943, and by 27 November extensive areas of the city had been reduced to rubble (nearly 3,800 dead, 10,000 injured, over 450,000 made homeless) by a series of five large-scale attacks. By March 1944 alone a further thirteen large-scale raids had occurred before the British night air-raids were supplemented by American day bombings (with at times more than one thousand bombers participating in a single raid).

Although extensive "air-raid protection" measures had been propagated soon after the National Socialist "seizure of power", when the war began only some 15% of the 2,000 public air-raid shelters planned for Berlin had been completed. The large bunkers (Zoo, Anhalt Station, Humboldthain, Friedrichshain, Kleistpark) offered relative safety to about 65,000 persons, while the majority of the population was obliged to take refuge in makeshift cellar air-raid shelters. In the summer of 1943 it was decided that those members of the population not essential to the maintenance of the wartime economy, particularly children, youths and the elderly, should be "evacuated" from the city. By the end of 1943 more than 800,000 Berliners (half of them children and youths) had been "evacuated"; in all some 1.2 million people eventually left the city. Entire classes of school-children were "evacuated" to the country with their teachers.

The year 1945 brought with it a further intensification of the air war. Often there were up to three air alerts a day. On 3 February, one of the most severe attacks of all destroyed large parts of the city centre and adjacent areas: nearly 3,000 deaths and more than 100,000 homeless were registered. The last air alert sounded on 21 April. After that began the Soviet Army's conquest of the city, prepared and supported by the Air Force.

Other German cities suffered relatively greater destruction and, in some cases, far more casualties than Berlin. Berlin, however, against which more than 300 bombing

4   Bombs over Kreuzberg, 1945.
On the lower right the Landwehrkanal and Urbanhafen are visible above the bombs; from left to right one can see the course
of the Spree River.

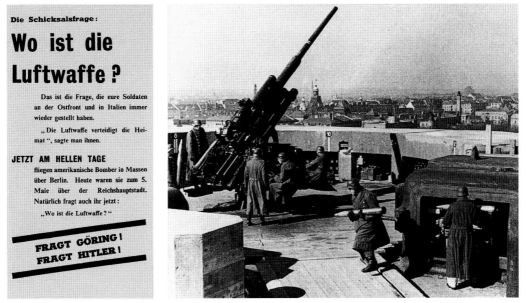

5 Front side of an American leaflet dropped over Berlin, 22 March 1944.

6 Air-raid exercise of the heavy anti-aircraft guns on the tower of the Zoo bunker, 16 April 1942.

missions had been flown, was the city in Europe that took by far the greatest number of bombs. In all, some 50,000 tons of incendiary, high-explosive, phosphorous and fragmentation bombs, aerial mines and delayed-action caps fell over Berlin. According to official statistics, at least 20,000 people died in Berlin as a result of air-raids.

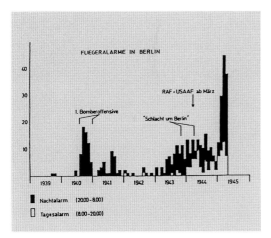

7 Air alerts in Berlin between 1939 and 1945.
The number of alerts does not directly reflect the significance of the bombing raids: the greatest destruction – with correspondingly high casualties – was wrought by the raids after the end of 1943.

Compilation of figures on aerial attacks and their effects on the civilian population, 1943–45.

The numbers in brackets name the victims among foreign forced labourers and prisoners of war.

No. of attack	Date	Killed	Injured	Homeless and evacuated	Missing
				1943	
[...]					
152. Air-raid	22.11.				
153. Air-raid					
154. Air-raid	to	3 758 (183)	9 907 (147)	454 056	574
155. Air-raid					
156. Air-raid					
157. Air-raid	26.11.				
158. Air-raid	2.12.	99 (3)	151 (6)	8 862	x
160. Air-raid	16.12.	628 (121)	968 (159)	30 063	60
161. Air-raid	24.12.	211 (16)	326 (23)	8 186	6
162. Air-raid	29.12.	260 (25)	509 (107)	4 012	52

No. of attack	Date	Killed	Injured	Homeless and evacuated	Mis-sing
1944					
163. Air-raid	2.1.	55 (7)	175 (8)	4 012	x
164. Air-raid	3.1.	143 (4)	204 (–)	9 943	4
168. Air-raid	20.1.	306 (29)	558 (55)	20 938	4
171. Air-raid	27.1.	413 (32)	426 (79)	19 945	46
172. Air-raid	29.1.	531 (17)	860 (5)	69 466	206
174. Air-raid	30.1.	582 (1)	908 (2)	82 980	633
26. Alert	5.2.				
177. Air-raid	15.2.	169 (x)	512 (x)	60 836	273
181. Air-raid	6.3.	86 (x)	57 (x)	2 245	17
182. Air-raid	8.3.	x	x	1 150	x
183. Air-raid	9.3.	76 (30)	173 (8)	2 000	x
43. Alert	19.3.	1	x	x	x
184. Air-raid	22.3.	70 (3)	185 (7)	8 000	125
186. Air-raid	24.3.	47 (x)	155 (x)	23 710	190
52. Alert	13.4.	1 (x)	1 (x)	x	x
193. Air-raid	29.4.	335 (34)	510 (28)	13 760	65
194. Air-raid	4.5.	169 (58)	284 (21)	17 573	150
195. Air-raid	8.5.	135 (x)	220 (x)	27 050	55
56. Alert	10.5.	13 (x)	175 (x)	x	x
198. Air-raid	24.5.	95 (12)	247 (13)	28 000	60
199. Air-raid	24.5.	4 (x)	14 (x)	420	x
200. Air-raid	24.5.	182 (16)	697 (25)	33 150	1
201. Air-raid	28.5.	4 (x)	22 (x)	450	9
205. Air-raid	10.6.	98 (x)	354 (x)	4 777	30
206. Air-raid	11.6.	47 (x)	104 (x)	1 350	60
207. Air-raid	12.6.	33 (23)	99 (17)	6 828	–
208. Air-raid	17.6.	– (–)	6 (x)	50	–
210. Air-raid	20.6.	No record			
211. Air-raid	21.6.	474 (x)	756 (x)	28 180	120
212. Air-raid	22.6.	39 (x)	102 (x)	2 270	56
213. Air-raid	25.6.	1 (x)	10 (x)	85	–
216. Air-raid	8.7.	23 (x)	97 (x)	5 600	81
217. Air-raid	11.7.	10 (x)	118 (x)	2 720	42
[…]					
253. Air-raid	23.10.	81 (x)	53 (x)	2 500	60
255. Air-raid	27.10.	– (–)	7 (x)	580	–
256. Air-raid	28.10.	– (–)	– (–)	162	–
257. Air-raid / 258. Air-raid	30.10.	1 (x)	10 (x)	2 298	1
259. Air-raid	1.11.	– (x)	– (x)	129	–
261. Air-raid	4.11.	4 (x)	9 (x)	2 206	–
262. Air-raid	15.11.	13 (x)	14 (x)	810	–
263. Air-raid	24.11.	92 (x)	25 (x)	2 728	3
264. Air-raid	27.11.	1 (x)	– (–)	476	–
265. Air-raid	5.12.	326 (80)	273 (30)	10 714	2
266. Air-raid	6.12.	1 (x)	18 (x)	448	–
267. Air-raid	9.12.	1 (x)	2 (x)	585	–
269. Air-raid	31.12.	10 (x)	41 (x)	1 265	–
1945					
271. Air-raid	2.1.	31 (x)	33 (x)	1 750	14
272. Air-raid	4.1.	– (–)	– (–)	130	–
273. Air-raid	4.1.	12 (x)	23 (x)	1 194	1
274. Air-raid / 275. Air-raid	5.1.	15 (x)	36 (x)	1 650	6
278. Air-raid / 279. Air-raid	14.1.	13 (x)	22 (x)	1 275	21
283. Air-raid	28.1.	4 (x)	17 (x)	401	–
284. Air-raid	29.1.	7 (x)	45 (x)	2 513	16
285. Air-raid	1.2.	33 (x)	63 (x)	1 470	100
286. Air-raid	2.2.				
288. Air-raid	3.2.	2 541 (x)	1 688 (x)	119 057	714
290. Air-raid	6.2.				
293. Air-raid	8.2.	10 (x)	15 (x)	1 208	–
297. Air-raid	14.2.	1 (x)	12 (x)	390	–
302. Air-raid	21.2.				
303. Air-raid	22.2.	1 (x)	15 (x)	602	–
304. Air-raid	22.2.				
305. Air-raid	22.2.	17 (x)	6 (x)	2 555	–
306. Air-raid	23.2.	4 (x)	9 (x)	2 816	60
307. Air-raid	24.2.	9 (x)	28 (x)	1 729	43
308. Air-raid	25.2.	– (–)	1 (x)	30	–
309. Air-raid	26.2.	636 (x)	389 (x)	71 283	519
[310. Air-raid to 313. Air-raid 26.2. to 28.2. No record]					
316. Air-raid	2.3.	– (–)	– (–)	280	–
320. Air-raid	5.3.	3 (x)	10 (x)	212	–
321. Air-raid	6.3.	4 (x)	3 (x)	69	–
323. Air-raid	8.3.	1 (x)	1 (x)	335	–
324. Air-raid	9.3.	No record			
325. Air-raid	10.3.	15 (x)	45 (x)	3 811	27
326. Air-raid	11.3.	21 (x)	41 (x)	6 836	17
327. Air-raid	12.3.	24 (x)	28 (x)	5 475	50
328. Air-raid	13.3.	– (–)	3 (x)	1 154	–
329. Air-raid	14.3.	17 (x)	12 (x)	3 420	24
330. Air-raid / 331. Air-raid	15.3.	7 (x)	17 (x)	1 666	6
332. Air-raid	16.3.	20 (x)	21 (x)	866	4
333. Air-raid / 334. Air-raid	17.3.	10 (x)	5 (x)	985	–
335. Air-raid	18.3.	336 (x)	357 (x)	79 785	226
336. Air-raid	18.3.	No record			
337. Air-raid	20.3.	15 (x)	12 (x)	903	6
340. Air-raid / 341. Air-raid	21.3. / 22.3.	20 (x)	48 (x)	3 344	77
342. Air-raid / 343. Air-raid	22.3.	1 (x)	6 (x)	2 685	–
344. Air-raid	23.3.	32 (x)	117 (x)	5 600	36
345. Air-raid	24.3.	44 (x)	68 (x)	923	32
346. Air-raid / 348. Air-raid	24.3. / 25.3.	7 (x)	1 (x)	1 013	21
349. Air-raid / 350. Air-raid	26.3.	7 (x)	21 (x)	1 120	4
351. Air-raid	27.3.	7 (x)	27 (x)	2 915	1
352. Air-raid	30.3.	340 (x)	62 (x)	9 980	5
353. Air-raid / 354. Air-raid	30.3.	15 (x)	24 (x)	2 200	1
356. Air-raid	3.4.	2 (x)	27 (x)	860	6
357. Air-raid / 358. Air-raid	3.4. / 4.4.	31 (x)	26 (x)	1 910	20
360. Air-raid	4.4.	22 (x)	11 (x)	180	17
365. Air-raid / 366. Air-raid	8.4.	7 (x)	20 (x)	2 025	3
367. Air-raid / 368. Air-raid	9.4.	7 (x)	23 (x)	1 140	5
369. Air-raid	10.4.	13 (x)	38 (x)	8 135	101
370. Air-raid	11.4.	24 (x)	65 (x)	5 012	42
371. Air-raid	12.4.	16 (x)	68 (x)	2 632	30
374. Air-raid	14.4.	7 (x)	8 (x)	4 315	127
375. Air-raid	15.4.	10 (x)	74 (x)	7 085	15
376. Air-raid / 378. Air-raid	18.4.	10 (x)	78 (x)	6 150	163

End of record

Berliner! Berlinerinnen!

Der Feind setzt den Luftterror gegen die deutsche Zivilbevölkerung rücksichtslos fort. Es ist dringend erwünscht und liegt im Interesse jedes Einzelnen, der nicht aus beruflichen oder sonstigen Gründen zum Verbleiben in Berlin verpflichtet ist (Frauen, Kinder, Pensionäre, Rentner usw.), sich in weniger luftgefährdete Gebiete zu begeben.

Hierzu bestehen folgende Möglichkeiten:

1. Wer Verwandte außerhalb Berlins hat, die ihn aufnehmen können, kann abreisen. Erforderlich ist, daß er sich bei seiner Kartenstelle eine Abreisebescheinigung ausstellen läßt. Hierzu sind sämtliche Lebensmittelkarten sowie die örtlichen Berliner Bezugsausweise mitzubringen. Auf Grund dieser Abreisebescheinigung erhält er von der zuständigen Ortswaltung der NSV. einen Freifahrschein.

2. Auch wer keine Aufnahme bei Verwandten außerhalb Berlins finden kann, darf ebenfalls abreisen, jedoch nur nach Orten in den für Berlin bestimmten Aufnahmegauen Mark Brandenburg, Ostpreußen und Wartheland. Auch in diesem Falle ist zwecks Beibringung einer Abreisebescheinigung durch die Kartenstelle die Vorlage sämtlicher Lebensmittelkarten und der örtlichen Berliner Bezugsausweise erforderlich. Das Quartier selbst wird durch die hiesige Ortswaltung der NSV. vermittelt, die einen Freifahrschein ausstellt.

3. Wer nicht gleich abreisen kann, aber Verwandte außerhalb Berlins besitzt, hat die Möglichkeit, sein Unterkommen bei seinen Verwandten schon jetzt vorsorglich festzulegen, indem er sich von seiner zuständigen Ortswaltung der NSV. eine Verwandten-Meldekarte besorgt und sie ausgefüllt zu seinen Verwandten schickt. Diese müssen auf der Karte ihre Bereitwilligkeit zur Aufnahme erklären und von der Ortswaltung des vorgesehenen Zureiseortes die Unbedenklichkeit der Aufnahme bescheinigen lassen. Die Karte ist der hiesigen Ortswaltung der NSV. zur Kenntnis vorzulegen und für den Fall der tatsächlichen Abreise aufzubewahren.

4. In jedem Falle empfiehlt es sich, einige Kleidungsstücke, kleinen Hausrat (Töpfe, Geschirr, Eßbestecke usw.), Bettzeug, mitzunehmen.

Die Transportkosten trägt der Bezirksbürgermeister (Quartierstelle).

Es ist verboten, unter Verzicht auf diese Möglichkeiten planlos zu reisen. Wer planlos reist, läuft Gefahr, am Zielort kein Quartier zu finden und muß mit Schwierigkeiten in der Lebensmittelversorgung rechnen.

Der Reichsverteidigungskommissar
für den Reichsverteidigungsbezirk Berlin
Dr. Goebbels
Gauleiter und Reichsminister

8 Goebbels' appeal to the Berlin population in his capacity as "Reich Defence Commissioner for the Reich Defence District of Berlin" regarding the evacuation of children and the elderly in particular, early August 1943.

9 People wanting to leave Berlin, at an S-Bahn station, February 1944.

Text 1

From a report of the SS Security Service [SD] on the in some cases inadequate evacuation of children, 10 February 1944.

10 February 1944
In order to reduce the relatively large number of children still living in areas subject to air-raids, in recent weeks the Party, Hitler Youth, the offices of Children's Rural Evacuation, the NSV and the schools have been carrying out publicity campaigns for school evacuations.
Unfortunately, despite these publicity actions a substantial portion of parents have proved unwilling to send their children away.
The following examples, which demonstrate the arguments and objections brought forward by parents against the evacuation of their children at these meetings, have been chosen from reports of actual parents' meetings:
"The parents of Primary Schools No. 28 and 29 were shown a film on a KLV (Children's Rural Evacuation) camp at the Passage Cinema in Neukölln. The young people present showed enthusiasm, but the mothers were reserved. When the speaker explained that the boys or girls might have to sleep on straw for a few days, but would not be awakened by sirens or have to seek out an air-raid shelter, the first interjection came: "But it's grand in the air-raid shelter!" When reminded that Berlin was a war zone, in which children had no business, various mothers called out "Neither do we!" When the speaker remarked that the mothers should be grateful that their children were in safety someone called out "But the children don't want to go". After appeals to mother love and the assertion that it was irrational to say one wanted to die together with one's children, the speaker was loudly contradicted, "No, it's right." To the statement that there was no school here in the city came the reply, "If not, then not." The statement that children under ten would be billetted with families since they were considered too young for camps was answered by loud laughter from the parent

10   The "little Zoo bunker" on the New Lake in the Tiergarten park, 1945.
The "little Zoo bunker", constructed between 1939 and 1941, served as the head anti-aircraft office for Berlin.
There were two other such above ground bunkers in Berlin, in Friedrichshain and in Humboldthain. They were built between 1940 and 1942 as "anti-aircraft turrets".
There were also other large bunkers, for example in Schöneberg or near Anhalt Station, which were used solely as air-raid shelters. Because the authorities expected a "blitz-krieg", air-raid protection for the civilian population was long neglected. Thus most Berliners depended upon the inadequate makeshift shelters in their own cellars.

When the speaker, who had dealt skillfully with the hecklers thus far, could offer no exact answer to the question of where the children under ten would go, the majority of parents left the meeting. The leader of the meeting was not able to prevent its dissolution by calling for a tribute to the Führer [*Führerehrung*].

Text 2

Journal entry by Ursula von Kardorff, describing the atmosphere in the Zoo bunker during a raid, 25 January 1944.

Recently I was in the Zoo bunker with Klaus for the seven o'clock alert. Eerie. The anti-aircraft fire had already begun, and a herd of human animals was running in the dark towards the entrances, which are small and much too narrow. People's torches went on and everybody was shouting: "Lights out!" Then the crowd pushed and shoved their way in – a wonder that everything went as smoothly as it did. The walls of the bunker, massive stone ashlars, are reminiscent of the set for the prison scene in Fidelio. An illuminated lift rides silently up and down, probably for ill people. The whole thing might have been invented by Ernst Jünger for his Capriccios. Snapping policemen and non-commissioned officers slowly drove the reluctant people up the stairs, to

11   Excerpt from the identity card of the Air-raid Warden Karl K. of Spandau, 1941.

12   Shortly before an air-raid; prams had to be left outside the public air-raid shelters, 1944/45.

Schutzraum 2
50 Personen
Ruhe bewahren!
Rauchen verboten!

13   In a public air-raid shelter during a raid, November 1943.

14 In the air-raid shelter under a house during an air-raid,
13 July 1943.

distribute them among the various floors. At each landing they all came to a stop. One woman had a screaming fit. She thought she was more likely to die upstairs. "I have a husband and son at the front", she shrieked. "I'm not going up there!" Finally she was taken away. There are spiral staircases in the turrets. This is where the courting couples sit – a travesty of a fancy dress party. When the batteries up above fire the building sways and people duck their heads as if a sickle were sweeping over them. Everyone is thrown together pell-mell: frightened rich people, weary women, threadbare foreigners carrying all their worldly possessions around in gigantic sacks, and soldiers looking quite awkward. If a panic were to break out here, God help us, I thought.

Text 3

Journal entry by Theo Findahl on an air alert that had occurred on the same evening, 22 November 1943.

The telephone call from Oslo came exactly at 6.15 pm. When I hung up the receiver, it was exactly 7.30 pm. Alert. Well, perhaps nothing will happen. I am alone in my flat in the Hansaviertel, at Klopstock Allee 33, so I have to make a round of the rooms to make sure all the lights are out, the bathtub is filled with water, and the windows are open so the air pressure doesn't shatter them. In the past week there have been warnings so often at precisely this time of evening, but

15   After the air-raid at Askanischer Platz, 3 February 1945. This air-raid was one of the most devastating, rendering over 100,000 people homeless. The American raid at midday was preceded by an English night raid.

16   Leaving the large Zoo bunker after the all-clear, February 1945.

17   After the bombing raid of 3 February 1945, near Anhalt Station.

18   Victims recovered after an air-raid, ca. 1944.

there hasn't been an attack yet. Goebbels has Berliners halfway convinced that the RAF won't manage to get all the way to Berlin, thanks to the city's excellent air defence. I don't feel like taking the little case with a set of underwear and toiletries with me, and walk alone through the pitch-dark streets to the Großer Stern, the old refuge where we, a whole troupe of colleagues and friends, congregate in the subway under the road whenever English bombers fly over Berlin.

Text 4

A schoolgirl from Prenzlauer Berg recalls her impressions of the air-raid of 18 March 1945, January 1946.

These reminiscences come from a collection of school essays from a girls' secondary school in Prenzlauer Berg.

The room is filled with chatter and laughter. But over everything lies a nerve-shattering tension. There, a close hit! The anti-aircraft guns begin to fire. The shocks become stronger and stronger. The chatter grows softer, and the laughter stops altogether. Suddenly, a deafening bang! The lights flicker, the room sways. Frightened, we all flinch. The old woman across from me begins praying softly. Sobbing, a child buries its head in its mother's lap. Its whining hangs in the air like the embodiment of our fear. Hit after hit! Each of us feels the nearness of death. Perhaps in three minutes, perhaps two, perhaps only one! The young woman next to me stares with dull eyes into the emptiness. Like all of us, she has given up on life.

Smoke penetrates through a small crack in the wall! It is a scarcely perceptible waft, and yet the musty cellar air soon stinks of smoke. A woman cries out. "We're done for!," she screams, grabbing her things and running to the door that leads to the back rooms. Many follow her. But when the room is black nobody can stand it anymore. The ground is still humming from the impact of the bombs. It is as if all Hell has broken loose. Then comes the news that the exit is blocked with debris. Right afterwards, though, a man shouts "It's burning above us, we have to get out!" Children scream, women cry; a fearful helplessness has gripped everybody. What will become of us? The smoke has penetrated this room as well. The air is sultry, and the burning smoke stings our eyes; we stand closely packed! The hand of death is over us.

"The emergency exits are blocked", says the air-raid warden. "We must wait until they are freed." "Wait, wait! We'll have suffocated by then" groans a young woman, whose child clings to her in fear. An old man has heart spasms. And we wait! We wait for death!

There, a draught of fresh air! One exit is free! Who can describe the joy one feels at having escaped death?

Everyone pushes to get out. "You must be quick about it!" call the guards. "There's a danger of collapse!" Nobody knows whether the attack is over yet, because all the alarm devices have been destroyed. We go up the stairs. It is burning over us, all around us.

Text 5

Journal entry by Theo Findahl on the air-raid on the evening of 23 November 1943.

From this spot it looks as if the whole city were on fire. The entire Hansaviertel behind the park is in flames. I must get home to see whether anything can be saved! In the Altonaer Straße the pipes have burst, and the street resembles an inland lake. It is impossible to reach Hansaplatz this way. The Tiergarten is like a jungle. Branches and stalks poke one in the face while one feels one's way over fallen tree trunks. Händelallee is a sea of fire. I press on and turn in to Klopstockstraße. The street is as hot as an oven; in a few places people are trying to salvage something, here and there pieces of furniture are catapulted onto the street, but most give up and let things burn. It is hopeless to get inside number 33; a scorching wind whips through the streets and the house is a whirlwind of fire. From the big house across the street, with the best cellar in the city, a band of distraught women staggers over, a half-grown girl screaming hysterically, but most of them are quite calm, as if half-dazed. As in a

19   The first page of the Air-raid Protection Incident Report issued by the "Leader of Technical Emergency Aid for the Spree Area" on the bomb attack of 6 October 1944, 13 October 1944.
Such "ARP Incident Reports" were compiled after every raid. The discriminatory separation of victims from among the foreign forced labourers and prisoners of war is striking. While Germans, both military and civilian, are described as "fallen" and "wounded", foreign labourers and prisoners of war were "killed" or "injured". ▶

Der Führer
TN-Bereichs Spree

Berlin-Lichterfelde, den 13.10.44
Haydnstraße 13-15
Fernruf: Sammelnummer 76 52 31

Ic.317- /44

Geheim

LS-Ereignismeldung

Luftangriffe am 6.10.44

I. Berlin

Schlußbericht
nach dem Stande vom 9.10.44

1. Abwurfmittel

1) Tagesangriff
- 1.000 Sprengbomben
- 100.000 Stabbrandbomben
- 1.000 Flüssigkeitsbrandbomben

2) Nachtangriff
2 Minenbomben
20 Sprengbomben

Unter den Sprengbomben bis jetzt 93 Blindgänger bzw. Langzeitzünder gezählt.

2. Personenverluste

1) Tagesangriff

		gefallen	verwundet schwer	verwundet leicht
Zivilbevölkerung:	Männer	100	54	130
	Frauen	51	15	67
	Kinder	8	1	4
Soldaten		13	2	2
Ordnungspolizei		5	3	5
		getötet	verletzt	
Fremdvölk. Arbeiter:	Männer	36	12	22
	Frauen	6	2	4
Kriegsgefangene		1	-	-
	insgesamt	220	89	234

Vermißte: noch etwa 30 Personen
Verschüttete: 88 Personen lebend,
137 " tot geborgen. (Diese Zahl ist in der Zahl der Gefallenen usw. enthalten.)

Obdachlose: etwa 6.200 Personen.

2) Nachtangriff

		gefallen	verwundet schwer	verwundet leicht
Zivilbevölkerung:	Männer	-	1	3
	Frauen	-	-	3
Soldaten		-	3	1
	insgesamt	-	4	7

20 Berlin Fire-Brigade putting out fires in Zimmerstraße in
Kreuzberg after an air-raid, 1944.

21   Concentrationcamp-inmates recovering a blind shell, 1944.
On the left two german policemen and a sergeant oft the
"Luftwaffe".

flash I see before me the pale, groaning French-woman three years ago in Bergues after the Germans had reduced the city to rubble, dragging herself along the walls of the houses. The best thing is to turn back as soon as possible and return to the park where the air is not so sharply redolent of soot and smoke – away from this place that was our home for three years!

Text 6

Description by Konrad Warner of the situation after the air-raid on the evening of 22 November 1944.

Soon after I joined them the burning stairwell above us collapsed. Our exit was blocked.
The cellar filled up more and more with smoke. We had to escape this hellish trap. People wandered past each other, unseeing. Sometimes one encountered an unfamiliar face and didn't know whether it belonged to someone from the house, to a neighbour or to some stranger intent on robbery. Others sat on their chairs and cots, exhausted and apathetic. We soaked our woolen blankets, scarves and handkerchiefs in the wash-basin to protect against fire and flying sparks.
Now we crawled through the hole in the wall into the air-raid shelter of the house next-door in order to go by subterrenean passages to an adjacent street which would take us to an underground station. These were the catacombs of the twentieth century. We dragged ourselves through various bomb cellars, crawling from one hole in the cellar wall to the next until we reached the last house in the next street, from which we had to go forward on the earth's surface. The old people were able to pass these small tunnels only with difficulty, babies and children were handed through, and suitcases pushed through. Above us the houses were ablaze, and we would never have made it through the streets.

1.2. The "Battle of Berlin"

At the end of 1944 and the beginning of 1945 National Socialist Germany's military situation was hopeless. To the west, American and British troops had been on Reich territory since the autumn of 1944. To the east, almost all allies had turned away from Germany, and after 12 January 1945 Soviet troops began their "assault on the Reich" from positions on the Weichsel. Since the Commander-in-Chief of the Western Allied forces, General Eisenhower, decided in March 1945 not to treat Berlin as a primary military target, the task of conquering the Reich capital was left to the Soviet Army alone.

The Red Army's superiority in January 1945 was impressive: the infantry outnumbered that of the German forces 9–11 to 1, and the artillery 10–20 to 1; the Allies also possessed air sovereignty, and German air defence was practically nonexistent. The "Third Reich's" political and military leaders were nonetheless unwilling to put an end to the futile fighting in order to prevent further bloodshed and needless destruction. On the contrary, they intensified the anti-Bolshevik propaganda and the reign of terror against soldiers and civilians who had ceased to share their hopes of "ultimate victory".

If one includes the reserves and rear-area services, at the beginning of the Berlin offensive on 16 April 1945 the Red Army had at its disposal 2.5 million soldiers, 41,600 units of heavy artillery, 6,300 tanks and 7,500 airplanes – i.e., one-third of the total capacity of the Soviet Armed Forces. In contrast, only some 100,000 inadequately trained soldiers, supplemented by units of the Peoples' Reserve [*Volkssturm*] and labour service, police and fire-brigades, were available to defend Berlin. Under the circumstances, defence was futile from the beginning. The fanatical resolve to defend the Reich capital "to the last man and to the last bullet" cost more lives on the German side alone than all the air-raids combined, and, particularly in the city centre, brought with it damages equal to those caused by years of bombing. The first Soviet City Commandant, General Bersarin, may have exaggerated when he said, "The Allies dropped 65,000 tons of bombs, we have fired 40,000 tons of grenades in two weeks!", but this does provide some idea of the extent of the city's devastation.

On 21 April the first Soviet units arrived in Berlin's northeastern suburbs. The actual final struggle began with the bombardment of strategic targets by Soviet fighter-bombers and the continuous shelling of the city's central districts. On 25 April the city was completely surrounded. In street battles that brought heavy casualties to both sides the Soviet troops advanced on the city centre on 28 April. On 30 April Soviet soldiers stormed the Reichstag and raised the Red Flag. Shortly thereafter Hitler committed suicide in the "Führer bunker" under the Reich Chancellery.

The "Battle of Berlin", which lasted from 16 April to 2 May, was one of the largest and bloodiest of the Second World War. The Red Army reported 200,000 dead, wounded and missing (including 100,000 alone in the battle of Seelow Heights east of Berlin). There are no precise casualty figures for the German side. The total number has been estimated at 50,000, including over 20,000 civilians.

Text 7

Hitler in conversation with Armaments Minister Albert Speer, 18 March 1945.

On 19 March, only one day after making this statement, Hitler gave the so-called "Nero" order calling for extensive destructive measures in the Reich. Through Speer's intervention the execution of this order could be largely prevented.

If the war is lost, the nation will be lost as well. It is not necessary to spare the basis for the German people's most primitive survival. On the contrary, it is preferable to destroy even these things. The nation has proved itself the weaker one, and the future belongs to the stronger eastern nation alone. Only the inferior will remain after this struggle anyway, for the good have fallen.

Text 8

The "Basic Orders for Preparing the Defence of the Reich Capital" issued by the Commander of the Defence District of Berlin General Hellmuth Reymann, 9 March 1945.

Only at the beginning of February did the German Army High Command begin to develop general guidelines for the defence of the city. A pronounced lack of militarily trained personnel and insufficient material resources meant that the plans that were developed were unrealistic and unenforceable from the very beginning.

Defence District Berlin   Berlin-Grunewald
Ia/op., No. 400/45 secret   9.3.1945
Basic
Orders
for
Preparing the
DEFENCE OF THE REICH CAPITAL

The principles of this order must become the spiritual property of each division leader (including leaders of the Peoples' Reserve [*Volkssturm*]). For the sake of uniformity, all preparations must remain within the framework of these principles.
[...]
A. General
[...]
2. Mission
The Reich capital will be defended to the last man and to the last cartridge.

3. Fighting Methods
The battle for Berlin will be conducted with all forces available for the immediate defence of the capital, not in the form of open battle but chiefly in the form of street- and house-to-house fighting. It must be conducted with
fanaticism
imagination,
with all means
of deception,
craft,
and cunning,
with planned
and spontaneous
aids of all kinds
on
above and
below the ground.
What is important here is to exploit mercilessly the advantages of being on our own soil and the presumed fear of most Russians faced with an unfamiliar sea of houses. Precise knowledge of place, the utilisation of the underground railway and sewer system, of existing communications, the excellent potential of houses for combat and concealment, the fortress-like extension of blocks of houses – particularly reinforced concrete houses – into bases of operation render the defenders invincible to any foe, no matter how superior numerically!
The enemy, who must not know a minute of peace, must burn and bleed to death in the tight network of pockets of resistance, bases and defensive blocks. Each house or base of operations lost is to be recaptured immediately by counterthrust. Shock-troops are to be led unnoticed to the enemy's rear using subterrenean passages, in order to surprise and destroy him from behind.
The prerequisite for a successful defence of Berlin, however, is that
every block of houses,
every house,
every storey,
every hedge,
every shell-crater
be defended to the last!
It is not important that every defender of the Reich capital have a perfect grasp of the techniques of military science, but rather that
every fighter
be inspired and permeated by
the fanatical will to
WANT TO FIGHT,
that he know that the world is watching this struggle with baited breath and that the battle for Berlin may decide the outcome of the war. [...]

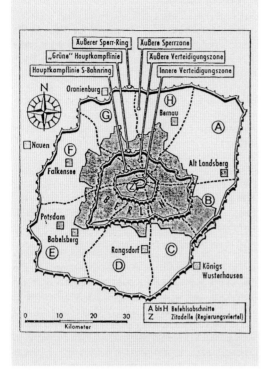

23 A man of the "Volkssturm" learning how to use the anti-tank grenade launcher, winter 1944/45.

The decree of 25 September 1944 creating the German Peoples' Reserve, which for propaganda purposes was not published until the anniversary of the Battle of the Nations in Leipzig on 18 October, called for the registration and induction of all "men capable of bearing arms" between the ages of 16 and 60. It was the responsibility of each district's gauleiter to set up and direct the Peoples' Reserve, while military training, arms and equipment were organised by the *Reichsführer SS* Heinrich Himmler in his capacity as commander of the reserve army. Only immediately before the onset of combat were the Peoples' Reserve units to enter the combat mission under the *Wehrmacht*. It is estimated that from the end of 1944 on a total of six million men were recruited for the Peoples' Reserve.

22   Outline of the plan of defence for Berlin according to the "Basic Orders", 9 March 1945.

24   Exhorting the Berlin population to hold out, 1945.

25 Men of the 405th battalion of the "Volkssturm" digging an anti-tank ditch on the road out of Mahlsdorf, 18 April 1945.

Text 9

Statement made by General of the Artillery Helmuth Weidling as a Soviet prisoner of war on the military situation in Berlin after 24 April 1945, 1946.

General Weidling directed military defensive measures against the Red Army from 24 April 1945 on as commander of the Defence District of Berlin. He died in 1955 as a Soviet prisoner of war.

The 24th of April had already convinced me that it was impossible to defend Berlin, and that it was also senseless from a military standpoint, since the German High Command did not have sufficient forces. In addition, the Commander did not have a single regular unit at his disposal in Berlin at the time, with the exception of the "Greater Germany" regiment and an SS brigade that was guarding the Reich Chancellery. The entire defence was handed over to the Peoples' Reserve, the police, the Fire-Brigade and various troops of the rear-area service and various administrative departments.

The city was divided into eight outer and one inner defence sector. Communication among the various sectors was poor. [...]

26 Anti-tank obstacles at the "Knee" (today: Ernst-Reuter-Platz), April 1945.

Berlin had food and munitions reserves for thirty days. Since the store-houses were on the outskirts of the city, however, supplying food and munitions became increasingly difficult the more the ring of Russians tightened around the defenders. On the last two days we had neither food nor munitions.

I think that the Peoples' Reserve, the police detachments, the Fire-Brigade and the anti-aircraft units consisted of about 90,000 men, not counting the troops of the rear-area services. There were also Peoples's Reserve units of the second mobilisation that joined the defence troops as the various firms were closed in the course of the battle. The LVI tank corps reached Berlin, that is, retreated to Berlin, with 13,000–15,000 men. It is impossible to give an exact figure of the number of people who defended Berlin, since I did not receive figures on the troop strength of the individual units under my command.

Chronology of Events between 16 April and 2 May 1945

16 April
Beginning of the Soviet offensive against Berlin.

19 April
The Red Army captures the Seelow Heights.
(Final occupation of the Ruhr by British troops.)

21 April
Street combat in Lichtenberg and Pankow.
The Red Army takes Weissensee.
Artillery bombardment of the government sector.

22 April
Colonel Ernst Kaether is appointed combat commander. The first issue of the morale-boosting newspaper, *Der Panzerbär* [The Armoured Bear] appears.

23 April
Fighting in Tempelhof, Steglitz and Zehlendorf.
The Red Army takes Köpenick, Lichtenberg and Pankow.
Service stops on the underground.

24 April
Fighting in Treptow, Neukölln, Friedrichshain, Prenzlauer Berg, Spandau and Reinickendorf.
General Weidling is appointed combat commander.

25 April
The Red Army takes Treptow and Neukölln.
The Soviet encirclement of Berlin is complete.
Service stops on the overground S-Bahn trains.
(American and Soviet units meet at Torgau on the Elbe.)

26 April
Fighting in Kreuzberg, Schöneberg, Wilmersdorf and Charlottenburg.
The Red Army takes Zehlendorf, Reinickendorf and Wedding.

27 April
Fighting in Tiergarten, at Alexanderplatz and at Hallesches Tor.
The Red Army takes Tempelhof, Schöneberg and Steglitz.

28 April
Street and house-to-house combat in Mitte.
The Red Army takes Kreuzberg, Wilmersdorf and Spandau.

29 April
The Red Army captures Anhalt Station and Potsdamer Platz.
Der Panzerbär appears for the last time.
(American troops take Munich.)

30 April
Fighting in Friedrichstraße.
The Red Army captures the Ministry of the Interior and the Reichstag building.
Hitler commits suicide.

1 May
People locked into the Reich Chancellery attempt to escape.
Armistice negotiations between General Krebs and General Chuikov.
Goebbels commits suicide.

2 May
The Berlin troops surrender.

27 Soviet IL-2 "Sturmovik" battle-planes on a mission over Berlin, April 1945.
On 16 April the Soviet Air Force began bombing raids on military targets in the city in support of ground troops. The British and Americans had stopped their own air raids.

An die Bevölkerung von Berlin!

Berlin ist von einem festen Ring der Truppen der Roten Armee eingekreist. Das Schicksal Berlins ist besiegelt. Die Rote Armee hat Zehntausende schwerer Geschütze und Salvengeschütze und Tausende von Bombern und Panzern zum Sturm herangeführt. Weiterer Widerstand wird die Einnahme der Stadt durch die Rote Armee nicht abwenden können. Er wird lediglich zur vollen Vernichtung der Stadt und zum sinnlosen Tode Hunderttausender deutscher Männer, Frauen und Kinder führen.

Jeder vernünftige Führer würde sich in einer solchen Lage zu sofortiger Kapitulation entschließen, um das Leben der Stadt und das Leben von Frauen und Kindern zu retten. Doch Ihr wißt sehr wohl: Von der verbrecherischen Hitlerbande ist so etwas nicht zu erwarten. Im Gegenteil, die Naziführer versuchen durch Drohungen und Schreckensmärchen über Greueltaten, die die Rote Armee angeblich an der deutschen Bevölkerung verübt, den Widerstand in die Länge zu ziehen. Dadurch geben sie die Stadt und die Bevölkerung der vollen Vernichtung preis.

Die Naziführer haben nichts zu verlieren. Diese Bande weiß, daß sie die verdiente Strafe erwartet. Ihr aber habt keinen Grund, Euch vor dem Einmarsch der Roten Armee in Berlin zu fürchten. Die Rote Armee führt keinen Krieg gegen die Zivilbevölkerung. Sie tut sogar den einfachen Mitgliedern des N. S. D. A. P. nichts, falls sie sich loyal zu der Roten Armee verhalten.

Berliner!

Ihr seid die Mehrzahl! Von Euch hängt es ab, das Ende der Schrecken näher zu bringen. Ihr könnt das retten, was noch zu retten ist.

Organisiert Euch in Widerstandsgruppen zum Widerstand gegen die Nazibande und zur Unterstützung der Roten Armee und handelt sofort!

1. Überzeugt alle Soldaten und Offiziere von der Notwendigkeit, den Widerstand sofort einzustellen!
2. Verbergt jeden Soldat und Offizier, der nicht weiterkämpfen will!
3. Verlaßt Eure Arbeitsstätten in den Rüstungswerken und bei den Befestigungsbauten!
4. Verlaßt den Volkssturm!
5. Sabotiert die Erfüllung der Befehle Hitlers und seiner Bande!

Duldet nicht die Zerstörung von Brücken, Transport- und Kommunaleinrichtungen! Merkt Euch diejenigen, die diese Niederträchtigkeiten durchführen:

Duldet nicht die Verminung von Gebäuden und Brücken! Merkt Euch die verminten Stellen und die Personen, die die Verminung durchführen.

Hißt überall weiße Flaggen als äußeres Zeichen Eurer Bereitschaft, den Widerstand einzustellen.

Kommt getrost über die Frontlinie in die russischen Stellungen. Hier seid Ihr in Sicherheit.

27. 4. 1945   Nr. 344

28 Red Army leaflet (front and back side), 27 April 1945.
The leaflet was distributed to the Berlin population from the air.

Text 10

Order from Hitler, published on 23 April 1945 in the military newspaper, *Der Panzerbär*.

Anyone who propagates or even condones measures that weaken our power to resist is a traitor! He is to be shot or hanged on the spot! This also applies in cases where such measures have supposedly been ordered on behalf of the gauleiter, Reich Minister Dr. Goebbels, or even in the name of the Führer.

Text 11

Excerpt from Helmut Altner's journal, 23 April 1945.

We are on the great road to Berlin. Lichtenrade passes by, then Mariendorf. No we are breathing city air. Along the street blocks of flats rise up into the sky. The inhabitants stand outside their doors. They shrink back as our steps echo loudly off the walls of the houses. Then they breathe again, we are Germans. [...]
Time pushes on, inexorably towards the final hour. Women press in from the south. Men hurry across the road, glancing around timidly. SS patrols drive their cars through the streets, stopping a man here, picking up a man there. The car drives off, motor singing. Members of the Peoples' Reserve, mainly in SS uniform, close the anti-tank obstacles. Hitler Youth walk the streets proudly with anti-tank grenade launchers. On our right is a large square. Ringed by the façades of bombed-out houses. Two SA men in uniform stand by a lamp-post. A civilian is hanging bound to a post. There is a red electric cable around his neck, which has bitten deeply into his flesh. His face is blue. His eyes are sunken deep in the sockets. Around his neck hangs a white cardboard sign. Written in shaky red letters, it reads: "I am Otto Meyer, I was too cowardly to fight for my wife and child. That is why I am hanging here. I am a rat." I feel a choking sensation. I would like to look away, and yet I cannot take my eyes off this terrible spectacle. The SA men are laughing and smoking. The dead man swings quietly in the wind. A civilian walking alongside us explains in a low voice why the soldier was hanged. He came back like us. Exhausted and war-weary he escaped the raging battle of extermination and encirclement before the gates of Berlin. He was young. His wife begged

him to stay. He gave in. Neighbours betrayed him. The SS picked him up. Before the eyes of his horrified wife, before the eyes of his child, he was murdered. First, though, he had to write the shameful sign with his own hands. The SS dictated the text, grinning. Then they strung him up. The wires cut into his neck and soon killed him. His wife lay unconscious on the ground. The SS drove away. The SA men took over.

Text 12

Journal entry for 28 April 1945 by Air Defence Assistant [*Luftwaffenhelfer*] Dieter Borkowski.

Drumhead courts martial had already been set up on 15 February 1945 by order of Reich Minister of Justice Otto Thierack. A diminution of fighting morale and the will to resist were to be prevented through terror against the German population.
The most notorious Berlin execution site was the Murellenschlucht in Spandau where death sentences against members of all ranks of the armed forces were systematically enforced. During the battle of Berlin soldiers and civilians were executed on the spot without any sort of trial.

29 Soviet artillery rocket launchers bombarding the Reich Chancellery from Asternplatz in Lichterfelde, late April 1945.
The salvo guns for rockets, known to Soviet soldiers as "Katyusha" and to German soldiers as "Stalin's organs", were muchfeared weapons in street-fighting as well because of the devastation they caused in the area of impact.

30   Soviet artillery and tank units in the Frankfurter Allee, end of April 1945.

31   Soviet infantry soldiers engaging in house-to-house combat, end of April or beginning of May 1945.

The shelling is now so punishingly thick that one can only move forward by springing from house to house. As I finally approached the Königstor I could see something curious from far away. On the shelter trenches before St Bartholomew's Church stood five men as stiff and silent as soldiers at drill while shells exploded all around them. Scarcely one hundred metres away, I called excitedly from the entryway of a house, "Take cover! Quick, into the trenches!" No answer, not a move. When I got closer I shrank back – the five men were dead. It was only from a distance that they appeared to be standing on the air-raid shelter. In reality they were hanging from the trees behind the shelter trenches. One of them had a sign on his chest: "We were too cowardly to protect Berlin from the Bolsheviks. We raised the white flag and betrayed Greater Germany and the Führer. For this we had to die!"

32   A flooded section of the north-south S-Bahn tunnel at the Landwehrkanal, after 1945.
The timepoint and cause of the explosion of the roof of the tunnel under the Landwehrkanal and the subsequent flooding of the S-Bahn shafts cannot be clearly reconstructed. It is probable that the explosion occurred on the morning of 2 May and was undertaken by retreating German units. Some one hundred bodies were recovered in the course of reconstruction work after May 1945. Speculations that there were thousands of casualties have proved untenable.

Text 13

Excerpt from the minutes of a briefing in the Führer's headquarters in the bunker of the Reich Chancellery, 27 April 1945.

Krebs: "In Berlin, the enemy has advanced far northwards. He is said to have advanced down Bülowstraße as far as the corner of Lützowstraße. Two enemy tanks are said to be on fire at the bridge at Hallesches Tor. Three companies that made a counter-attack have been encircled at Moritzplatz. Jannowitzbrücke unchanged. The enemy has come closer to Alexanderplatz. To the northeast largely in check. Unpleasant breach at Humboldthain Station. Anti-aircraft turrets encircled here. Seesaw battles at Westhafen docks. The enemy is said to have been riding around with assault boats. Enemy tanks are standing north of Witzleben Station. Our own tanks are advancing against them. In the Grunewald the Reich Labour Service holding with assault guns and keeping contact with right and left. The bridges at Pichelsdorf and Stößensee are holding. Enemies have advanced to near the trotting racetracks at Ruhleben, but are held up in the south."
Hitler: "One cannot occupy a city of millions with 400 tanks. They'll disappear."
Krebs: "It has been largely substantiated that the enemy's intentions in the past six days must have been as follows:
1. sealing off on a large scale
2. sealing off on a small scale, which has succeeded in the West;
3. now they will press on to Potsdamer Platz, Alexanderplatz and Charlottenburg Station in order to try to divide the city centre into separate sections."
Hitler: "We must keep a number of assault guns in readiness here in the centre as a central reserve. – The only thing that is crippling us is that we do not know exactly what is happening and have no exact reports and are dependent upon chance information. We must keep pushing."

Text 14

Journal entry by Chief of the Air Force General Staff, General Karl Koller, 22 April 1945.

20.45: Christian [Chief of Air Force Operations Staff, General Vice Marshal Eckard Christian]

Lesen und weitergeben!

Der Panzerbär

29. April 1945

KAMPFBLATT FÜR DIE VERTEIDIGER GROSS-BERLINS

Heroisches Ringen

Bei Tag und Nacht neue Eingreifkräfte herangeführt

Der Kampf um den Stadtkern entbrannt

Entlastungsangriffe laufen

Aus dem Führerhauptquartier, 28. April.

Das Oberkommando der Wehrmacht gibt bekannt:

In dem heroischen Kampf der Stadt Berlin kommt noch einmal vor aller Welt der Schicksalskampf des deutschen Volkes gegen den Bolschewismus zum Ausdruck.

Während in einem in der Geschichte einmaligen grandiosen Ringen die Hauptstadt verteidigt wird, haben unsere Truppen an der Elbe den Amerikanern den Rücken gekehrt, um von außen her im Angriff die Verteidiger von Berlin zu entlasten.

In dem inneren Verteidigungsring ist der Feind von Norden her in Charlottenburg und von Süden her über das Tempelhofer Feld eingedrungen. Am Halleschen Tor und am Alexanderplatz hat der Kampf um den Stadtkern begonnen. Die Ost-West-Achse liegt unter schwerem Feuer.

Fliegende Verbände unterstützen die Kämpfe unter aufopferndem Einsatz der Besatzungen. Trotz stärkster Jagd- und Flakabwehr wurden bei Tag und Nacht Eingreifreserven gelandet und Munition abgeworfen. Unsere Jagd- und Schlachtfliegerverbände vernichteten in den letzten vier Tagen 143 Flugzeuge, 58 Panzer und über 300 Fahrzeuge.

Im Raum südlich Königs Wusterhausen setzten Divisionen der 9. Armee ihre Angriffe nach Nordwesten fort und erwarteten sich während des ganzen Tages konzentrischer Angriffe der Sowjets gegen die Flanken. Die vom Westen angesetzten Divisionen warfen den Feind in erbittertem Ringen auf breiter Front zurück und haben Ferch erreicht.

Westlich Berlin wurde die Linie Brandenburg—Rathenau—Kremmen gegen alle feindlichen Angriffe behauptet.

Im Raume von Prenzlau warfen die Sowjets neue Panzer- und Infanterieverbände in den Kampf und erzwangen unter starkem Schlachtfliegereinsatz tiefe Einbrüche.

Im nordwestdeutschen Raum kam es gestern nur zu örtlichen Kämpfen. In Bremen hält der Kampfkommandant mit dem Rest der tapferen Besatzung den Nordostteil der Stadt.

An der Donau brach der Feind in Regensburg und Ingolstadt ein. Zwischen Dillingen und Ulm setzten die Amerikaner ihren Vorstoß nach Süden fort. Kämpfe sind in Mindel und im Guenztal im Gange.

Die Armeen in Italien setzten sich hinter dem Po und Tessin ab.

Während die Sowjets im Südabschnitt der Ostfront sich auf starke örtliche Vorstöße beschränkten, setzten sie ihre Angriffe im Raum Brünn mit starken Kräften fort und konnten trotz zäher Gegenwehr der Besatzung in die Stadt eindringen.

Nordwestlich Bautzen, wo bei Meißen die Verbindung mit der Westfront gebildet an der Elbe hergestellt

Der längere Atem

Seit fünfeinhalb Jahren lodert die Fackel des Krieges in Europa. Ihr verzehrendes Feuer hat nach Polen ganz Europa, nach diesem Erdteil schließlich noch zwei weitere erfaßt, Asien und Amerika.

Deutschland mußte einerseits die Ketten abzustreifen versuchen, die ihm in Versailles auferlegt waren und ihm jede Lebensmöglichkeit nahmen. Es hat dies seit 1933 in dem denkbar engsten Rahmen getan und peinlichst vermieden, dabei den Kreis der unmittelbar betroffenen Gebiete, d. h. die deutsche Lebens- und Interessenzone zu überschreiten.

Wenn unsere Feinde behaupten, Deutschland habe eigennützige Machtziele verfolgt und die Unabhängigkeit und Freiheit der kleinen Nationen bedroht, so haben England und Amerika sehr bald durch ihr Verhalten bewiesen, daß ihnen in Wirklichkeit nicht nichts an der Freiheit dieser kleinen Nationen gelegen ist, sondern daß sie selbst bereit waren, diese an Stalin zu verkaufen, ja,

wurde, sind unsere Truppen zum Angriff nach Norden angetreten.

Sicherungsfahrzeuge der Kriegsmarine versenkten östlich Gotenhafen ein sowjetisches Schnellboot und schossen ein weiteres in Brand.

Schwächere amerikanische Kampfverbände führten am Tage Angriffe gegen Orte in Süddeutschland. In der Nacht herrschte über dem Reichsgebiet nur geringe feindliche Kampftätigkeit.

Kleinstunterseeboote versenkten aus dem stark bewachten feindlichen Nachschubverkehr zwischen Themse und Schelde zwei vollbeladene Schiffe mit 8000 BRT.

sie für ihre eigenen imperialistischen Ziele auszubeuten.

Mehr noch! Während die von Deutschland besetzten Feindländer durchaus auskömmlich leben konnten, zum Teil sogar einen fühlbaren wirtschaftlichen und sozialen Aufschwung nahmen, ächzen die "befreiten" Bundesgenossen unter der Hungersnot, Desorganisation und Ausbeutung durch die Engländer und Amerikaner. Besonders groß aber sind die Leiden der Neutralen und jener Völker, die sich den jüdisch-plutokratischen und bolschewistischen Drahtziehern auf Gedeih und Verderb unterwarfen.

Deutschland ist durch den Verrat klug geworden, dem es 1918 zum Opfer fiel. Es weiß, daß alle Versprechungen der Feindseite nichts anderes bedeuten als den Versuch, unser Volk wiederum völlig wehrlos zu machen und es damit der wirtschaftlichen Ausbeutung, persönlichen Versklavung und völkischen Vernichtung auszuliefern.

Zu verlieren haben wir nichts mehr. Wir haben alles verloren und würden durch Kapitulation uns selbst, unsere Zukunft, Frau und Kind preisgeben. Wohl aber haben wir die Chance, uns zu behaupten und einst dann Existenz, Familienleben und unseren sozialen Staat wieder aufzubauen, in dem wir einen noch größeren Wohlstand erreichen werden, als wir ihn vor diesem Kriege bereits genießen konnten.

Dies ist ein fernes, aber ein reales Ziel. Wir wollen es stets vor Augen behalten, wenn die Gegenwart heute Anforderungen an uns stellt, die uns fast unerträglich erscheinen mögen, wenn unser Todfeind uns Wunden schlägt, aus denen das Blut unserer Besten fließt.

In Berlin, in den rauchenden Ruinen der Reichshauptstadt

33 The final issue of the military newspaper *Der Panzerbär*, 29 April 1945.

came to see me. His report and his message: "The Führer has collapsed, he regards the struggle as hopeless now. He does not want to leave Berlin, however, but to stay in his bunker and defend Berlin. When the Russians come he intends to take the consequences and shoot himself. Keitel, Jodl, Bormann, Dönitz and Himmler, the last two by telephone, have tried to change his mind and convince him to leave Berlin, because he can no longer lead from there. But it was all in vain. The Führer has ordered his files, documents and papers to be brought from his rooms to the courtyard to be burned. That is happening at this very moment. The Foreign Minister also appeared, but Hitler didn't want to see him. He called for Goebbels, his wife and the six children, who are all sitting in the bunker with him now."

Why?, I ask him. Christian answered: "They will kill the children, then the adults will commit suicide."

34   Hitler viewing the destroyed Reich Chancellery, 27 April 1945.
To his left is his adjutant *SS Obergruppenführer* Julius Schaub.

35   Entrance to the bunker in the garden of the Reich Chancellery just after the end of the fighting, 2 or 3 May 1945.
On 16 January Hitler transferred his headquarters to the "Führer bunker", which he never left after March 1945. He directed operations for the defence of Berlin from there until his suicide on 30 April.

36 The staged raising of the Red Flag over the Reichstag building, 2 May 1945.
The photographer Yevgeny Khaldeiij had been working for the photo department of the TASS news agency since 1942, documenting events at the front. His effectively staged photos of the raising of the Red Flag over the Reichstag building are especially famous.

37 White sheets hanging on a Berlin house as signs of surrender, 2 May 1945.

38 German and Soviet soldiers killed during the final days of fighting, lying amidst the rubble, early May 1945.

1.3. The Double Capitulation

With the insistence on "unconditional surrender", formulated by the United States and Britain at the Casablanca Conference on 24 January 1943 and adopted by the Soviet Union on 1 May 1943, the Allies had declared the complete military and political subjugation of the "Third Reich" to be their foremost war aim. Separate negotiations, which, in light of impending defeat, segments of the National Socialist leadership favoured in order to isolate the Soviet Union, were thus doomed to failure from the beginning. The "Anti-Hitler Coalition" retained its stability despite obvious conflicts of interest.

In Berlin, General of the Artillery Helmuth Weidling, who had been appointed "Commander of the Defence District of Berlin", was well aware of the hopelessness of the military situation, but nevertheless followed Hitler's orders that the troops remaining in the city should continue to fight. Only after Hitler's suicide on the afternoon of 30 April were serious efforts made to end the war. In the early morning hours of 1 May, General Hans Krebs, the last Army Chief of General Staff, tried to negotiate a cease-fire with the Soviet Colonel-General Chuikov, which was however rejected. One day later General Weidling sent an offer of surrender, which was immediately accepted. At one o'clock in the afternoon of 2 May, in Chuikov's staff command post at Schulenburgring 2 in Tempelhof, Weidling formulated the order to cease all fighting in Berlin.

The capitulation of the Reich capital did not, however, mean the war was over. Admiral of the Fleet Dönitz, whom Hitler had named as his successor, tried at first to avoid a total surrender in order to continue the fight against the "Bolshevik mortal enemy". Thus it came to a series of partial surrenders to the Western Allies. The German Army had already surrendered in Italy on 28 April, followed by the Army Group Southwest on 4 May. On 4 May, at Lüneburg, the German armed forces in Holland, northwest Germany and Denmark also surrendered to the British Commander-in-Chief Field Marshal Montgomery.

Surrender negotiations began on 7 May in Rheims, at the headquarters of the Commander-in-Chief of the Allied Forces, General Eisenhower, but were only concluded after Eisenhower threatened to resume the strategic air war and hand over German prisoners of war to the Soviet Union. The Act of Military Surrender was finally signed by Colonel-General Jodl and Admiral-General von Friedeburg, so that the surrender came into effect at 11.01 p.m. on 8 May.

Since what was signed in Rheims was only an abbreviated version of the Act of Military Surrender originally drawn up in July 1944, Stalin took the opportunity to demand that the whole procedure be repeated with the full text at Soviet headquarters in Berlin-Karlshorst. The signing, dated 8 May, actually took place on 9 May at 12.16 a.m. This document, too, dates the capitulation as becoming effective at 11.01 p.m. on 8 May.

The Second World War in Europe was now over, bringing to an end the National Socialist reign of terror and violence.

Berlin, 2. 5. 45.

B e f e h l.

Am 30. 4. 45. hat sich der Führer selbst entleibt und
damit uns, die wir ihm die Treue geschworen hatten, im
Stich gelassen.
Auf Befehl des Führers glaubt Ihr noch immer um **Berlin**
kämpfen zu müssen, obwohl der Mangel an schweren **Waffen**,
an Munition und die Gesamtlage den Kampf als sinnlos erscheinen lassen.

Jede Stunde, die Ihr weiterkämpft, verlängert die entsetz-
lichen Leiden der Zivilbevölkerung Berlins und unserer
Verwundeten. Jeder, der jetzt noch im Kampf um Berlin

fällt, bringt seine Opfer umsonst.
Im Einvernehmen mit dem Oberkommando der sowjetischen
Truppen fordere ich Euch daher auf, sofort den Kampf ein-
zustellen.

(Weidling)
General der Artillerie
und
Befehlshaber Verteidigungsbereich Berlin

39 General Helmuth Weidling's order to the Berlin troops to
surrender immediately, 2 May 1945.
The order, tape-recorded on 2 May 1945 at the headquarters
of the Soviet General Vassily Chuikov at Schulenburgring 2 in
Tempelhof, was played over loudspeakers to the population of
Berlin.

40 General Weidling leaving the bunker at the Reich Chancellery by the Voßstraße exit, 6 May 1945.
Soviet propaganda presented this photograph as depicting
Weidling's capture on 2 May. It was actually taken during a
"tour of inspection" of the destroyed Berlin by German officers
who were Soviet prisoners of war.

41   A spontaneous victory celebration by Red Army soldiers in front of the Reichstag on 2 May 1945.

Text 15

Journal entry for 2 May 1945 by the Red Army's war correspondent, Michael Guss.

I glance at the clock: on 2 May 1945 at 6 a.m. General Weidling, Commander-in-Chief for the Defence District of Berlin appeared at Chuikov's command post, together with his staff, and surrendered. [...] General Weidling is wearing trousers that are much too short and long stockings and is sitting at a square table in the middle of a small room in the modest flat of a low-level employee. The room is in shadow because the windows have been boarded up. Beside him sits Air Marshal Woytasch ret., face to face Air Marshall Schmid-Dankward. In the corner is the Major I brought along, sitting with his elbows resting on his knees and his chin on his hands, as if paralysed. Across from Weidling sits his Chief of Staff, Colonel of the General Staff von Duvfing. [...]

I enter the room, make a general bow and sit down off to the side. Spasskiij and Mednikov /two Soviet radio reporters/ bring in the equipment and set it up, and Weidling asks whether I understand German; then those present continue their conversation. The colonel, robust and broad-shouldered, who is wearing pince-nez, paces back and forth and reports on what he saw this morning in the various districts of Berlin when he brought the order to cease resistance. "Terrible!" he said. "Just a week ago everything was intact, and now!"

And then he /General Weidling/ read out his order in a monotonous, calm voice, pronouncing each word exactly. After following the recording over his headphones, Spasskiij asked him to begin again, and turned on the set. The Germans sit rigidly in their seats. The only sound in the room is Weidling's matter-of-fact voice.

42   Provisional assembly camp for German wounded and prisoners of war in Unter den Linden, early May 1945.
In the first days after the capitulation, a lack of accomodation
meant that German prisoners of war had to sleep in the open
air in assembly camps.

43   Marshal Georgi K. Zhukov (third from the right), Deputy
Commander-in-Chief of the Soviet Armed Forces since August
1944, in the inner courtyard of the Bendlerblock, headquarters
of the German Army's High Command on 2 May 1945.

44   Route column of german prisoners of war, among them
many very young soldiers, early May 1945.

45   Field Marshal General Wilhelm Keitel (in the middle with marshal's baton) and the German delegation, General Hans-Jürgen Stumpff (on the left) and admiral Hans-Georg von Friedeburg (third on the right), at Tempelhof Airfield, 8 May 1945.

46   The Soviet delegation (left foreground Marshal Zhukov) receiving the surrendering Germans in Berlin-Karlshorst on 8 May 1945.

47   Keitel signing the declaration of unconditional surrender, 9 May 1945.

The signing took place at 12.16 a.m. on 9 May; the document is however dated 8 May, the day when the fighting ended.

Text 16

The English-language text of the Act of Military Surrender of Berlin-Karlshorst, 8 May 1945.

ACT OF MILITARY SURRENDER

1. We the undersigned, acting by authority of the German High Command, hereby surrender unconditionally to the Supreme Commander, Allied Expeditionary Force and simultaneously to the Supreme High Command of the Red Army all forces on land at sea, and in the air who are at this date under German control.

2. The German High Command will at once issue orders to all German military, naval and air authorities and to all forces under German control to cease active operations at 2301 hours Central European time on 8th May 1945, to remain in the positions occupied at that time and to disarm completely, handing over their weapons and equipment to the local allied commanders or officers designated by Representatives of the Allied Supreme Command. No ship, vessel, or aircraft is to be scuttled, or any damage done to their hull, machinery or equipment, and also to

machines of all kinds, armament, apparatus, and all the technical means of prosecution of war in general.

3. The German High Command will at once issue to appropriate commanders, and ensure the carrying out of any further orders issued by the Supreme Commander, Allied Expeditionary Force and by the Supreme High Command of the Red Army.

4. This act of military surrender is without any prejudice to, and will be superseded by any general instrument of surrender imposed by, or on behalf of the United Nations and applicable to GERMANY and the German armed forces as a whole.

5. In the event of the German High Command or any of the forces under their control failing to act in accordance with this Act of Surrender, the Supreme Commander, Allied Expeditionary Force and the Supreme High Command of the Red Army will take such punitive or other actions as they deem appropriate.

6.   This Act is drawn up in English, Russian and German languages. The English and Russian are the only authentic texts.

Signed at Berlin on the 8. day of May, 1945

[signed] Friedeburg [signed] Keitel [signed] Stumpff
        On behalf of the German High Command

[signed] Tedder	[signed] Zhukov
On behalf of the	On behalf of the
Supreme Commander	Supreme High
Allied	Command of the
Expeditionary Force	Red Army

At the signing also were present as witnesses:

[signed] de Lattre de Tassigny	[signed] Spaatz
General, Commander	General, Com-
in Chief	manding United
First French Army	States Strategic
	Air Force

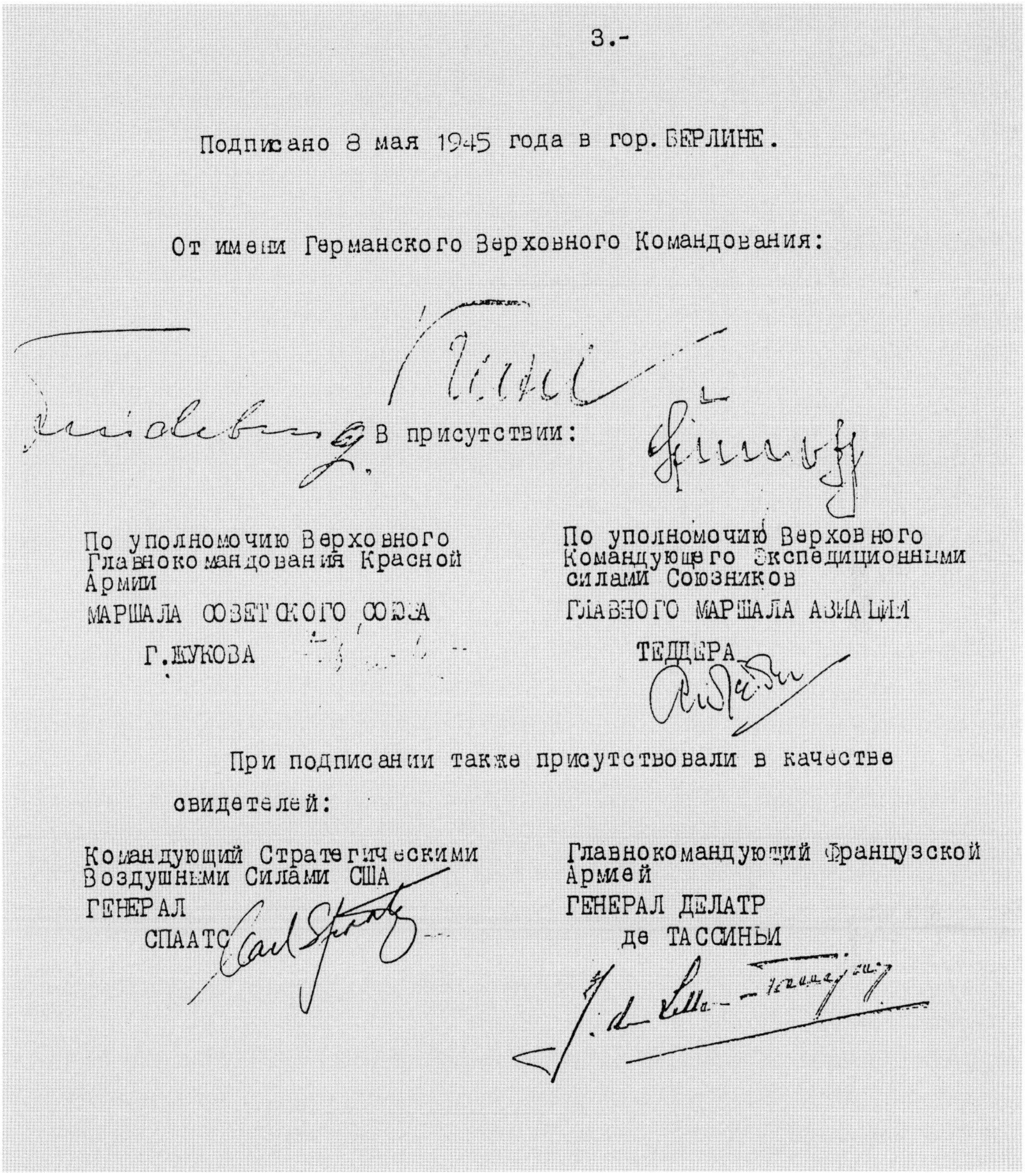

3.-

Подписано 8 мая 1945 года в гор. БЕРЛИНЕ.

От имени Германского Верховного Командования:

В присутствии:

По уполномочию Верховного
Главнокомандования Красной
Армии
МАРШАЛА СОВЕТСКОГО СОЮЗА

Г.ЖУКОВА

По уполномочию Верховного
Командующего Экспедиционными
силами Союзников
ГЛАВНОГО МАРШАЛА АВИАЦИИ

ТЕДДЕРА

При подписании также присутствовали в качестве

свидетелей:

Командующий Стратегическими
Воздушными Силами США
ГЕНЕРАЛ
СПААТС

Главнокомандующий Французской
Армией
ГЕНЕРАЛ ДЕЛАТР
де ТАССИНЬИ

48 The signatures of the Russian-language text of the Act of
Military Surrender, 8 May 1945.

1.4.   The Experience of War

During the final months of the war Berliners' lives were marked not only by the continual air raids but also by the rapidly growing fear of the city's capture by Soviet troops. Scarcely a day and not a night went by without air-raid warnings and in the city's central districts the devastation reached unimaginable proportions. Undisturbed sleep was a thing of the past, and those people with access to a somewhat secure cellar still had to worry not only about their worldly goods but above all about the safety of their closest relatives and friends.

Even if one's house or flat was not completely destroyed, everyday life was a series of ever-new improvisations, black-outs, cut-off heating and water, a deteriorating food supply and the destruction of most forms of transport. To be sure, people conscientiously continued to go to work, but the prerequisites for actually doing anything once there were increasingly absent. People who had been "bombed out" were given temporary shelter and rations. They were joined by the rapidly growing numbers of refugees moving westward before the Red Army.

Considering the extreme stresses and strains to which they were subject, the physical and mental robustness of the Berlin population was remarkable. Despite constant danger to life and limb, the massive destruction of normal living conditions and the prospect of a wholly uncertain future, most displayed an extraordinary capacity to bear suffering and a strong will to survive. National Socialist ideology played only a minor role here in the final months of the war. People were weary of war, and few believed in "wonder weapons" or "final victory" anymore. Among older members of the Peoples' Reserve, for example, enthusiasm was low and "defeatism" common. There were, however, still fanatical Party members who mercilessly pursued remarks or behaviour critical of the regime, and segments of the "Hitler Youth" prepared even now to die for "Führer, Folk and Fatherland". In April and May over 5,000 suicides were registered of Berliners who preferred not to outlive the "Third Reich".

We do not know the total number of Berliners who died as a result of the effects of war. Not only had 300,000 men been inducted into the Army, but 1.2 million people had also been "evacuated" from the city (so that of the 4.3 million people living in Berlin at the beginning of the war only 2.77 million were still in the city). The total losses among the civilian population remaining in Berlin are estimated at about 50,000. Women, children under five years and men over 60 years of age were overrepresented here. As large as this number is, it appears rather low in light of the severity of bombing raids and the intensity of the "Battle of Berlin". As a percentage of population, other German cities suffered far greater losses than Berlin.

49   Notices on the whereabouts of the former residents of a bombed-out house at the corner of Hauptstraße and Hähnelstraße in Schöneberg, early 1945.

50   A message left for relatives and friends on the ground floor of a bombed-out house near Potsdamer Platz, February 1945.

Text 17

Journal entries for 25 and 26 January 1944 by Ursula von Kardorff.

25 January 1944
[…]
The guests will be coming soon. The preparations are finished. The three Frenchmen, who just invited Klaus and me for a bottle of champagne, are the happiest. No air-raid warning in sight. Prospects are good since it's foggy in England. The dining room looks almost as it did in the old days. We polished the parquet as best we could, we've set up a kind of bar and hung blinds, which Mama once painted with flowers, before the cardboard window-panes. Now the doorbell is ringing. I must end now.

26 January 1944
Utterly exhausted. Our party lasted until morning. A friend of Thilenius', Count Widmann, who had just arrived from Prague, said: "So this is how you live among the ruins, dancing on the volcano, and we, who know nothing of bombs, scarcely dare to laugh anymore! The Czech musicians played splendidly. When we found out that they were students Hülsen passed around a plate for money. I believe he collected several hundred marks.

We danced like the possessed. As if someone were standing behind us all with a hunting-whip, as if it were the last time. "Decline of the West" was what we christened the party. The melody *"Bei mir biste scheen"* must have been played twenty times. Herr Remde from the St Pauli Bar next-door, whom we had also invited, provided the red wine.

Schwab, whose father died in prison three months ago, Jutta, whose siblings were burnt alive, Dr Meier, whose father starved to death in a camp – all of them joined in. Everybody wanted to forget his burdens and mourning for a few hours. Joy is also a giver of warmth in these times. We all live only for the moment, but more intensely than ever.

The day after tomorrow a van is coming to take the furniture to Lychow.

Text 18

Theo Findahl's observations on everyday life in the destroyed city, 1945.

Only in the last stage of aerial warfare did it seem that the Berliners finally realised the senselessness and hopelessness of all attempts to rebuild the city in its old form. They became more modest and restricted themselves to attempting to make the ruins as livable as possible. And something strange occurred in the course of this work: before our eyes a small town began to grow up on the remnants of the metropolis. Around the areas destroyed by bombs the industrious ants scurried and hurried, toiling to organise little cells in the piles of wreckage. Unbelievable how many people still lived in the city, how many rooms a city of several million inhabitants had had that were used for something else than living. The gapingly empty first-storey windows in were bricked up and new panes set into the smaller openings, all in a severely practical style. Saving material was the main thing. Particularly enterprising people painted the new walls in light colours, and behind the spotless little windows flower-pots stood before pretty curtains. Whether it was a shop, a pub or a private flat behind the facade, the picture had something of a small town idyll, of a dollhouse, graceful, old-fashioned and cosily German, as in the days of the petty princelings.

51   The belongings of people who have been bombed out in front of a house in Berlin, 1945.

Text 19

Karl Friedrich Borée's description of working conditions at a bank during the bombing raids in the final months of the war, 1954.

For all their unpleasantness, conditions at the bank were not without a certain comedy. The employees, from the head-clerks on down to the stenographers, developed an ant-like zeal to remedy the continually renewed damage. Clearing away debris – which they simply threw out the windows – sweeping, and boarding up windows was their job; they brought the necessary tools and material from home. People developed into specialists, and they were passed around. I couldn't tell: was this the touching German mania for activity and order, was it fear of losing a job or of unwelcome duties, or did they simply enjoy throwing themselves into something other than the usual office round? The courtyard rang with pounding and clanking, but also with cheerful voices.

The whole place in all its shamelessness emitted the ghostly noise of an idling machine. A hollow sound buzzed through the building. One ran down to the cellar to fetch one's files, typewriter and adding machine, then ran back down with them when an early warning sounded. Then came the lunch-break (or an air-raid). In many rooms, work had to stop altogether when the lights went out. The post arrived only in random spurts. Surely this was the case in all businesses and ministries, but obviously nobody had the courage to inform the highest authorities that work in Berlin nowadays was only for show; perhaps those in high places didn't want to admit it either, so that the exodus of government offices and economic centres would not cause a general panic. Naturally there were still some very conscientious people. One day I encountered one departmental head, who was wont to work in the air-raid shelter, doing business with the Estonian government, which no longer existed. The Middle Eastern department corresponded with business partners in Persia long since behind the front.

Finally, entire departments were rendered homeless because the place where they had sat was now in the open air. The hallways filled with rainwater, which dripped down the marble staircases. Head-clerks, forwarding clerks, and stenographers sat shoulder-to-shoulder at long tables. A makeshift stove heated with wood scraps stretched its black pipe right across the room and out the boarded-up window. A few tiny oil-lamps burned with a smoky flame. If anybody had to use the telephone he went into the irreparable next-door room where the phone had happened to survive; it sat on the ground amidst the rubble.

Text 20

Excerpt from Report No. 21 by the "Department of Army Propaganda of the OKW" on the mood of the Berlin populace in the period between 28 February and 6 March 1945, 9 March 1945.

/From reports of individual observations/

23. Executions by firing squad:
In the S-Bahn it was reported that a number of soldiers have been shot as deserters recently. In future, it was said, they will be shot on the spot where they are captured. This is supposed to demonstrate to soldiers and the population how summarily those who break their oath to the Führer will be dealt with. In the Friedrichstraße, it is said, such a shooting has already been carried out.

52 A woman gathering the remains of her belongings in the ruins of her flat, 1945.

24. Communist Agitation:
At Schöneberg Station on 27 February two women coming from Wannsee were chatting about their experiences during the journey. One of them was outraged: "Just imagine, when I was travelling recently from Beelitz to Wannsee, somebody had written 'Kill the Führer!' in a second-class compartment" – apparently the railway employees do not think it necessary to remove such scribblings.

25. Conduct of a Reichsbahn employee:
The little posters printed in blue ink with pictures, text and verses appealing to the population to work harder are hanging in all Berlin stations. These were removed by an eastern female worker on 25 February between 9.00 to 9.30 a.m. When questioned about this, the man with the red cap replied brusquely: "What's the point of that muck! Who needs it?"

Text 21

Excerpt from Report No. 25 by the "Department of Army Propaganda of the OKW" on the mood of the Berlin populace in the period between 30 March and 7 April 1945, 10 April 1945.

Although they usually maintain an outer calm, the mood of the Berliners could hardly sink any lower. It is not the Berliners' way to lose heart and give up easily, but in general people see no way out anymore. And thus they frequently conclude, rationally, that continuing the struggle will only prolong the bloodshed unnecessarily. Their war-weariness is plainly apparent here. People are afraid of renewed severe air-raids and of the coming Soviet assault. Since there is no longer any hope of a turn for the better, the will to defend the city is minimal, and people are asking themselves what the point of all this is. People are facing whatever comes with a certain fatalism expressed as black humour, which certainly hides a good bit of desperation. Women see no sense in leaving Berlin now. Where should they go? No place is safe. And it is all just fate! People keep asking how the leadership can justify its hopes of a positive outcome now. That the Allies might split up before crushing Germany is considered out of the question. If any hope is expressed at all, it is that the British and Americans will reach Berlin before the Soviets. To be sure, the Berliners will stand their ground as before, but it is the general view that, unless some miracle should occur, the war is lost.

53   Tram traffic in Schöneberg at the intersection of Kurfürsten-, Luther- and Keithstraße during the winter of 1944/45.

Text 22

From the Reich Security Main Office's "Reports of Important Events Pertaining to the State Police ", No. 1, on youth cliques, 2 June 1944.

The report shows how wartime conditions opened up new social spaces, in this case for young people, and challenged the National Socialist authorities to take appropriate counter-measures.

2 June 1944

In Berlin 24 youths were arrested who early in 1944 had joined together to form a clique called "Knee-deep". They met almost daily in a café in north-east Berlin. They danced and "jived" to jazz music. One member of the clique let them use his absent parents' flat for rowdy parties where they drank excessively and committed moral outrages with girls. They also assaulted members of the Hitler Youth, tearing off their badges and harrassing them. They usually wore their hair long.

Two members of the clique who were Jewish half-breeds of the first degree [*Mischlinge ersten Grades*] were committed to a labour education camp; twelve boys were sent before a judge of the Juvenile Court.

Text 23

Excerpt from a report by the SS Security Service's Branch II in Wilmersdorf to the Security Service's Main Command for Berlin concerning the mood of the Berlin populace, 17 April 1945.

The basic feeling is that the war has been lost. Peoples' morale has declined accordingly. The few optimists are considered mad; one nonetheless has the impression that even the pessimists are clutching at every available straw. What is certain is that, rationally, nobody can go along anymore, and that the belief in a turn for the better, if it ever existed, is sinking fast. ...

The closer the fronts advance, the greater the worry about whether the Berlin populace can be saved from starvation. As a consequence most people are doing what they can to find food. [...] For lack of a destination, far fewer individuals are leaving Berlin. In contrast, all sorts of government offices and leading figures are hurrying to save themselves. In many offices no work has

been done for the past six weeks. This has become a new source of disquiet that has infected the population, which is speaking quite openly of sabotage. Party offices are disappearing, mainly to Bavaria, the better ones to Landshut and Berchtesgaden. It is said that the Führer and his loyal followers plan to entrench themselves in the latter town if the worst comes to pass. The Ministry of Labour was transferred to Eisenach for a time, but then returned and has now moved on to Bavaria too. Many Reich offices, such as the Reich Office of Metals and the *RAM* [Foreign Ministry] have sent a number of employees on leave or dismissed them altogether.

Text 24

Konrad Warner's account of his experiences at an "Air-raid Damage Office" in January 1944.

On Wednesday morning I went to the Air-raid Damage Office to pick up our Relief Entitlement documents. The office was housed in a theatre. When I arrived it was indescribably crowded. The people obliged to queue here for hours were all telling their stories. Some had had their houses or flats destroyed by H.E. bombs. They had been unable to salvage anything. Others' flats had burned so quickly that they had barely managed to escape with their lives. One person told of burst pipes and floods, the next of people buried alive and mutilated, and all spoke of war, death and extermination.

It became more and more crowded, so that at last we forgot the war and began to protest. It turned into quite a little rebellion. The man issuing documents climbed up on a chair and gave a speech to the people, like they used to do in Parliament. People interrupted him with heckling and insults. He began all over again explaining why it was taking so long to serve people.

The Relief Entitlement document recorded the names of all family members and the damaged or destroyed home. It said that the paper would not be replaced if lost, and that it was only valid for one month in the Reich capital. It was signed by the Lord Mayor. Inside in bold-faced type: "No employed person may leave Berlin! He will be housed here and continue working!"

With this certificate one can get ration cards and special allocations of cigarettes, fruit and candies, wine and soup at one's Ration-card Issue Office. Now one had to return to the Ration-card Issue Office. Many people claimed that they had

54   People who have been bombed out reporting and register-
ing their losses at the "Air-raid Damage Office" in 1944.

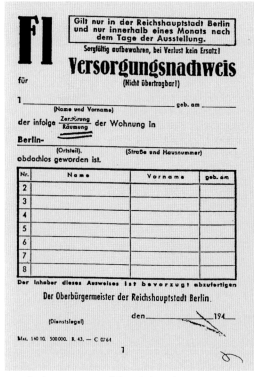

55   The first two pages of the Relief Entitlement [*Versorgung-
snachweis*] document the bombed out received at the "Air-raid
Damage Office", 1944/45.

lost their ration cards and identification cards for other purchases, although this was not the case at all. In this way they were able to live on double rations for two weeks until the new card period began. Anybody would need them after all that effort. Then I went to the issuing office with a big cloth and received sandwiches and the special allocations, which they were giving away for free.

Text 25

Food rations for the 74th allocation period (9 – 29 April 1945) for persons entitled to normal rations and for children up to six years of age per person and day (figures rounded off), 28 March 1945.

56 Bomb-damage claimants receiving a hot meal at a field kitchen on 26 November 1943.

	Persons entitled to normal maintenance	Children
1. Bread	243g	143g
2. Meat	36g	14g
3. Fats	18g	18g
4. Processed cereals	11g	11g
5. Sugar	8g	18g
6. Artificial Honey	—	6g
7. Cheese	3g	3g
8. Curds	6g	6g
9. *Ersatz* coffee	5g	5g

Text 26

Letter from the head of Ration-card Issue Office 10 in Oberschöneweide to the District Mayor of Köpenick, Mathow, concerning supply problems and the resulting disgruntlement among the public, 16 April 1945.

The shortening of bread rations in the 73rd allocation period aroused great anger within all segments of the population. This anger was further increased when the NSV [National Socialist Welfare] issued extra bread ration cards, but only to those citizens who had already received extra bread rations in the 71st period. Mothers of children over six years of age appeared at the Ration-card Issue Office and demanded that we stamp those coupons that were excluded from the supply. When the officials refused, as they had to, the mothers chided them, and the employees

of the Ration-card Issue Office had to listen to some very unkind words. What is more, as of 2 April 1945 whole milk was no longer being supplied to children over the age of six, while the ration cards were still valid until 8 April. There were some particularly sharp words about this. The mothers cried "are our children supposed to starve?" and a few also called out "wait 'til the Russians get here". In my opinion a number of these incidents were caused by the fact that the NSV simply passed on applicants they could not help to the Ration-card Issue Offices, in order to be rid of them. Since they could not be helped here either, even our polite refusals were interpreted as ill will.

Four employees were immediately set to work making out the necessary vouchers for supplying households with coal for cooking. In the first days of issue there was quite a throng. People had to wait 60-90 minutes. Now, however, the stream has been directed into orderly channels.

Since four employees had to be withdrawn from their normal duties a slight backlog has arisen in the issue of purchase permits for shoes and textiles.

There is, naturally, a high degree of tension as a result of the enemy's approach to the Reich capital.

Text 27

Excerpt from Report No. 25 by the "Department of Army Propaganda of the OKW" on the supply situation in the period between 30 March and 7 April 1945, 10 April 1945.

The special bread distribution caused a good deal of bad blood. The organisation of this distri-

Der Luftterror unserer Feinde fügt der Bevölkerung schwere Schäden an Hab und Gut zu.

Die Versorgung der Bombengeschädigten mit den notwendigsten Gebrauchsgütern gehört daher zu den vordringlichsten Aufgaben.

Wer sich zu Unrecht als Bombengeschädigter ausgibt und sich unter Vorspiegelung falscher Tatsachen Vorteile erschleicht, handelt gegen die Volksgemeinschaft.

Die Sondergerichte haben wiederholt gegen derartige Volksschädlinge Todesurteile und langjährige Zuchthausstrafen ausgesprochen.

57 Announcement concerning fraudulent bomb-damage claims, February 1944.

bution was a complete failure, and the *NSV* welfare centres' treatment of applicants aroused great outrage. [...]
The suburban population is highly displeased, since they have not received special allocations and were not eligible for the special bread distribution either.-
The shutting-off of the gas supply has aroused great uneasiness. People are asking how the responsible authorities imagine that neighbourhood assistance is supposed to function when entire blocks of flats or streets depend solely on gas stoves. Quick and sensible action must be taken here.
All the housewives are complaining about the non-allocation of washing agents, since no soap powder has been available for some time now. [...]
There is great dissatisfaction with the public transport situation. Pity all those poor working citizens who have to change once or several times to reach their places of employment. Waiting and more waiting has become the sad slogan for these fellow citizens. In the trains it is also quite apparent that Berliners are becoming increasingly irritable and nervous.

58 Sign warning looters, 1945.
Particularly during the final months of the war, looting and theft became common in the periods of confusion immediately following air-raids.

Text 28

Journal entry by Konrad Warner on thefts during air-raids, January 1944.

I often heard about robberies and thefts during the raids. Friends of mine found a stranger's corpse in their cellar, a young man. He had probably been out stealing because a cabin-trunk they managed to salvage showed signs of attempts to break the lock. The chap apparently collapsed from smoke inhalation and died. Other people had their bags stolen from their cellars or off the street where they had just set them down for a moment. One of my acquaintances, in whose house only the upper storeys had burnt out, had all his linen, shoes and clothing, wine, schnapps and cigarettes stolen right out of the cupboards. In a ladies' lingerie shop one of the owners told me: "I was helping to put out a fire across the street because nothing had happened at our place. And then I helped with the salvage work. When I came home in the morning my entire stock had been cleared out."

59   People waiting to fill their buckets at a water pump, 1945.
The old water pumps which existed almost everywhere in Berlin
became particularly important after the drinking water pipes
were severely damaged by numerous bomb attacks.

Text 29

Journal entry for 29 April 1945 by seventeen-year-old Liselotte G., on the atmosphere before the entry of the Red Army into Berlin.

Some hundred suicides are said to have occurred on this first day in Friedrichshagen. It is a blessing that there is no gas, or even more people would have killed themselves; we might be dead too. I felt such despair! [...] This is what my German Fatherland has come to, without rights, completely at the mercy of foreign powers. But this is what the German people want, they must always submit to somebody, be ground under somebody's heel, otherwise they don't feel right. Once it was Hitler, now it is Stalin's slave-nation. Where is the freedom I long for? Is it never to be ours again? Oh, if Schiller or Kant had experienced these times. If only Dad were here, he would protect us from the enemy mob. Why don't you come?
I wonder if Frau L. is still pure, or whether they have violated her too?

60   Improvised bread-selling on the street shortly after the bomb attack of 3 February 1945.

61   Refugees and homeless people near Lehrter Straße railway station, 1945.

62   Two old men in a debris-littered street, May 1945.

63 Berlin women watching the entry of Soviet T-34 tank convoys at the corner of Yorckstraße and Mehringdamm in Kreuzberg, beginning of May 1945.

64 Shortly after the capitulation – Berliners are making their way through the ruined city between Soviet soldiers and military vehicles, May 1945.
Civilians wear white armbands as signs of surrender.

Text 30

Table giving an overview of the suicide rate in Berlin in 1945.

Time Period	Suicides
Year	
1929	1,678
1932	2,262
1938	2,108
Monthly Average	
1929	140
1932	187
1938	176
1945	
January	117
February	199
March	238
April	3,881
May	977
June	367
July	340
August	263
September	196
October	188
November	154
December	137
Total	7,057
Monthly Average	588

Text 31

Journal entry by Hermann Kasack on his encounter with Soviet soldiers on 27 April 1945.

When we walked out the front door we saw a machine gun set up in the gateway between the narrow front gardens with its muzzle pointed at the broadside of the empty street. The gunners were crouched on the steps. When asked where to go we were told: "To the lawn". The interpreter stayed by the machine gun. I understood. We crossed the street very slowly. On the sandy path before the lawn my wife hugged me again, and I kissed her. "It's all over", I said. "Yes", she said. Somebody asked, "Are we going to be shot now?" – "Yes", I said. I saw that half a dozen graves had been dug in the lawn. How quickly such things happen. We stood next to each other in the middle of the grass, our faces towards our house. So this is how it is, I thought. Time stood still. After a while we were told through the interpreter to go to the opposite side of the street. We turned around, and nobody said a word ..

From the moment that we stepped onto the lawn to be shot, I belonged to the dead. That this death had not been carried out did not make it any less valid ..

Text 32

Journal entry by nineteen-year-old Sabine K. on her recollections of the day of the capitulation in Berlin, 2 May 1945.

I unfortunately could not write any more yesterday. I'm always on the run anyway, since a Russian could come up here at any moment, then I quickly jump under the bed in the little room; it's true that they rape all the girls and older women too. But that comes later.

65 Just after the conquest of Berlin – everyday life in the destroyed city, May 1945.

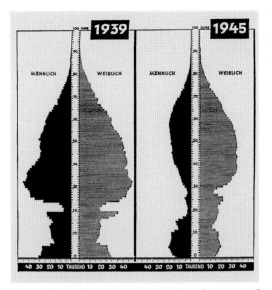

66 The effects of the war on the age and gender structure of the Berlin population, 1949.

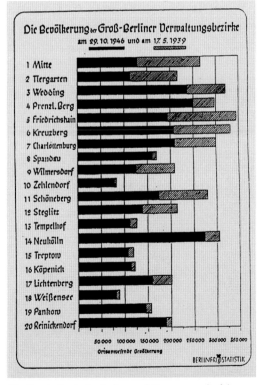

67 The decline in the Berlin population as a result of the war, 1947.
It is striking that the rate of decrease in the population varies greatly from district to district: while in some the number of inhabitants was halved, in others it remained almost constant. The areas hardest hit by the air-raids also experienced the greatest drop in population.

Text 33

The proportional fall in Berlin's population as a result of the war by district, 1947.

Administrative district Sector	Fall in population from 17 May 1939 to 29 October 1946 in %
1. Mitte	52,2
2. Tiergarten	47,2
5. Friedrichshain	44,7
9. Wilmersdorf	39,4
6. Kreuzberg	38,5
11. Schöneberg.	38,1
12. Steglitz	35,3
7. Charlottenburg	30,7
3. Wedding.	27,4
17. Lichtenberg	19,9
4. Prenzlauer Berg . . .	16,6
13. Tempelhof	10,9
14. Neukölln	9,9
15. Treptow	9,6
18. Weißensee	9,1
16. Köpenick.	6,1
19. Pankow	6,1
20. Reinickendorf	5,9
10. Zehlendorf	4,3
8. Spandau	3,5
Greater Berlin	26,6
of which	
Soviet Sector	26,3
American Sector	26,7
British Sector.	31,7
French Sector	19,2

68   Life among the ruins, late May 1945.

69   The sidewalk café at the Hotel am Zoo on Kurfürstendamm, late May 1945.

1.5. The Destroyed City

The destruction wrought by the air war and the fighting after mid-April 1945 changed the city of Berlin – its buildings, squares, streets, bridges and parks, indeed its entire urban structure – radically and violently. The Berlin the National Socialists left behind was, as one study called it, "the largest continuous ruin in Germany and Europe". According to conservative estimates, there were some 55 million cubic metres of debris, but the figure was probably closer to 80 million. "Berlin. The rubble heap near Potsdam", Bert Brecht called it after his return from the USA.

An investigation by the Berlin Central Office of Statistics in 1947 found that of the city's 1.5 million flats almost one-third were uninhabitable; of 5.2. million rooms in the city the figure was almost 40%. Surprisingly, damage was significantly less severe in the industrial sector, so that, measured against 1936 production levels, Berlin's industry was working at about 75% capacity in May 1945. In the central city over one-third of the streets were impassable. Most of the bridges in the city centre had been blown up by German troops during the "Battle of Berlin" and were unusable. The underground and elevated railways were at a complete standstill, and scarcely a bus or railway car had escaped undamaged.

The destruction affected the city's districts very differently. The outlying districts had been targetted much less than the central areas. In the Tiergarten district, for example, some 60% of the buildings were considered uninhabitable, while in Pankow the figure was only 20%. The district of Mitte was hardest hit because of the concentration there of government and administrative offices, which were defended until the last. Here Soviet artillery fire and street-fighting left their mark along with the bombs.

Especially painful was the destruction of many major buildings which particularly reflected Berlin's present and past. These included the palaces and churches, the Philharmonic hall and many theatres, the newspaper publishing quarter and large publishing houses, the imposing hotels, Unter den Linden, Wilhelmstraße, Pariser Platz, Leipziger Platz and Potsdamer Platz. The Zoo and the Tiergarten park had also been destroyed. In the latter, bombs, shelling, fires and subsequent clearing had reduced the number of trees from 200,000 to 7,000.

"This is the second Carthage" remarked Harry Hopkins, a longtime advisor to the American President, after flying over Berlin in 1945. Other observers were also felt moved to compare Berlin with the ruins of antiquity. In November 1945 the American war correspondent and Berlin expert William L. Shirer wrote of "the picture of a metropolis destroyed to the point of unrecognizability". Just after the end of the war, a writer argued in the *New York Times* that the annihilation of Berlin might usher in a renewed civilisation process in Germany. The assertion that "very few people would mourn the disappearance of this unpleasant parvenu among the European capitals" is scarcely surprising, considering the crimes for which the German Reich and with it, the capital, were responsible.

70   Anhalt Station in Kreuzberg, ca. 1945.

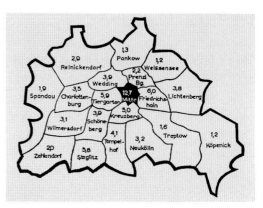

71   The volume of debris in the various districts according to the Berlin Statistical Year Book for 1952 (in millions of cubic metres).

Gebäudezustand nach Beendigung der Kampfhandlungen
Mitteilungen des Hauptvermessungsamtes

Verwaltungsbezirk — Sektor	Von den Gebäuden waren						leicht beschädigt, unbeschädigt		Gebäude insges.[1]
	total zerstört		schwer beschädigt		wieder- herstellbar				
	Zahl	vH	Zahl	vH	Zahl	vH	Zahl	vH	
1 Mitte	3 573	34.6	1 758	17.0	1 580	15.3	3 392	32.9	10 321
2 Tiergarten	2 429	32.2	1 673	22.2	1 150	15.2	2 291	30.4	7 543
3 Wedding	1 666	19.3	736	8.5	1 055	12.3	5 110	59.4	8 608
4 Prenzlauer Berg	689	10.4	460	7.0	725	10.9	4 745	71.6	6 625
5 Friedrichshain	2 179	27.0	1 496	18.5	1 046	12.9	3 317	41.0	8 088
6 Kreuzberg	2 346	26.0	1 250	13.9	1 364	15.1	3 942	43.8	9 009
7 Charlottenburg	1 461	17.7	1 400	16.9	411	5.0	4 996	60.4	8 268
8 Spandau	888	5.1	766	4.4	484	2.8	14 932	86.5	17 266
9 Wilmersdorf	1 085	16.9	902	14.0	1 101	17.2	3 336	51.9	6 424
10 Zehlendorf	722	5.5	835	6.3	1 553	11.8	10 064	76.1	13 220
11 Schöneberg	729	8.8	1 823	22.0	1 319	16.0	4 398	53.2	8 269
12 Steglitz	1 984	11.5	3 045	17.7	1 707	9.9	10 496	60.9	17 232
13 Tempelhof	1 072	8.4	1 274	9.9	2 499	19.5	7 961	62.2	12 806
14 Neukölln	1 331	7.5	774	4.3	1 874	10.5	13 853	77.7	17 837
15 Treptow	581	4.4	466	3.6	431	3.3	11 308	86.7	13 045
16 Köpenick	533	4.7	237	2.1	585	5.2	8 395	74.3	11 299
17 Lichtenberg	1 832	8.2	318	1.4	1 279	5.8	18 792	84.4	22 267
18 Weißensee	719	7.4	39	0.4	577	5.9	8 440	86.3	9 775
19 Pankow	407	2.9	292	2.1	619	4.4	12 467	89.6	13 920
20 Reinickendorf	1 453	6.2	583	2.5	1 489	6.3	19 730	84.0	23 478
Groß-Berlin	27 679	11.3	20 127	8.2	22 848	9.3	171 965	70.1	245 300
davon Sowjetischer Sektor ..	10 513	11.0	5 066	5.3	6 842	7.2	70 856	74.3	95 340
Amerikanischer Sektor	8 184	10.4	9 001	11.5	10 316	13.2	50 714	64.7	78 373
Britischer Sektor	5 863	14.8	4 741	12.0	3 146	8.0	25 555	64.7	39 501
Französischer Sektor ..	3 119	9.7	1 319	4.1	2 544	7.9	24 840	77.4	32 086

[1]) Einschl. der unerkundeten Gebäude, insgesamt 2681 oder 1.1 vH aller Gebäude.

72   Statistical survey by the Central Surveyor's Office on the condition of buildings after the end of fighting in Berlin on 2 May 1945, 1946.

Text 34

From the chapter *"Am Alexanderplatz"* in Alfred Döblin's autobiographical *"Schicksalsreise"* of 1949.

Döblin (1878-1957), a physician who published the famous Berlin novel *Berlin Alexanderplatz* in 1929, emigrated to the USA via France in 1933 and returned to Germany in 1947/48 as an officer of the French occupation forces.

The city again. We see the sad rows of skeletal houses, the empty façades, all that fire and the furies of war have left behind. Yes, something did happen here, I saw it once again. This was the spectre's primary theatre. It was here that crime spread, that the people let themselves be lulled, here were singing youth, enthusiastic onlookers. It rolled through the streets in waves, splashing off the walls of the buildings, which have now fallen on their foreheads. Just try to avoid thinking about judgment here. The people who lived here then certainly did not participate by the millions. All they did was to watch the celebration of the witches' sabbath. But then their houses collapsed and people were killed. Such terrible verdicts are issued by history's court. The streets. This is all so removed from what went before. It is no longer the city I once knew. But it has been brought home to me in a new way: struck and marked by a divine blast. During the discussion I also said: you need to sit among the ruins for a long time, to let them get to you, and experience the pain and the judgment fully. Yes, this is very much my business.

73 The destroyed gasometer in Bayreuther Straße (today: Welserstraße) in the Schöneberg district, 1945.
Viktoria-Luise-Platz is in the background.

Text 35

The English journalist Isaac Deutscher in a report on the destroyed Berlin for "The Observer" newspaper, 1946.

When the buildings lose their deceptively solid appearance, Berlin evokes the impression of a miraculously well-preserved ruin of classical antiquity – like Pompeii or Ostia – on a gigantic scale. The emptiness of many streets intensifies the similarity to an excavated city.

Text 36

Compilation of data on the extent of destruction in Berlin in May 1945 according to statistics reported by the Berlin municipal authority [*Magistrat*] in the years 1945-1947.

The Extent of Destruction in Berlin in May 1945

1. Housing:
Of 1,562,000 flats only 370,000 had remained undamaged. [...] In Berlin-Mitte, for example, 60.7% of housing had been destroyed, and in Friedrichshain 54.3%.

2. Public Services
37 out of 38 gas tanks had been damaged. The eight gasworks, 50–60% destroyed, had stopped working. The gas mains were 99.9% inoperable.
Not a single one of the city's ca. 100,000 electric or gas streetlamps was functioning.
The 19 waterworks were, to be sure, only partially destroyed, but 2,000 defects in the pipe system cut off the water supply. The 87 pumpworks of the city's drainage system were out of order; 60% had been destroyed. The pipe system had 3000 defects.[...]
122 out of 188 post offices had been seriously damaged. The telephone system's 46 exchanges were out of commission; alongside the defects in the exchanges themselves many cables had also been interrupted.

3. Transport
Of 4,300 km of streets 1,350 were destroyed, particularly the arterial and exit roads.
Of 166 larger highway bridges 122 had been destroyed.
Of 153,000 motor vehicles only 115 were in running order.

95% of the tram system's overhead contact lines were no longer intact.
2,739 of 2,832 tram cars, 1,056 of 1,101 underground railway cars, and 649 of 667 buses were damaged.

4. Public Health
The 366 public health offices, clinics and other institutions were not spared by the war. Of 33,000 hospital beds, 24,000 were unusable. Not one of the city's 400 ambulances was operational.

5. Education and Culture
Of 649 school buildings 149 had been completely destroyed, 147 severely damaged, 292 slightly damaged, and 81 had been put to other uses. Of 22,730 classrooms some 20,000 had been destroyed. Many university and technical college buildings had been heavily damaged, along with their valuable equipment. Of 106 public libraries many had been bombed and burnt out.[...]
The museums had all been affected by air-raids and street combat. During the final days of the war, in particular, the SS had entrenched themselves in the city centre's museums, using them as pockets of resistance.
19 theatres and concert halls had been completely and 13 partially destroyed. Of some 400 cinemas only 20 were open.

6. Sport
Only 38 of Berlin's 416 gymnasiums survived.
Of 151 athletic grounds 40 were severely damaged and 111 could be reopened after some time.
9 of 12 indoor swimming-pools had been largely destroyed.

7. Industry, Commerce and the Trades
In the motor industry, only 3% of machine tools survived. With much labour and patience some 25% of the machines salvaged from the rubble could be made usable again. [...]
The war had spared only 1,000 hotel beds out of 24,000. In the catering trade 9,500 of 12,000 firms had been destroyed. Of the ca. 1,600 cleaning establishments [laundries, dyeworks, etc.] 1000 were no longer in business.
Of 19 covered markets 8 had been destroyed.
The retail trade had also been very hard hit: of 1,829 chemist's shops only 372 were open, of 3,312 soap shops 1,017, of 788 paint and wallpaper shops only 40, of 853 shops for medical, photographic, and x-ray supplies 70, of 1,650 radio and electric shops 800 and of some 600 furniture and woodworking firms ca. 200 were still serving the public.

74   The ruins of the Ministry of Propaganda at Wilhelmplatz 8–9 in 1946.

Parts of the new complex built in the Thirties are visible in the background.

Text 37

The English writer Stephen Spender's impressions of the destruction in Berlin in 1945.

The Reichstag and the Chancellory are already sights for sightseers, as they might well be in another five hundred years. They are scenes of a collapse so complete that it already has the remoteness of all final disasters which make a dramatic and ghostly impression whilst at the same time withdrawing their secrets and leaving everything to the imagination. The last days of Berlin are as much matters for speculation as the last days of an empire in some remote epoch: one goes to the ruins with the same sense of wonder, the same straining of the imagination, as one goes to the Colosseum at Rome.

75   A view from the west of the New Reich Chancellery in Voßstraße, completed in 1938/39 under the direction of Albert Speer, 1945.

Text 38

Journal entry for 3 November 1945 by the American CBS correspondent William L. Shirer.

How can one find words to convey truthfully and accurately the picture of a great capital destroyed almost beyond recognition; of a once almighty nation that ceased to exist; of a conquering people who were so brutally arrogant and so blindly sure of their mission as the master race when I departed from here five years ago, and whom you now see poking about their ruins, broken, dazed, shivering, hungry human beings without will or purpose or direction.

76   The main building of Berlin's Technical University in July 1945.
The building, with its 33,600 square metres of floor space, was severely damaged by a bomb attack in 1943. The partially destroyed south wing was rebuilt after 1950.

77   The ruins of the former Royal Palace in May 1945.
After the Berlin Palace lost its function as the residence of the
Hohenzollerns in 1918 large segments were let to various users,
mainly museums. After the National Socialists took power in
1933 the Reich Chamber of Visual Arts resided in a transverse
wing of the Palace.

The Palace compound was severely damaged by the bombing
of 3 February 1945 and by artillery fire during the conquest of
Berlin. On 30 December 1950 the last portion of the building
left standing, the Eosander portal, was blown up.

78   The Hotel Kaiserhof at Wilhelmplatz, ca. 1945.
The "Kaiserhof" had been Hitler's Berlin headquarters before
the National Socialists assumed power in 1933.

79   St Hedwig's Cathedral in Berlin-Mitte, 1945.

80   The façade of the destroyed synagogue in Lindenstraße in Kreuzberg, 1949.
Of 29 Berlin synagogues listed in a post-war statistic only nine had been damaged as a direct result of war. The remaining 20, including the Lindenstraße synagogue, had sustained varying degrees of damage during the pogroms of 9 November 1938 ("Reichskristallnacht").

81   The Philharmonic hall in Bernburger Straße, May 1945.

Text 39

Gottfried Bermann Fischer in a letter to his wife Brigitte after his return to Berlin, 1947.

The old centre of Berlin, Wilhelmsplatz with the Kaiserhof, the Ministry of Propaganda... the Reich Chancellery are bizarre ruins – Friedrichstraße, Leipzigerstraße, Potsdamerplatz are completely dead, the occasional cyclist – a pedestrian, whose footsteps echo loudly through the wasteland, in broad daylight. A gust of wind blows white clouds of dust in your face.
Potsdamer [Platz] Station a high wall with the main staircase and nothing behind it ... The Kurfürstendamm a glorified village street. The facades are still standing. People crawl out of the debris from someplace ... At Wittenbergplatz the true horror begins. Nothing remains there but a great wilderness of rubble, in which one wanders streets so foreign that after a while one no longer knows where one is at all ... The Tiergarten is a sort of refuse pit with allotment gardens.
Over all this bustle gleam the ghostly Hohenzollerns, who have outlasted everything, and whom for some ungodly reason nobody has cleared away. Diana sits lonely upon her horse, solitary and abandoned, to her right the mighty Russian monument, behind it the burnt-out Reichstag with its hidden dome, and behind that the Victory Column with the Tricolore and the Union Jack ...

82 Hertie Department Store (until 1935 Hermann Tietz department store) at Alexanderplatz, 1945.

Text 40

From the chapter "Am Alexanderplatz" in Alfred Döblin's autobiographical "Schicksalsreise" of 1949.

The underground brought us to Alexanderplatz in the afternoon. Everything is still recognizable, but silenced. [...] I still know this square. I already knew it before the mighty Tietz Palace had even been erected yet, the same palace that has now been knocked down, dome and all. (The building looks like a man whose neck has been broken with a blow and his skull shoved down into his chest.) No, all of this is history, it is past. Here, like the Friedrichstraße, Lützowplatz, Stettin Railway Station, everything is smashed and trampled. A human settlement that took centuries to build – destroyed. Much effort was devoted to the matter. They assembled riches, but were unable to master the whole. In the end everything collapsed. But the destruction did not proceed from this place and its people. Here peaceful life pulsated, as human life does, with all its frailties, vices and depravity. This sank down and was sacrificed, the houses, shops, cafés, the restaurants, the little hidden hotels, Aschinger's, and with them all the objects that make everyday life worth living. There was nothing excessive or violent here. And if this has all declined and fallen now, decaying into mere masonry, the submarine that destroyed everything in its wake still did not come from here.

Text 41

Excerpt from Arnold Zweig's 1948 "Fahrt durch die Ruinenstadt".

Nobody who walks through the ruined city of Berlin with his eyes and heart open can escape the realization that this is the backkick of total war. It was here that it was unleashed: a hundred thousand throats yelled their assent in the Sport Palace – and so a hundred thousand houses here are reduced to rubble, including that very Sport Palace. Berlin paid dearly for Hitler's and Goebbels' rhetorical sport.

83 The destroyed Deutschlandhalle, the roof of which had been removed, after 1945.

84 The remains of the burnt-out Sport Palace in Potsdamer Straße, 1945.
The Sport Palace was not only the scene of spectacular sporting events such as six-day races or boxing matches, but also served as a venue for National Socialist propaganda events.

85 The devastated Friedrichstraße looking southwards, July 1945.

86   An AEG (*Allgemeine Elektrizitäts Gesellschaft*) generator
factory, July 1945.

Text 42

**From the article *"Deutsches Bekenntnis"*
by Johannes R. Becher, which appeared in
the journal *Aufbau* in September 1945.**

Half a room floats at a dizzying height above the
abyss of a debris-choked courtyard, hopelessly
solitary in the ruined wasteland of a neighbourhood put to death, with table, piano, sofa, chairs
and two walls hung with paintings: unaware that
the merest gust of wind could sweep all away
into the void. Eerily, from the backdrop of a
burnt-out and dead world, a woman steps
through an invisible back-door onto the stage,
and, holding a watering-can before her, feels her
way towards the table; a balcony, too, over the
rubble realm, as if raised up for a moment, and it
is as if it were bowing down again, suspended.

Text 43

Losses of flats and rooms in Berlin as a direct result ot war according to 1947 statistics.

District	Flats on 1.1.43	Flats on 13.4.46	Decrease in %	Rooms on 1.1.43	Rooms on 13.4.46	Decrease in %
Mitte	96.430	44.195	54,2	291.423	113.632	61,0
Tiergarten	75.215	37.063	50,7	248.572	102.221	58,9
Wedding	121.826	83.729	31,3	324.632	210.779	35,1
Prenzlauer Berg	113.468	89.672	21,0	329.302	241.328	26,7
Friedrichshain	132.779	65.334	50,8	354.821	164.079	53,8
Kreuzberg	129.487	76.505	40,9	368.395	188.693	48,8
Charlottenburg	102.673	63.327	38,3	392.568	209.372	46,7
Spandau	57.167	49.406	13,6	190.146	150.721	20,7
Wilmersdorf	72.738	41.596	42,8	324.264	150.448	53,6
Zehlendorf	26.153	20.353	22,2	129.695	85.738	33,9
Schöneberg	93.641	60.168	35,7	370.759	197.341	46,8
Steglitz	72.100	39.769	44,8	305.752	143.938	52,9
Tempelhof	45.303	35.658	21,3	168.949	114.902	32,0
Neukölln	113.640	96.328	15,2	339.386	270.477	20,3
Treptow	42.364	36.190	14,6	139.681	111.778	20,0
Köpenick	43.547	38.432	11,7	155.231	118.349	23,8
Lichtenberg	69.748	50.179	28,1	222.529	145.506	34,8
Weißensee	31.558	26.606	15,7	100.283	77.996	22,2
Pankow	53.520	48.812	8,8	187.002	150.465	19,5
Reinickendorf	69.284	61.936	10,6	241.610	193.340	20,0
Total	1.562.641	1.065.258	31,8	5.185.000	3.140.603	39,4

87   Bayerischer Platz in Schöneberg, ca. 1946.
The *Bayerische Viertel* (Bavarian Quarter) in Schöneberg, a purely residential area, was largely destroyed by several bomb attacks.

88   Tiled stoves left standing in the ruins of a house in Berlin-Mitte, November 1947.

89   Gleisdreieck elevated railway station, 1946.

Text 44

Report of 1947 by Dr. Walther Schneider, First Director of the *BVG*, on the destruction and reconstruction of Berlin's municipal public transport.

War damage to public transport was no less severe than the destruction of the city itself. The underground, which lies relatively close to the road surface, experienced a number of tunnel collapses to which only makeshift repairs could be made during the war and which, at the end of the war, brought the entire underground rail system to a halt. In addition, blasts to an underground intersection between the railway lines and the Landwehrkanal in the final days of the war meant that a large portion of the tunnels on the most important central underground lines were completely under water. As to the trams, the overhead contact lines suffered most, since 95% of them had collapsed by the end of the fighting. The bus system was most affected by the loss of the vehicles, which was also great in the tram and underground railway. Aside from the diversion of a large number of omnibuses for directly military purposes, the vehicles were also so severely damaged by bombs and fire that by the end of the war only 18 of 800 omnibuses were operational. If one also considers that the tram and omnibus depots as well as the workshops for

all three transport systems suffered heavy damage and that Berlin Transport's [*BVG*] central administrative offices had been totally destroyed by bombs, fire and water, one must see that by the end of the war, in late April and early May 1945, we were left with an immeasurable field of debris and a public transport system at a complete stillstand.

Text 45

Journal entry for 31 October 1945 by the American CBS correspondent William L. Shirer.

But, ah, Berlin this morning! The utter wasteland where once stood the proud capital of the regime that Hitler said would last a thousand years! [...]
It had happened before, of course. Babylon and Carthage. And had not Rome been sacked by the Germanic barbarians? But I don't think there has ever been such destruction on such a scale as this.

90   The remains of Admiral-Scheer-Brücke at Humboldthafen,
1945.

91   The collapsed Stubenrauchbrücke over the Teltowkanal in
Tempelhof, September 1945.

2. The Legacy: The Capital of the "Third Reich"

2.1. The Destruction of Cities on Orders from Berlin

The destruction of Berlin by Allied air and ground troops was preceded by the destruction of numerous European cities by the German armed forces. The planning and command centres for these campaigns of destruction were based, either directly or indirectly, in Berlin.

It had become apparent even before the Second World War that the industrialisation and technologisation of warfare would signal a new quality of destruction and annihilation for civilian as well as military populations. To this day, the small Basque city of Guernica, destroyed by the German Air Force's "Legion Condor" on 27 April 1937, remains a symbol of the inhumanity of modern warfare.

The German war of conquest against Poland in September 1939 had already been characterised by massive aerial attacks on urban population centres: within a few days the German Air Force dropped almost 6,000 tons of bombs on Warsaw, which was severely destroyed. The final destruction of the city occurred in October 1944 after the Warsaw Uprising. German warfare led to the destruction of a number of cities in the west as well: Rotterdam's city centre was completely demolished on 14 May 1940, and French cities, including Paris, Marseilles, Dijon, Lyon and St Etienne were bombed in order to demoralise the population.

In August and September of 1940 the "Battle of Britain" was supposed to prepare the way for a German invasion of Great Britain ("Operation Sea Lion"). After the plans for invasion were deferred, the German Air Force increasingly began to bomb residential areas as well. Alongside continuing assaults on central London, the bombing of Coventry on 14-15 November 1940 and the so-called "Baedeker blitz" on militarily insignificant cultural centres such as Canterbury, Bath and York in particular represented a radical departure from the forms of warfare common up to that point. After the loss of air sovereignty to the British and American Air Forces, from the summer of 1944 on the German Air Force began to deploy V1 flying bombs and later also remote-controlled V2 rockets against English cities, particularly London. Recent estimates suggest that the air war against Britain claimed some 60,000 civilian lives; between July 1940 and July 1941 alone 350,000 houses were registered as uninhabitable.

While the German Army still attempted to justify the destruction of cities in Western Europe with military constraints, this was no longer considered necessary during the war against the Soviet Union. Countless Soviet cities were completely razed by air-raids and artillery fire. In the context of the ideological war of annihilation German troops worked together with Special Units of the SS and SD (Security Service) to destroy numerous smaller towns as well. In Leningrad, whose population was systematically starved out, over 800,000 people died despite the ultimate success of resistance to the blockade.

Last but not least one must recall the cities that fell victim to "punitive actions" against resistance activities. Lidice in Czechoslovakia in 1942 and Oradour-sur-Glane in France in 1944 are two sites that remain symbols of this massacre and devastation.

Text 46

Excerpt from an Air Force General Staff order of 10 September 1939 regarding the bombing of Warsaw.

The assault is to be regarded as retaliation for the crimes committed against German soldiers and has as its objective the annihilation of the "Waterside". It is important that the first attack achieve massive destruction in the densely-populated districts of the city.

Text 47

From a telex sent by Flight Commander seconded for special duty [*Fliegerführer z.b.V.*] Brigadier General Wolfram von Richthofen to the Air Force General Staff, 23 September 1939.

1. Assault on Warsaw discussed with Army Group and 8th Army leading the action. Communication with 8th Army secured.
2. Army intends to approach the inner city in a 2-stage frontal attack in the south and northwest, to isolate it and force surrender through shelling and starvation.
[...]
4. If the Flight Commander seconded for special duty is so instructed, all efforts will be made to obliterate Warsaw altogether, all the more so because in future only a border customs office.
5. Urgently request ultimate possibility of fire and terror attacks as a large-scale effort. For this a Heinkel III squadron with combat landing field Grojek necessary. Intend He 111 squadron to drop only incendiary bombs, dive bombers and K.G. 77 H.E. bombs. The latter day and night.
[...]

Text 48

From the personal journal of Colonel Otto Hoffmann von Waldau, Chief of Operations for the Air Force Operations Staff, 25 May 1940.

The attack of 2 brigade and dive bomber groups turned South Rotterdam into a pile of rubble that would stand up to any comparison with Warsaw. The total surrender of Holland followed after only 2 hours. The case of Holland was closed.

Text 49

From a memorandum of 30 June 1940 by Chief of the Armed Forces Operations Office [*Wehrmachtführungsamt, WFA*] of the Armed Forces High Command Brigadier General Alfred Jodl on the continuation of the war against England.

The German expectation that, after the surrender of France, the English government would seek to negotiate proved unrealistic. For this reason the military leadership began preparations for a landing on the British Isles under the code-name "Sea Lion". The Air Force was accorded a prominent role in preparations for the landing. After plans for operation "Sea Lion" were deferred in September 1940, the Air Force increased its air-raids on English population centres.

Chief of the *WFA*   30.6.40

The continuation of the war against England.

If political means cannot achieve the desired end, England's will to resist must be broken by force
a) by the fight against the English motherland

92   The destroyed St Lawrence's Church in Rotterdam, 1940.
The bombing of Rotterdam by the German Air Force was
intended to effect a more rapid surrender of the Dutch troops.
The assault brought the air war to a new level in that – in contrast to Warsaw in 1939, which the Polish government had
declared a military stronghold – for the first time a city not
declared a military object was bombed.

93   Coventry Cathedral after the bombing of 14 November
1940, 9 December 1940.
Although the night raid on Coventry in the English Midlands –
code-named "Moonlight Sonata" – was conceived primarily as
an assault on the city's numerous armaments plants, mainly
civilian targets were hit and destroyed. In Germany the complete destruction of urban settlements was known henceforth by
the cynical term "coventrying".

94 The destroyed city centre of Sevastopol after its capture by the German Army, 2 July 1942.
During a siege lasting 250 days, Sevastopol was under constant artillery fire and bombardment. The siege and storming of the city was repeated in 1944 – this time by the Red Army.

95 Bombed-out houses and businesses in London, photographed from St Paul's Cathedral on 16 May 1941.

b) by the extension of the war on the periphery. There are 3 possibilities for a:

[...]

2.) terror attacks against English population centres

[...]

If we succeed in neutralising the aircraft industry plants concentrated around London and Birmingham the English Air Force can no longer be renewed. This would mean the end of England's capacity for military action against Germany, since the English fleet's blockade effect no longer has any capacity to decide the outcome of the war. This first and foremost objective of the campaign against England is supplemented at the same time by the campaign against the English storage dumps as well as import and export by sea and in the harbours.

Together with propaganda and occasional terror attacks -portrayed as retaliation – this increasing deterioration of the English food supply will cripple and finally break the people's will to resist, thus forcing the government to surrender.

[...]

[signed] Jodl

Text 50

From a speech by Hitler on the bombing of English cities, given at the opening of Wartime Winter Relief in Berlin's Sport Palace on 4 September 1940.

And if the British Air Force is dropping two or three or four thousand kilograms of bombs, then we will drop 150,000, 180,000, 230,000, 300,000, 400,000, one million kilograms a night. If they declare that they will make massive assaults on our cities, then we will eradicate their cities!

Text 51

Excerpt from the war diary of the High Command of the 6th Army concerning German actions against Soviet cities, 20 October 1941.

The Army Group South conveys the Führer's following declaration of intent:
It would be irresponsible to risk the lives of German soldiers to save Russian cities from the danger of fire or to feed their populations at the

96   A small town in Russia, ca. 1942.
Since the houses were typically built of wood, only the brick chimneys were left standing.

97 Recovering victims of German artillery fire in Leningrad, 1941.
The city of Leningrad, which was completely cut off from all land routes by German and Finnish siege troops, had to receive its supplies from September 1941 until 1943 over the water or ice of southern Lake Ladoga. About one-fourth of the city's 3.2 million inhabitants died of starvation or disease. The city was only liberated in January 1944, after 900 days under siege.

expense of the German homeland. The chaos in Russia will increase accordingly the more the population of Soviet Russian cities flees towards the Russian interior. The cities are thus to be worn down with artillery fire before their capture, and their populations made to flee. All commanders are to be notified of these measures.

Addition of the Army High Command (AOK):
The conduct of the troops in case of fires has been dealt with in the Commander-in-Chief's instructions of 10.10.41 on conduct in the Eastern Area. Artillery fire is to be used in fighting near the cities of Kharkov and Belgorod, including inhabited districts of the cities. The flight of the population eastwards is to be promoted during and after the occupation of the city.

Text 52

From Army Chief of General Staff General Franz Halder's notes on Hitler's plans for Moscow and Leningrad, 8 July 1941.

12.30 Report to the Führer
[...]
2. The Führer is determined to raze Moscow and Leningrad in order to prevent people remaining there whom we would have to feed during the winter. The cities are to be destroyed by the Air Force. Tanks must not be used for this purpose. "A national catastrophe that will rob not merely Bolshevism but also Muscovitism of its centres".

Text 53

Report notes of the Department of National Defence in the *OKW/WFSt* on the destruction of Leningrad, 24 September 1941.

Secret Commando Matter
Department of National Defence
F.H.Qu., 21.9.41
09119/41 gKdos. (I Op.)
6 copies
6th copy

Report notes Leningrad

Possibilities:
1. Occupy the city, i.e., proceed as we have done with other large Russian cities:
To be rejected because we would then be responsible for provisions.

98   The ruined marketplace in Warsaw's old town after the systematic destruction of the entire city centre, late 1944.

2. Tightly cut off the city, preferably with an electric fence guarded by machine guns:
Disadvantages: of some 2 million people the weaker ones would starve to death within the foreseeable future, while the stronger would secure all food for themselves and survive. Danger of epidemics which would spread to our front. It is also doubtful whether our soldiers can be expected to shoot at the women and children who try to escape.
3. Remove the women, children and old people through gateways in the ring of encirclement and let the rest starve to death:
[...]
It is recommended that:
[...]
b) We begin by hermetically sealing off Leningrad, and then crush the city with artillery and air attacks so far as possible (at first only limited Air Force personnel available!).
c) After the city has been softened up by terror and incipient starvation a few gateways will be opened and the helpless released. As far as possible evacuation to the Russian interior. The rest will automatically disperse throughout the country.

d) The rest of the "fortress occupants" will be left to their own devices over the winter. In the spring we will enter the city (if the Finns do so first we will not object), take those still alive to the Russian interior or prisoner, blow up the remaining buildings and turn over the area north of the Neva to the Finns.

[signed] von Loßberg

Text 54

From the interrogation on 29 January 1946 of General Heinz Guderian by the Polish public prosecutor Jerzy Sawicki, who was admitted as counsel to the International Military Tribunal at Nuremberg.

The military uprising against the German occupation forces, which was organised in late summer 1944 by the Polish "Home Army" under the command of General Tadeusz Count Bór-Komorowski, had been discussed beforehand with the government in exile in London and with the Western Allies. Faced with superior German numbers and a lack of support from the Soviet troops who had advanced to just before Warsaw, the "Home Army" surrendered on 2 October 1944. The German troops reacted by systematically destroying entire districts of the city, as they had done after putting down the Warsaw Ghetto uprising in April and May 1943.

The razing of the city centre, purportedly ordered out of military necessity, but actually part of the German Army's "scorched earth" policy, was carried out by systematic explosions and the shelling of individual buildings and streets.

(Pr.= Prosecutor; D. = Defendant Guderian)

Pr. Hadn't you heard that after the civilian population left Warsaw the city was flattened and that regular military units participated in this?

D. We erected military fortifications because Warsaw was on the front line. In those places where it was necessary to create open terrain for the artillery entire blocks of houses had to be destroyed.

Pr. Aren't you aware that one street after another was razed to the ground?

D. I knew about it from a photo album which Fegelein showed me at Hitler's headquarters. But this was not done on my orders, and was never my intention. I admit that this measure was not justified by any military necessity. The erection of fortifications, which was dictated by such necessities, was in itself terrible enough for Warsaw, but it was not excessive. Military necessity called for the creation of a defensive position on the Weichsel. This became unavoidable at the point when Warsaw was incorporated into the front line.

Pr. What did Fegelein say to you when he showed you the album?

D. He showed it to the *Führer* and said, "Here is the album. I do not know who took the pictures, but they reflect the current situation in Warsaw". The album contained shots of all the destruction.

Text 55

Journal entry by the Governor-General of Poland, Hans Frank, 5 August 1944.

20.05 The Governor-General sends the following telex to Reich Minister Dr Lammers:

...

The greater part of the city of Warsaw is in flames. Burning down houses is the surest way to rob the insurgents of hiding-places. The German special troops [*Einsatztruppen*] began combat action at three sites in the outlying districts at about 10 this morning. This has not yet had any perceptible effect on the city centre, in the sense of an improvement in the situation of the Germans in the area surrounded by barricades.

In the city, with its millions of inhabitants, the misery is unimaginable. After this uprising and its suppression Warsaw will have rightfully reverted or submitted to the fate it deserves – total annihilation. ...

99   A V-2 strikes in the London district of West Hampstead on 17 March 1945.
In the face of threatened defeat, the so-called retaliation weapons [*Vergeltungswaffen, V-Waffen*] were supposed to effect a turning-point in the war. Since the summer of 1944 the undifferentiated and – from a military standpoint – unsuccessful air war against England had been fought with V-1 missiles. The bombardment of London with V-2 missiles in 1945 had at most psychological significance, since the Allies were expecting further revenge attacks using new "wonder weapons", including chemical warfare.

2.2. Berliners and Nazi Rule

Unlike Munich or Nuremberg, Berlin was a city in which the National Socialists initially had trouble establishing themselves. Berlin was never a major electoral centre for the NSDAP; it was a "red" city in which Social Democrats and Communists dominated elections. Even on 4 March 1933, when the NSDAP received nearly 44% of the national vote in the Reichstag elections, the figure in Berlin was only 34.6%. In middle-class districts, however, the alliance of National Socialists and German Nationalists managed to achieve clear majorities.

After the successful "seizure of power", the systematic and brutal elimination of all political opponents, Berlin quickly became a city in which Hitler and the National Socialist movement could dramatise their power and celebrate their triumphs. Berlin was the central stage for the "Third Reich's" self-presentation. On "Führer's birthday", the 20th of April, the "day of national labour", the first of May, for state visits or major political events such as the "anschluss" of Austria, the people of Berlin were at once cheering backdrop and active participants in the demonstrations, parades and rallies. The corrupting effects of power and success were visible even in those segments of the population initially sceptical of or hostile to the Nazi system.

Even under the double grip of terror and propaganda, elements of urban life survived in Berlin, managing to escape the political stranglehold at least to some extent. During the 1936 Olympics, in particular, these elements were used for propaganda purposes in order to present a cosmopolitan image to the outside world. Thus for a time even openly anti-Semitic slogans and measures were avoided.

The beginning of war in 1939 aroused as little jubilation in Berlin as elsewhere in Germany. The militarily successful "blitzkrieg" actions, however, turned public opinion around. In 1940 enthusiasm for the victory over France gripped even those who up until then had rejected Hitler's war policy as an irresponsible adventure. Once again, as in 1936 and 1938, the Berlin population largely identified with the apparently victorious "Third Reich". Despite impressive initial military successes there was no such approval of the war against the Soviet Union and by Stalingrad, at the latest, a final disenchantment had set in. When Goebbels declared "total war" in February 1943 those who cheered him were not "the Berliners" but hand-picked fanatical National Socialists, of whom, to the bitter end, there was no shortage in Berlin.

Berlin was the capital of the "Third Reich", but also the centre of the German Resistance, from early working-class resistance to the attempted coup of 20 July 1944. Even persecuted Jews were not wholly without helpers: of some 5,000 Jews who went "underground" in the city, about 1,400 managed to survive with the assistance of non-Jewish neighbours and friends. The Peoples' Court [Volksgerichtshof] and Reich Court Martial [Reichskriegsgericht] wreaked havoc among the opponents of National Socialism. Over one thousand victims of Nazi terror ended their lives in the execution shed at Plötzensee Prison alone.

Text 56

The Reichstag elections of 6 November 1932 and 5 March 1933 in Germany and Berlin (in %)

	Election of 6 November 1932		Election of 5 March 1933	
	Germany	Berlin	Germany	Berlin
NSDAP	33.0	25.9	43.9	34.6
DNVP	8.3	11.3	8.0	10.9
KPD	16.8	31.0	12.3	24.4
SPD	20.4	23.3	18.3	21.7
Zentrum	11.9	4.4	11.3	4.9
Sonstige	9.8	4.1	6.2	3.5

Text 57

The writer Hans Sahl recalls his experiences in the spring of 1933.

I didn't sleep at home anymore, I went to the cinema four or five times a day, I lived at the cinema, in department stores and cafés, went home every once in a while, made sure that nobody had been there yet, burnt papers or threw them in the wc, pulled them out again because it was stopped up, ran across the roof garden to the house next door because I thought I heard the doorbell. Somebody had told me that my name was on a blacklist. He ought to know since he was now one of those people who looked at blacklists out of old affection, which however would not last long, and tried to warn his former friends.

I went once again to the "Romanisches Café" where those who had been "blown in" sat and were surprised to find themselves still there, reading the newspaper and playing chess. They sat there like creatures frozen in attitudes, waiting to be swept or cleared away. It seemed that they had lost their identities and were waiting for new ones that would save their lives. Some of them consulted train schedules, bent over maps or wrote letters to relations who had emigrated to America and made something of themselves. Lucky the man with an uncle in Amsterdam, a nephew in Shanghai, or a cousin in Valparaiso. I had no relations abroad. My family had stayed home and earned their bread honestly. [...]

I rang up my mother and we met at a café at Roseneck. I passed her my keys under the table and asked her to get me a few things from my flat, underwear, my passport, my holdall. She asked no more questions; she knew what was what.

Text 58

The writer Kurt Hiller on his committal to the Berlin concentration camp "Columbiahaus" in the spring of 1933, 1935.

After the National Socialist "seizure of power" the former military prison in Columbiadamm housed one of the so-called "wild" concentration camps in which opponents of the regime were incarcerated and tortured. Later the Gestapo in Prinz Albrecht Straße used the building as an additional "*Hausgefängnis*".

We have to line up in a dim narrow hallway, place all our belongings in our hat or cap on the floor in front of us: wallet, watch, pocket-knife, pencils, purse, even the ring from our fingers, collar and tie, handkerchief, belt, shoelaces. An SS chap steps in front of each of us, close, almost nose to nose. I look at mine, analytically; he roars "Look at the ground, pig!" His neighbour, grinning, asks to change places with him. A gigantic mongrel of a sportsman steps up, sarcastic expression, pointy nose, a bit too small, reddish on the bottom. He smiles: "I have a weakness for soft noses" and jabs me four or five times in the face with all his boxer's force at close range so that I go all woozy and blood spurts in great gushes out of my nose. They push me into the office, I turn over my belongings and they take down my vital statistics. Then they kick me into a cell. I fall onto a straw mattress, bloodied. The door bangs shut. [...]

Before I truly recover my senses they drag me out again and hurry me into a spacious room. Its walls are hung with whips and switches; the space in the middle is taken up by a large square clean-scrubbed table; [...] I have to bend over the table; four chaps press my hands to the edges and hold my feet still. The one who has stripped down steps up behind me with an enormous whip; [...] Twenty-five lashes. After the fifth or sixth I was sure I wouldn't survive and started screaming. That spurred them on; sarcastic remarks. After about the twentieth I screamed that I was about to faint. After the twenty-fifth they took a break. I fell down, somebody dragged me up. They ordered me to let down my trousers and underwear, and I had to bend over the table again on my stomach. They grab hold of my joints, push my head with so much force against the scrubbed table top that it too might have been flat in front, pull up my shirt, and then came another twenty-five.

Text 59

Journal entry by the Berlin physician Helga Narthoff, 1 April 1933.

Anti-Jewish boycott.
This day is burnt into my heart with letters of flame. That something like this is still possible in the twentieth century. Young boys in uniform carrying signs reading "Don't buy from Jews", "Don't go to Jewish doctors", "Only traitors buy from Jews", "The Jew is lying and cheating incarnate" are standing in front of all Jewish shops, lawyers' offices, doctors' surgeries, and flats. Doctors' name-plates on the houses have been scrawled over and in some cases damaged, and the people watched open-mouthed and silent. They must have forgotten to paste over my plate. I think I would have become violent. It was only in the afternoon that a boy came to my flat and asked "Is this a Jewish business?" "This isn't any kind of business", I replied, "It's a doctor's surgery. Are you ill?" After these ironic words the boy disappeared without posting himself before my door. To be sure, many patients who had appointments never came. One lady rang up to say that she could not come today and I said that it would be best if she did not come back at all. I myself made a point of buying in shops with sentries outside. One of them wanted to keep me from going into a small soap shop, but I pushed him aside, saying "I'll spend my money wherever I want". Why doesn't everybody do the same? The boycott would have been over quickly. But people are a cowardly lot; I noticed that long ago.

Text 60

The French Ambassador in Berlin (1931-1938) André François-Poncet on his impressions of the 1936 Olympics.

In the history of the Nazi regime the ceremonies for the Olympics in Berlin in August 1936 represent a high point, a pinnacle, if not an apotheosis for Hitler and the Third Reich. In a certain respect they recall Napoleon's days in Erfurt in 1808. Weary of the upset caused by the occupation of the Rhineland, which aroused fears that a general conflagration was to engulf humanity once again, people were relieved to give in to the relaxing of tension; they allow themselves to be lulled by the impression that an evil dream has broken, and hope for the advent of better times in the bosom of peace, now that Germany has

100   National Socialist mass rally in the Lustgarten, May 1934.

realised its declared objective of throwing off the chains of Versailles.
Hitler has forced himself on Europe as an extraordinary personality. He not only spreads fear and loathing, but also arouses curiosity and wins sympathy. His reputation is growing. The power of attraction he exudes extends beyond the borders of his own country. Kings, princes and famous guests come to the capital, less, perhaps, to attend the coming sporting contests than to meet this man who will be shaping the future, who appears to hold the continent's fate in his hands, but also to see this Germany which he has transformed and revitalised with irresistable force. And the whole world is thrilled by the perfect organisation, the absolute order and discipline, cultivated with extravagant generosity.
It is, indeed, a grand picture.

Text 61

Journal entry by the American CBS correspondent William L. Shirer on the reaction of the Berlin population to the occupation of Sudetenland by the German Army on 27 September 1938.

BERLIN, September 27
A motorized division rolled through the city's streets just at dusk this evening in the direction of

the Czech frontier. I went out to the corner of the Linden where the column was turning down the Wilhelmstrasse, expecting to see a tremendous demonstration. I pictured the scenes I had read of in 1914 when the cheering throngs on this same street tossed flowers at the marching soldiers, and the girls ran up and kissed them. The hour was undoubtedly chosen today to catch the hundreds of thousands of Berliners pouring out of their offices at the end of the day's work. But they ducked into the subways, refused to look on, and the handful that did stood at the curb in utter silence unable to find a word of cheer for the flower of their youth going away to the glorious war. It has been the most striking demonstration against war I've ever seen. Hitler himself reported furious. I had not been standing long at the corner when a policeman came up the Wilhelmstrasse from the direction of the Chancellery and shouted to the few of us standing at the curb that the Führer was on his balcony reviewing the troops. Few moved. I went down to have la look.

Hitler stood there. and there weren't two hundred people in the street or the great square of the Wilhelmsplatz. Hitler looked grim, then angry, and soon went inside, leaving his troops to parade by unreviewed. What I've seen tonight almost rekindles a little faith in the German people. They are dead set against war.

Text 62

Journal entry by William L. Shirer giving his impressions of the victory celebrations in Berlin after France's surrender on 18 July 1940.

BERLIN, July 18
For the first time since 1871, German troops staged a victory parade through the Brandenburg Gate today. They comprised a division conscripted from Berlin. Stores and factories closed,

101   Mass rally in the Lustgarten, 1 May 1936.

by order, and the whole town turned out to cheer. Nothing pleases the Berliners – a naïve and simple people on the whole – more than a good military parade. And nothing more than an afternoon off from their dull jobs and their dismal homes. I mingled among the crowds in the Pariserplatz. A holiday spirit ruled completely. Nothing *martial* about the mass of the people here. They were just out for a good time. Looking at them, I wondered if any of them understood what was going in in Europe, if they had an inkling that their joy, that this victorious parade of the goosesteppers, was based on a great tragedy for millions of others whom these troops and the leaders of these people had enslaved.

103   Spectators in Berlin's Olympic Stadium before the beginning of the final match between FC Schalke 04 and Rapid Vienna for the German football championship on 22 June 1941.
In the early morning hours of the same day the war against the Soviet Union began with a German attack.

Text 63

Journal entry by Ruth Andreas-Friedrich, 19 September 1941.

Berlin. Friday, 19 September 1941
It has happened. The Jews are outlaws. Marked as outcasts with a yellow star of David which

102   Unter den Linden on Sunday, 26 July 1936 during the Olympics.

each of them must wear on the left side. We would like to scream out loud for help. But what is the use of screaming? Those who could help us do not hear. Or perhaps they do not want to hear. "Jew" is written in Hebraic letters in the middle of the yellow star of David, "Jew" mock the children when they see someone walking the streets with such a star. Andrik tells two such brats that they should be ashamed of themselves and boxes their ears a few times before they can stop him. The people standing around smile approvingly. Like sinners caught in the act the two boys slink off. Thanks be to God! The majority of the population is not happy with the new regulations. Almost all the people who encounter us are as embarrassed as we are. And even the children's mockery has little to do with serious anti-Semitism. They mock because they think it will be fun. Fun that costs nothing because it is at the expense of the defenceless. There isn't much difference between pulling the legs off a fly, pinning butterflies, or hurling insults at Jews.

Text 64

Excerpt from a January 1940 report on the mood of the public for the Social Democratic Party of Germany [*Sopade*].

Party members living underground in Germany regularly prepared reports on the mood of the German population for the Party's leadership in exile.

It is still almost impossible to gain a uniform impression of the mood of the Berlin populace. It is interesting to note that despite the rising prices of food and drink, the declining quality of beer and the use of *ersatz* foods, restaurants and cafés are doing a booming business. At certain times of day it is nearly impossible to find an empty seat. The cinemas are also extraordinarily full. This phenomenon is an expression of the fatalism that has become widespread. People want to spend their money because it makes no sense to save anymore, and they don't want to sit at home because they need diversion. Should Germany win, they say, it won't do us any good, we won't be any better off than now. Should Germany lose, we may be much worse off. Basically, whatever happens it doesn't really matter.

Text 65

Journal entry by Ursula von Kardorff, 6 October 1943.

Our greenish-pale porter, with her pointy nose and dark cap, who looks like a figure out of Breughel, says: "Just let the Russians come, they won't do anything to us little people. At least the war will be over then."

Text 66

Security Service [SD] report of 22 February 1943 on the reactions of the German population to Goebbels' speech at the Berlin Sport Palace on 18 February 1943.

In the *Meldungen aus dem Reich* (Reports from within the Reich) the "Security Service of the *Reichsführer SS*" kept the Party leadership informed about the domestic political situation, particularly the mood of the German population.

No. 361, 22 February 1943
According to the reports before us, the speech by Reich Minister Dr Goebbels was heard by a large proportion of the population, despite its sudden and rather late announcement. In addition, the repetition of the broadcast, its publication in the press and the lively discussion of its contents has

104 Summer holidays at Wannsee Beach, 7 July 1942.

105   Pedestrians before a site map of the Eastern Front hanging in a showcase of the Scherl publishing company, 12 July 1941.
Little flags mark the advance of, and the areas of the Soviet Union occupied by, the German Army.

ensured its penetration into broad segments of the population. All reports agree that its effect has been unusually great and all in all very positive. Those Germans whose morale had sunk with reports of the most recent developments on the Eastern Front, particularly the alarming news of Kharkov's evacuation were practically longing for a clear account of the situation. The speech by Reich Minister Dr Goebbels, despite its very open exposition of the seriousness of the situation, had a calming effect and revived public confidence and trust in the military leadership. Dr Goebbels succeeded in developing an enthusiasm and a "martial mood" in the Sport Palace which conveyed itself to those listening on the wireless.

Text 67

Security Service report on "the breakdown in the attitudes of the population", 8 July 1943.

The available reports generally indicate that, under the impression of the aerial terror against West Germany, and also the feared material superiority of the enemy powers in the coming land operations, as well as the incalculability of further military developments and of an end to the war, many Germans are downhearted and often nervous. This general situation is affecting not merely the mood of the population, but recently has also been exhibiting phenomena that point to an incipient change in individual aspects of the basic attitude of the population. The following, among others, are mentioned as indicators in the reports:

1) The spreading of rumours of all kinds has increased greatly in recent months. To the extent that these involve surmises about impending military operations and the like, the openness of the people to rumour is understandable. What is more worrisome is the fact that even the most nonsensical and vicious rumours concerning leading men in the Party and government spread so quickly and remain in circulation for weeks and months. [...]

2. The attitude towards political jokes is similar. Since Stalingrad the telling of seditious and nasty jokes, even about the person of the Führer, has increased significantly. [...]

3. Another phenomenon which, according to the reports, can no longer be considered merely one of mood, is the widespread enthusiasm for criticising the State and Party leadership. Many Germans have been vigorously attacking the performance of individual government or Party offices ("The Party has failed", "the administration is in chaos") and have encountered little or no direct disagreement with such statements. Most people either say nothing or even agree. A segment of the population apparently no longer considers attacks on the institutions of the Party or State or their personnel to be any of their affair, but rather have distanced themselves internally. [...]

4. The reports also indicate that listening to foreign radio stations has apparently increased greatly in past months. [...]

5. The attitude of a large portion of Germans towards other enemy propaganda has also undergone a change. Leaflets dropped during air-raids are being picked up by Germans and discussed. [...]

6. In several reports the fact that a large proportion of Germans are expressing their fears about the outcome of the war openly and in an undisciplined manner is also regarded as a sign of the deterioration in attitudes. People are losing control in this regard and expressing their doubts about victory without considering the effects of such utterances on other people, particularly soldiers on leave from the front. [...]

106   The Berlin Sport Palace during Goebbels' speech of 18
February 1943 proclaiming "Total War".

7. According to businessmen and civil servants who are in contact with the public, the use of the German salute has decreased strikingly in recent months. It has also been noted that many comrades have stopped wearing their Party badges.

8. Reports from areas under aerial attack emphasise that it is difficult to determine whether certain phenomena should be regarded as a result of the low spirits and nervousness prevailing there or as indicating a more general deterioration of public attitudes. [...]

Text 68

Gestapo report on the activities of "German People's Radio" [*Deutscher Volkssender*], 10 September 1943.

The illegal German People's Radio, run mainly by members of the communist resistance, called on the German people to resist the Nazi regime and was also used to help organise resistance activities.

Reich Security Main Office
Department IV
Report of important events of state police interest
No. 2
10 September 1943
Enemy propaganda
On 2 September 1943 German People's Radio broadcast a report on the negative effects of recent air-raids on employees of Berlin factories. The prevailing unrest is increasing particularly among workers on the night shift. It was reported, among other things, that: "On the anniversary of the outbreak of the war protests against the continuation of the war took place in many plants. In workers' conversations hatred of Hitler and of his war is becoming more widespread. A number of armaments plants report passive resistance among the workers. Word of mouth campaigns encourage workers to leave their workbenches and anti-Hitler slogans such as 'Make peace, overthrow Hitler!'; 'Stop producing weapons and munitions!'; 'Practice passive resistance!'; 'Prepare mass strikes, prevent a fifth winter at war!'; and 'War criminals to the gallows, save Berlin, stop the war!'" are seen more frequently on the walls of buildings.

2.3.   The Addresses of Power and Terror

Berlin was the centre of the "Third Reich". Berliners may have been more sceptical of National Socialism than other citizens of the Reich, but that does not change the fact that National Socialism found its strongest expression in Berlin. This was primarily the result of the successful enforcement after 1933 of centralist notions of the state. The dualism of national [*Reich*] and state [*Länder*] ministries disappeared; the Prussian ministries were fused with the Reich ministries. Berlin, however, was the centre not only of state power, but also of the NSDAP's party administrative offices, which, with few exceptions, were transferred to the Reich capital after 1933. Finally, under the leadership of *Reichsführer-SS* Heinrich Himmler, Berlin also became the site of the SS state, which was centred around an apparatus of persecution composed of state and SS agencies.

The new rulers emphasised continuity. On 21 March 1933, "Potsdam Day", Hitler styled himself as Bismarck's heir, and German nationalist politicians and bureaucrats, whose authoritarian domestic policies and expansionist foreign policy ambitions had not been satisfied by the Weimar Republic, accepted Hitler as the repository of their hopes. "Wilhelmstraße", the German Reich's government quarter, felt quite comfortable in its swastika décor.

The hopes for German renewal in the spirit of Bismarck soon proved illusory. Without the rule of law, the Prussian sense of duty degenerated into criminal collaboration. This was already visible in the architecture of Wilhelmstraße, the centre of Prussian-German power. Where the National Socialist government created its own buildings, in the Air Force Ministry, which was constructed in 1935-36 or the New Reich Chancellery, which was completed in 1939, the naked will to power and world domination triumphed. The architecture of intimidation contrasted strikingly with the rather modest atmosphere that had characterised Wilhelmstraße up to that point. The New Reich Chancellery and Air Force Ministry give an idea of how Berlin would have been remodelled after victory in the war. Until that point, the headquarters of terror hid behind friendly, venerable or inconspicuous façades. The Chief of Security Police and Security Service resided in the baroque Prinz-Albrecht-Palais, the Gestapo used a former school of applied arts, the General Manager of Industrial Conscription [*Generalbevollmächtigte für den Arbeitseinsatz*] organised forced labour throughout Europe from the Berlin offices of the Thuringian state government, and ministerial civil servants served the terror regime from behind neo-classical façades.

Massive bombing and the "final battle" destroyed most of the buildings in which power was concentrated in the "Third Reich". This destruction brought a German and European reign of terror to an end.

107   Hitler is shown the New Reich Chancellery by Speer (to his right) on 7 January 1939, two days before its official opening.

108   The microphone room in the Propaganda Ministry, 1933. The mark of Goebbels' propaganda was his grasp of the mass media. He controlled not only the radio, but also the press and film. The most conspicuous characteristic of his world-view was a fanatical hatred of Jews. Not only was he a driving force behind the 1938 November pogrom, but he considered having made Berlin "Jew-free" his "greatest political achievement". The more difficult Germany's position in the war became, the stronger was Goebbels influence. As "General Manager of the Total War Effort" [*Generalbevollmächtigter für den totalen Kriegseinsatz*] from July 1944 on he tried to mobilise the last reserves. Appointed Reich Chancellor by Hitler's testament, he had his six children killed the day after Hitler's suicide and then committed suicide, together with his wife Magda, on 1 May 1945.

Text 69

Excerpt from Hitler's speech in the Sport Palace to construction workers who had participated in the building of the New Reich Chancellery, 9 January 1939.

I am here as a representative of the German people! And when I receive someone in the Reich Chancellery, then it is not as the private individual Adolf Hitler that I do so, but as the leader of the German nation, and thus it is not I but through me Germany that receives him. And for that reason I want these rooms to be equal to the task. Each individual has helped to create a work of architecture that will survive for hundreds of years and that will be a monument to our age. The first building of the new great German Reich!

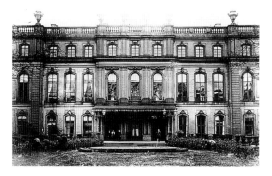

109   Prinz-Albrecht-Palais, Wilhelmstraße 102, ca. 1928.
The transfer of SS institutions from Munich to Berlin also required a new headquarters for the Security Service of the SS (*SD*), which was headed by Reinhard Heydrich. The baroque Prinz-Albrecht-Palais, which during the Weimar Republic had

served as a guesthouse for high-ranking state visitors, was chosen. After the consolidation of the Gestapo and the police force in the Security Police (*Sipo*) in 1936, which represented a step in the centralisation of the National Socialist apparatus of repression, the Reich Security Main Office (*RSHA*) was founded on 27 September 1939, adding the *SD* to the already existing Sipo. The head of the *RSHA* was Reinhard Heydrich. The Prinz-Albrecht-Palais was to remain his headquarters and that of his successor Dr Ernst Kaltenbrunner. The *RSHA* (Prinz-Albrecht-Straße 8) was not only the main instrument of political persecution, but also of racist annihilation policies. At the so-called Wannsee Conference on 22 January 1942, Heydrich secured for himself centralised control over the murder of the European Jews. Within the framework of the *RSHA* the Reich Criminal Police Office [*Reichskriminalpolizeiamt*] was responsible for the deportation of Gypsies.

Heydrich died on 4 June 1942 as the result of an assassination attempt in Prague. Kaltenbrunner was sentenced to death at the Nuremberg war crimes trials and hanged on 16 October 1946.

110   Leipziger Platz and Leipziger Straße, ca. 1928.
The administrative offices of the Four-Year Plan were concentrated in and around Leipziger Platz.
Leipziger Platz 6-9: Reich Commissioner for Price Formation.
Leipziger Platz 11: Forestry Operations Group.
Leipziger Platz 7 and Leipziger Straße 110-111: Food Operations Group [*Geschäftsgruppe Nahrung*].
Leipziger Straße 3: General Department, Currency Operations Group [*Geschäftsgruppe Devisen*].

Leipziger Platz and Leipziger Straße housed not only the offices of the "Four Year Plan", but also others under the leadership of Hermann Göring, such as the Reich Forestry Office (Göring was Reich Superintendant of Forestry and Game [*Reichsforstmeister* and *Reichsjägermeister*]) at Leipziger Straße 2 and Leipziger Platz 10 and 11 and, after 1936, the monstrous Reich Air Force Ministry at Leipziger Straße 7.

111 Reich Air Force Minister and Air Force Commander-in-Chief Hermann Göring inspecting a parade in front of the Reich Air Force Ministry in Wilhelmstraße, 1937.

The Reich Air Force Ministry (with 2,000 offices) was erected in 1935-36 by Ernst Sagebiel in the typical style of National Socialist intimidation architecture. From 1939 on, the Air Force Ministry sought to put into practice Hitler's wish to "wipe out" enemy cities. It is thus all the more surprising that this building survived the bombing of Berlin almost unscathed and was used after the war as the "House of the Ministries of the GDR" and, after 1990, as the offices of the *Treuhand*, then as seat of the ministry of financial affairs. As Air Force Commander-in-Chief Göring was both powerful and vulnerable; the failure of supplies to the enclosed 6th Army at Stalingrad as well as of air-defence against enemy bomber squadrons strongly damaged his reputation. As the "number two man in the state", he was the main defendant in the Nuremberg trials. He avoided execution by hanging by taking poison on 15 October 1946.

112 The Army High Command at Tirpitzufer (today: Reichpietschufer) 72-76 on 31 May 1936.

Next to the swastika flag the former imperial war flag [*Reichkriegsflagge*] is flying to commemorate the anniversary of the Battle of Skagerrak.

Since 20 August 1934 soldiers of the German Armed Forces had been required to swear a personal oath of loyalty to Hitler. Misgivings among the generals were directed at Hitler's military dilettantism, not his strivings for expansion. At the same time as Hitler took over the high command on 4 February 1938, the former Office of the Armed Forces [*Wehrmachtamt*] became the High Command of the Armed Forces [*Oberkommando der Wehrmacht, OKW*], headed by the future General of the Army [*Generalfeldmarschall*] Wilhelm Keitel. The OKW took over operations from the Reich Ministry of War, which was abolished at the beginning of 1938, and Keitel had ministerial rank. It was also Keitel who saw to the dissemination of the spirit of National Socialism within the Army. Not only in the *Waffen-SS*, but also in the Army itself the "political soldier" developed, i.e., a soldier whose actions were no longer guided by international military law, but by the enforcement of National Socialist ideology. Keitel, like Alfred Jodl, Chief of the Army Operations Staff [*Wehrmachtführungsstab*], was condemned to death at the Nuremberg trials and executed on 16 October 1946.

2.4. Dictatorship and Violence

When Adolf Hitler was named Chancellor of the German Reich by Reich President v. Hindenburg on 30 January 1933, few people had any idea of what this really meant. Many assumed that Hitler would mismanage himself out of office after a few months like so many governments before him. The National Socialists, however, were not about to risk the power that had just been handed to them. The "Reichstag Decree" and "Enabling Law" abolished the Weimar Constitution for all practical purposes and SA street terror, which was now given a free hand, intimidated political opponents. The National Socialists created, with Dachau, the first government concentration camp, and allowed the SA to open its own camps. The murder of Röhm on 30 June 1934 and the ensuing reduction in the SA's power appeared to signal the end of the terror that had accompanied the "seizure of power", and gained Hitler the renewed support of the middle class, which had been annoyed by the actions of the SA. The Röhm affair, however, by no means meant a return to legality – on the contrary. When Hitler retroactively declared the murders of 30 June 1934, which had claimed the lives not only of SA leaders but also of conservative and moderate opponents of Hitler, such as General Schleicher and the head of "Catholic Action", Erich Klausener, to have been legal measures necessary to ward off a "state emergency", he made it absolutely clear that he, as "Führer", was above the law.

With the waning of street terror, the systematic and cold-blooded terror of the Secret State Police [Gestapo] and SS Security Service showed itself more openly. When Himmler assumed office as Chief of the Prussian Gestapo in 1934 the apparatus of repression was systematically expanded. It culminated in 1939 in the founding of the Reich Security Main Office, whose competence extended beyond political repression to encompass racist persecution as well.

The creation of jobs in the armaments industry in preparation for war, improvements in social policy as well as foreign policy successes (the march into the de-militarised Rhineland unaccompanied by sanctions, the return of the Saar by plebiscite, the "anschluss" of Austria) ensured increasing support for the system among the population, particularly since the one-party dictatorship permitted no legal opposition that might have publicly criticised these policies. Sufficiently anchored in the population, the National Socialists were able to carry their violence outwards, and to make accomplices of the Germans who had initially been the victims of Hitler's dictatorship. If in the first years of the dictatorship those confined in concentration camps were almost exclusively German, by 1945 90% were non-Germans. The function of the concentration camps also changed. Whereas the first camps were mainly geared to the intimidation of political opponents, during the war concentration camps were used as an almost inexhaustible reservoir of slave labour. At the same time they served the policy of racist extermination. The industrial complex at Auschwitz-Monowitz was the most extreme example.

Text 70

Except from the Reich President's "Decree for the Protection of People and State", 28 February 1933.

Taking the Reichstag fire as a pretext, the decree suspended the basic rights guaranteed by the Weimar Constitution. Although only the Communists are mentioned as enemies of the state, the Reichstag fire decree served as a general legal basis for persecuting all political opponents and also for the imposition of "protective custody", i.e., for incarceration in a concentration camp. In the scholarly literature the decree of 28 February 1933 has been called with good reason the "Third Reich"s' actual "constitutional charter".

§ 1

Articles 114, 115, 117, 118, 123, 124 and 153 of the Reich Constitution are suspended until further notice. As a result restrictions of the rights to freedom of speech, including freedom of the press and freedom of association and assembly, intervention in the secrecy of the post, telegraph and telephone, the ordering of house searches and confiscations as well as restrictions on property will be allowed, including those outside of the legal limits otherwise imposed.

[...]

Text 71

Excerpt from the Reich President's "Decree for Defence Against Perfidious Attacks on the Government of the National Rising [Nationale Erhebung]", 21 March 1933.

On 20 December 1934 this decree was replaced by the "Perfidy Law" [Heimtücke-Gesetz].

§ 3

(1) Anyone deliberately making or spreading an untrue assertion or a crudely distorted assertion based on fact that is liable to severely damage the well-being of the Reich or one of its states or the reputation of the Reich government or a state government or the parties or associations behind these governments will be punished, so long as other regulations do not call for a more severe penalty, by up to two years' imprisonment and, if the allegation was made or spread in public, with imprisonment for no less than three months.

[...]

Text 72

Excerpt from the "Law for the Redress of the Suffering of People and Reich" [-Gesetz zur Behebung der Not von Volk und Reich], 24 March 1933.

The so-called "Enabling Law" [Ermächtigungsgesetz] abolished the Weimar Constitution for all practical purposes without formally suspending it.

Article 1

Laws may also be passed by the Reich government without going through the procedure set down in the Reich Constitution. This also applies to the laws indicated in Article 85 para. 2 and Article 87 of the Reich Constitution.

Article 2

The laws passed by the Reich government may deviate from the Reich Constitution so long as they are not concerned with the institution of the Reichstag and the Reichsrat as such. The rights of the Reich President remain unaffected.

113 The Reichstag in session on 24 March 1933 in the Kroll Opera House, which served as an alternative meeting place after the parliamentary building was destroyed by fire on 27 February 1933.
Hitler is at the speaker's podium. Reichstag President Göring is observing the members of parliament through binoculars. With the exception of the Social Democrats, all of the parliamentary parties present voted in favour of the Enabling Law. The Communists, under prosecution because of the Reichstag fire, were no longer able to participate in this session of parliament.

114 The Jewish lawyer Dr Michael Siegel being driven through the streets by SA men in Munich in March 1933. Dr Siegel was forced to wear a sign reading: "I shall never complain to the police again". He had lodged a complaint with the police about the treatment of his client, the Munich department store owner Uhlfelder, who had been taken into "protective custody". Dr Siegel succeeded in emigrating from Germany in 1940. He died in 1979 in Lima, Peru, aged 96.

Text 73

Excerpt from the "Law Prohibiting the Rebuilding and Founding of Parties" [*Gesetz gegen die Neubildung von Parteien*], 14 July 1933.

This law provided the legal basis for one-party dictatorship. The parties of the Weimar Republic, with the exception of the NSDAP, had either been crushed (KPD), prohibited (SPD) or had dissolved themselves.

§ 1
The only existing political party in Germany is the National Socialist German Workers' Party.

§ 2
Anyone undertaking to maintain the organisational unity of another political party or to form a new political party will, so far as other regulations do not call for more severe punishment, be punished by up to three years at hard labour or by imprisonment between six months and three years.

Text 74

Excerpts from the law of 10 February 1936, concerning the Secret State Police [Gestapo].

The authority of the Gestapo was regulated by three laws, those of 26 April 1933, 30 November 1933, and 10 February 1936. In this third Gestapo law § 7 is particularly important, since it represents the legal construction of a space outside the law.

Law of 10 February 1936, concerning the Secret State Police

The Ministry of State has resolved to pass the following law:
§ 1.
(1) The Secret State Police has the task throughout the entire State of investigating and fighting all attempts to endanger the State; to gather and evaluate the results of the investigations; to inform the State Government and to keep all other authorities [*Behörden*] abreast of important developments and to supply them with suggestions. The Head of the Secret State Police in cooperation with the Minister of the Interior will determine which specific tasks will be carried out by the Secret State Police.
[...]
§ 7.
Orders and concerns of the Secret State Police are not subject to the scrutiny of the courts of administration [*Verwaltungsgerichte*].

Text 75

Excerpts from an article of 15 April 1936 by Reinhard Heydrich on "Combatting Enemies of the State".

Reinhard Heydrich, SS Major-General [Gruppen-führer], Head of the Prussian Secret State Police Office, Berlin:

Combatting Enemies of the State
[...]

National Socialism no longer proceeds from the State, but from the People. The Führer already indicated this tendency in "*Mein Kampf*". He refers to the State as a "means to an end", and "an institution for the nation [*Volkstum*] in question" designed to preserve and promote a "community of physically and mentally similar beings". Accordingly, we National Socialists recognise only the enemy of the People. He is always the same person, remains eternally unchanging.
[...]

Jewry as such is, naturally, isolated as the Jewish race and Jewish people by the Nuremberg Laws. This prevents the direct influx of Jewish blood into the national body [*Volkskörper*]. The indirect influence of Jewish thought, however, has by no means been eradicated once and for all. On the one hand many people, particularly in the sciences and the intellectual world, remain unconsciously infected by Jewish, liberal and Masonic residues. On the other hand, our own German history has demonstrated that the Jewish objective always remains the same: to rule the world through a more or less visible Jewish upper class. And if National Socialist policy has made the ground in Germany domestically unfruitful, the Jew will switch to the economy and foreign policy. In the economy he may always count on the cooperation of egoistic and treacherous elements. In foreign policy the Jew operates with those organisations that are already totally under his control: Bolshevism and the Masonic lodges which are still intact abroad.

The Communist, principally recruited from international criminals, and working with all means of modern technology, is particularly dangerous, because he must be regarded at the same time as a spy for Soviet Russia. This means that the anarchist criminal is also the most dangerous aggressor against the elements of national defence.

The Masonic lodges, in Germany as elsewhere, were never anything more than auxiliary organisations of Jewry. They had as their goal the gradual and imperceptible bending of the character and intellect of German men to Jewish purposes.

Except for a few incorrigibles, most people recognise the threat that Jews, Communists and Freemasons pose to the State and People and approve of their treatment as enemies of the State and People with all the consequences. One still frequently encounters a good deal of misunderstanding, however, in regard to a further enemy of the State and People, the politicising occupants of Church office.
[...]

In conclusion it may be said that:

National Socialism regards the enemy of the State as an enemy of the People. All expressions of anti-State forces always lead back to the enemy of the People, and are supported, guided and determined from thence. The enemy of the People can only be properly opposed when his methods and means are grasped intellectually. This task is fulfilled by the Secret State Police and Security Service of the SS, whose model cooperation thus provides an example of the unity of State and Party.

Text 76

Excerpt from "Reports from within the Reich" [*Meldungen aus dem Reich*], 23 October 1939.

The "Reports from within the Reich" were compiled by the Security Service of the SS (SD) using a large network of informants. The "Reports" served a dual function: they were intended to inform the leadership of the actual mood within the population, but were also reports of occurrences and opinions that were considered "dangerous to the State" and passed on to the Gestapo.

The curate Riedesel in Königsberg, who is an adherent of the Professing Front, said in a sermon in connection with the parable of the Good Samaritan: "A wounded man is lying in a ditch, an elegant automobile with a man in a handsome uniform drives by, the man holds several State or Party offices. He offers no help to the injured man because it would waste precious time. Another automobile comes by, also offering

115   I.G. Farben's Buna Works at Auschwitz-Monowitz, 1945.

no assistance. Only the third, a Jew in a ram-shackle vehicle, takes pity on the wounded man and picks him up". (State Police already notified.) [...]

Text 77

Excerpt from the "Disciplinary and Punishment Regulations for the Prison Camp" at Dachau, 1 October 1933.

The first state concentration camp was opened at Dachau near Munich on 22 March 1933. In the summer of 1933, *SS-Oberführer* Theodor Eicke became the camp's commandant. His regulations for the camp became a model for other camps because Eicke was named Inspector of Concentration Camps and thus had the opportunity to apply the methods he developed at Dachau more generally.

Tolerance is weakness. Recognising this to be true, ruthless action will be taken wherever the interests of the Fatherland make it necessary. The decent citizen [*Volksgenosse*] who has been incited will not come into contact with these penal provisions. To the politicising agitators and intellectual fomenters of whatever stripe, however, we say take care that you aren't caught, otherwise we will take you by the throat and silence you with a taste of your own medicine. [...]

§ 8

The following persons are to be punished with fourteen days of strict confinement and 25 lashes at the beginning and end of their sentence:

Anyone who leaves or enters the prison camp without an escort, or, without authorisation, joins a labour crew that is marching out,

anyone who expresses in letters or other communications negative opinions about National Socialist leaders, the State and government, official authorities or institutions, who glorifies Marxist or liberal leaders or November parties, who reports occurrences in the concentration camp,

anyone who keeps prohibited objects, tools or cut-and-thrust weapons in his quarters or in straw mattresses.

Text 78

Excerpt from a report by Reich Minister of Justice Dr Otto Thierack on a discussion with Himmler concerning "Extermination through Labour", 18 September 1942.

2. Release of asocial elements from prisons to the *Reichsführer-SS* for Extermination through Labour. All those in security custody [*Sicherheitsverwahrten*], Jews, Gypsies, Russians and Ukrainians, Poles serving sentences of over three years, Czechs or Germans serving over eight years according to the decision of the Reich Minister of Justice. The worst asocial elements among the last will be removed first. I will keep the Führer apprised of this via Reichsleiter Bormann.

Text 79

Letter from Dr Otto Ambros, Deputy Director of the I.G.-Farben Company in Ludwigshafen, to the Directors Dr ter Meer and Dr Struß concerning the erection of the Buna Works at Auschwitz, 12 April 1941.

Dr Otto Ambros   12 April 1941/S1
I.G. Farben Industries   Ludwigshafen a.Rh.
                              Telephone 6498

Dr ter Meer, Director
Dr Struß, Director

I.G.- Frankfurt

Gentlemen,
   Enclosed please find the reports on our regular building meetings, which take place once a week under my chairmanship.
   They will show you how things are organised and in particular the beginning of our activities in the east.
   The constituent founding meeting, which went satisfactorily for the most part, took place on

7 April in Kattowitz. Certain objections by petty bureaucrats could be dealt with quickly.

Dr Eckell did an excellent job there and our new friendship with the SS is proving to be quite a blessing.

On the occasion of a dinner held for us by the Camp Commandant we were able to arrange all further measures affecting the truly excellent involvement of the concentration camp on behalf of the Buna Works.

I remain, with all best wishes,
Yours faithfully,
Otto Ambros

Enclosure

116   The Wilhelmsgymnasium at Bellevuestraße 15, headquarters since 1935 of the Peoples' Court [*Volksgerichtshof*], no date.

The Peoples' Court had to vacate the former Prussian Parliament because the Reich Air Force Ministry was able to enforce its claim on the building. The former parliament was now called the "House of the Flyers" [*Haus der Flieger*]. The Peoples' Court found a new home at Bellevuestraße 15, using the former secondary school as a court-house until 3 February 1945 when bomb damage rendered it unusable. The President of the Peoples' Court, Roland Freisler, was killed in the air-raid of 3 February 1945. The conspirators of 20 July 1944 were not tried in Bellevuestraße, but rather in the plenary assembly hall of the Superior Court of Justice [*Kammergericht*] in Elßholzstraße in Schöneberg. In order to establish the jurisdiction of the Peoples' Court in this case, the accused officers had first to be expelled from the Army. Otherwise the Reich Court Martial [*Reichskriegsgericht*] would have had jurisdiction.

Text 80

Excerpts from the First Ordinance supplementing the Reich Citizenship Law, 14 November 1935.

§ 4

(1) A Jew cannot be a citizen of the Reich. He has no right to vote; he may not hold public office. [...]

§ 5

(1) Anyone descended from at least three racially fully Jewish grandparents is a Jew. [...]
(2) A citizen of mixed blood [*Mischling*] descended from two fully Jewish grandparents will also be considered a Jew if
a) he was a member of the Jewish religious community at the time when the law went into effect or became a member thereafter,
b) he was married to a Jew when the law went into effect or did so subsequently
c) he is the product of a marriage to a Jew as defined in para. 1 which was contracted after the Law for the Protection of German Blood and German Honour went into effect on 15 September 1935 (*Reichsgesetzbl.* I p. 1146),
d) he is the product of extramarital relations with a Jew as defined in para. 1 born out of wedlock after 31 July 1936.

Text 81

Death sentences and Executions (excluding military tribunals), 1914–1945.

	Death sentences	Executions
First World War	141	94
Weimar Republic	1,132	184
"Third Reich"	ca. 16,000	ca. 12,000
Italy (1.7.1931–10.8.1944, i.e., from the introduction to the abolition of the death penalty)	156	88

2.5. War Crimes

War in itself is a crime. To this extent it was only logical to put the accusation of "conspiracy against the peace" at the top of the list of charges at the Nuremberg war crimes trials. But it was not only the "Third Reich's" preparation for and unleashing of war that was criminal, but also the way in which the war was conducted. At issue here were not the excesses that occur in any army during wartime, but rather a conscious and organised suspension of all ties to international law. Even before the invasion of Poland, Hitler had postulated that it was not right but victory that mattered. Many of his generals agreed with this assessment. In an army order General Hoth remarked, referring to the war against the Soviet Union, that the struggle could only end with the annihilation of one side; there could be no settlement.

Annihilation was meant in an all-encompassing sense. After 1939, Germany's aims were not simply military victory and the establishment of hegemony in Europe, but rather the reorganisation of the continent along racist lines. The German Army not only conquered large areas in which German civilian agencies could set up their racist order, but also itself participated in the decimation of those people deemed "racially inferior":

the murder of Polish prisoners of war and civilians during the "Polish campaign", the death of millions of Soviet prisoners of war, in part deliberately caused, in part through negligence, the murder of countless civilians under the pretence of combatting partisans. The shooting of Jews and Gypsies as "retaliation" for the killing of German soldiers by Yugoslav partisans, the shooting of hostages generally and the destruction of entire villages everywhere in occupied Europe – all this occurred with the authority of the German Army leadership.

War crimes, however, included not only deeds committed during battle and by the military administration, but also those acts of violence that military victory made possible: the expulsion of the local population from the annexed territories, as in Poland, the mass murders committed by the Special Units first in Poland and then, above all, in the Soviet Union, the abduction of local populations for slave labour in Germany.

Towards the end of the war, the National Socialists' criminal notion of war was turned against the German people itself. In Hitler's eyes, the German people had failed and thus forfeited its right to exist. His "Nero Decree" of 19 March 1945, which foresaw the application of the "scorched earth" principle to Germany, would have made continued existence after the inevitable surrender even more difficult. The Germans, however, did not follow their leader and choose self-destruction. All they could hope for was that, after the war, the victors would not treat them as they had treated their vanquished for five and a half years.

Text 82

Excerpts from Hitler's *Mein Kampf*, Volume 2, 1927.

On the other hand we National Socialists must cling steadfastly to our foreign policy objective, namely, of securing for the German people the land it deserves on this earth. [...] Germany will either become a world power or cease to exist. To become a world power, however, it needs that size which, in the present age, will give it the required significance and its citizens life. [...] If we speak of new land in today's Europe, however, we can only be thinking of Russia and the bordering states under her rule.

Text 83

From Hitler's secret memorandum on the Four-Year Plan, August 1936.

I set the following tasks here:
I. The German Army must be operational within four years.
II. The German economy must be prepared for war within four years.

Text 84

Excerpt from Colonel Hoßbach's notes on a conference involving Hitler, the Minister of War, the Foreign Minister and the supreme commanders of the Army, Navy and Air Force concerning preparations for war held in the Reich Chancellery on 5 November 1937.

If one begins the following explanations with the decision to risk the use force, then the questions "when" and "how" remain to be answered. One may distinguish among three cases here:

Case 1: Time period 1943-1945
[...]
No one knows today what the situation will actually be in 1943-45. All that it clear is that we cannot wait any longer.
The large armed forces with the necessity of securing their maintenance and the aging of the movement and its leadership on the one hand, and the prospect of sinking standards of living and birthrates on the other leave no other choice

but to act. Should the Führer still be alive, it is his unalterable wish that the German problem of space be solved by 1943-45. In cases 2 and 3 action before 1943-45 would be considered.

Case 2:
If social tensions in France were to grow to such a crisis of domestic politics that the French Army would become absorbed by the latter and be unavailable for warfare against Germany, the time would be ripe to move against Czechoslovakia.

Case 3:
If France were to become so deeply involved in war with another state that it could not proceed against Germany.

Text 85

Excerpt from notes taken of an address by Hitler on 22 August 1939 to Army commanders concerning the initiation of war against Poland.

Poland's annihilation primary. Goal is the removal of living forces, not reaching a particular line. Even if war breaks out in the west, annihilation of Poland remains primary. Quick decision because of season of year.
I will provide a propagandistic pretence for starting a war against Poland, however incredible. Afterwards nobody will ask the victor whether he told the truth or not. In initiating and pursuing a war what counts is not right but victory.
Close hearts to pity. Proceed brutally. 80 million people must have their due. Their existence must be secured. The stronger is in the right.

Text 86

Report by Karl Schoepke, employee of the Main Office for Ethnic Germans [*Volksdeutsche Mittelstelle*], on the forced evacuation of Poles in 1940, 1946.

One evening a Polish village was surrounded by a group of SA men who were leading the action. A few ethnic Germans [*Volksdeutsche*] had also been forcibly incorporated into the commandos. The village was encircled and shortly after midnight the people were driven from their beds. Then they were ordered to pack a bag of up to

30 kg and be ready to travel within one-half to three-quarters of an hour. The place was terribly ravaged. Pictures of saints and crucifixes were smashed and thrown out with the rubbish. The Poles had to drive to the district town in their own vehicles and were put behind barbed wire there.

Ethnic Germans who had been brought in from elsewhere were already waiting in the district town. These ethnic Germans were loaded into the same vehicles in which the Polish families had arrived. Naturally the ethnic Germans were appalled by the terrible things they found there.

Text 87

Mass executions of Polish civilians and prisoners of war from 1 to 4 September 1939.

These actions continued throughout the war against Poland. Crimes claiming fewer than twenty-five lives do not appear in this selection.

Day of execution	Place	District/Village	Voivodeship	Murdered by	Number of victims	Remarks
1.9.	Zimnowoda	Kłobuck	Kielce	Army	41	106 farms burnt down
1.9.	Torzeniec	Ostrzeszów	Poznań	*PiBat. SS*	34 (every 2nd man)	Village "pacified"
1./2.9.	Wyszanów	Wieruszów	Łódź	Army	59	Village "pacified" 20 farms burnt down
1./2.9.	Parzymiechy	Kłobuck	Kielce	Army	75	
2.9.	Łaziska	Tychy	Śląsk	Army	37 (some burnt alive)	Village "pacified"
3.9.	Świekatowo	Świecie	Pomorze	Army	26	Village "pacified" Victims chosen during Mass
3.9.	Nierada/Zrębice	Częstochowa	Kielce	Army	25	
3.9.	Kamieńsk	Piotrków Trib.	Łódź	Army/ Police	30 (most killed by butt stroke)	
3./4.9.	Imielin	Tychy	Śląsk	Army	28	
3./4.9.	Złoczew	Sieradz	Łódź	Army	200	Village burnt down- (80%: 248 farms)
4.9.	Katowice	Katowice	Śląsk	Army/ Free Corps	750 (mainly former participants in the Silesion uprising and boy scouts)	
4.9.	Zarki	Mysków	Kielce	Army	102 (among them 90 Jews)	
4.9.	Opatowiec	Pinczów	Kielce	2.1. Div. (XV AK, 10. A)	45 (Polish prisoners of war)	
4.9.	Orzesze	Tychy	Śląsk	Free Corps	32	
4.9.	Częstochowa	Częstochowa	Kielce	Army/ Police	300 ca.	
4.9.	Kruszyna	Radomsko	Łódź	Army	38	
4.9.	Folwarki	Piotrków Trib.	Łódź	Army/SS	28	20 forms burnt down
4.9.	Szczawno	Sieradz	Łódź	Army	32	

Text 88

Excerpt from Martin Bormann's notes on a conversation between Hitler and Hans Frank, Erich Koch, Baldur v. Schirach and himself concerning the relationship of the Germans to the Poles, 2 October 1940.

The Führer must emphasise once again that the Poles can only have one master, the German; two masters may not exist side by side, and thus all members of the Polish intelligentsia must be killed. This may sound harsh, but it is the law of life.

117 Forced evacuation of Poles in Wartheland, no date.
The original caption reads: "Polish camp at the Gelsendorf distribution point". The photo was taken for the SS Main Office [*Hauptamt*] "Reich Commissioner for Strengthening Germanism" [*Reichskommissar für die Festigung deutschen Volkstums*]. The Reich Commissioner was Heinrich Himmler.

Text 89

Excerpts from the economic policy guidelines for the Economic Staff East, Agricultural Group, on cutting off Russian industrial centres from the grain belt, 23 May 1941.

This means: at all events, sealing off the black earth regions must make more or less high surpluses available to us. The consequence is non-delivery to the entire forest zone including the significant industrial centres of Moscow and Petersburg.
[...]
The upshot of all this is that the German administration in this region may endeavor to lessen the effects of the famines that are sure to follow and to speed the process of naturalisation. One may endeavor to cultivate these areas more intensively, extending the areas of cultivation for potatoes and other high-yield crops important for consumption. Famine cannot be averted there by these means. Tens of millions of people will become superfluous in this region and will have to die or migrate to Siberia. Attempts to save the popula-

tion from starvation by using surpluses from the black earth zone can only occur at th expense of supplying Europe. They limit Germany's staying power in the war, and Germany's and Europe's resistance to a blockade. This must be made absolutely clear.

Text 90

Excerpts from the Army High Command's Decree concerning the treatment of political commissars of the Soviet Army [*"Kommissarbefehl"*], 6 June 1941.

In the struggle against Bolshevism, the enemy cannot be expected to behave according to the principles of humanity or international law. The political commissars in particular can be expected to treat our prisoners with [...] hatred, cruelty and inhumanity.
It must be clear to the troops that
1.) In this struggle, mercy and consideration for international law are misplaced when dealing with these elements.
[...]
2.) The political commissars are the inventors of barbarian Asian fighting methods. They must thus be combatted immediately and unquestioningly with all due severity.
Thus when captured during combat or resistance they are to be disposed of immediately by arms.
The following regulations also apply:
[...]
2.) [The commissars] are to be separated from prisoners of war immediately, i.e., on the battlefield. [...] These commissars will not be recognised as soldiers; the protection of prisoners of war under international law does not apply to them. After separation they are to be disposed of.

Text 91

Excerpt from Hitler's decree as Commander-in-Chief of the Army concerning military jurisdiction in the war against the Soviet Union, 13 May 1941.

Acts committed by members of the German Army and its support forces against enemy civilians must not necessarily be prosecuted, even in those cases where the act is a military crime or offence.

Text 92

Excerpt from Operational Order No. 8 from the Chief of Security Police and Security Service, concerning the guidelines for commandos to be assigned to prisoner of war and transit camps, 17 July 1941.

Top Secret!
Berlin, 17 July 1941
Department IV

Guidelines
for the Commandos of the Chief of Security Police and Security Service that will be assigned to the prisoner of war camps [*Stalags*].
[...]
The Commandos will work independently by virtue of special authority bestowed upon them and according to the general guidelines they were given within the framework of the camp rules. It goes without saying that the Commandos will keep in the closest contact with the camp commander and with the intelligence officer assigned to him.
The task of the Commandos will be the political scrutiny of all camp inmates and the selection and further treatment
a) of those among them who are unacceptable for political, criminal or other reasons,
b) of those persons who can be utilised for the reconstruction of the occupied territories.
[...]
Most importantly, those persons belonging to the following categories must be identified:
all significant state and party functionaries, particularly
professional revolutionaries,
Comintern functionaries,
all important party functionaries of the C.P. of the Soviet Union and its sub-organisations in the central, district and regional committees,
all peoples' commissars and their deputies,
all former political commissars in the Red Army,
the leading personages of the central and intermediate echelons within the state agencies,
leading personages within the economic sphere,
the Soviet Russian intelligentsia,
all Jews,
all persons identified as agitators or fanatical communists.
As already mentioned, it will be no less important to identify all persons who may be put to use in the reconstruction, administration and management of the conquered Russian territories. [...]

118   Sergeant Matveii Artemovich Timokhov, captured by the Germans in November 1943, in the district military hospital for prisoners of war and civilians in Dorogobush on 26 August 1944.

No executions may be carried out within the camp or its immediate vicinity. If the camps are located in the *Generalgouvernement* very close to the border, prisoners singled out for special treatment are to be transported if possible to formerly Soviet Russian territory.
If executions should become necessary, for reasons of camp discipline, the commander of the Special Unit must contact the camp commander on the matter.

Text 93

Letter sent by the *Reichsführer-SS* to the Higher SS and Police Leader for the Ukraine Hans-Adolf Prützmann, concerning the destruction of evacuated areas, 7 September 1943.

Reichsführer-SS	Field Command Post
Tgb. No. 1741/43 geh.R.	7 September 1943
RF/En	Top Secret

To the Higher SS and Police Leader
of the Ukraine
Kiev

7 copies
7th copy

Dear Prützmann,
General of the Infantry Stapf has special orders regarding the Donez region. Get in touch with him immediately. I am expecting you to do your level best. We must ensure that when areas in the Ukraine are evacuated, not a human being, a farm animal, a hundred-weight of grain, or a railway track is left, that not a house is standing, that

BEKANNTMACHUNG

Aus einem Aufruf Aufständischer aus Rasina geht die Ermordung des am 19. 11. 42. in Kupci bei Brus entführten deutschen Soldaten hervor.

Gemäss Ankündigung wurden 30 weitere Kommunisten und Draža Mihajlović – Anhänger erschossen.

Am 15. 12. 42:
1. Kokić Borislav, Abiturient, geb. 30. 9. 22. Leskovac,
2. Petrović Djorgje, Arbeiter, geb. 10. 10. 24. Precina,
3. Popović Jovanka, Lehrerin, geb. 1. 6. 12. Sarajevo,
4. Stojković Anna, Studentin, geb. 19. 11. 20. Šabac,
5. Stijković Borivoje, Bauer, geb. 1914 Gor. Presnica,
6. Djordjević Ilija, Bauer, geb. 20. 2. 20. Zdravinje,
7. Evac Vojislav, Volkssänger, geb. 16. 8. 14. Drenova,
8. Tiegermann Stefan, Schlosser, geb. 13. 5. 05. Bela Crkva,
9. Brković Ratomir, Arbeiter, geb. 15. 4. 20. Kos. Mitrovica,
10. Andjelković Živojin, Buchdrucker, geb. 25. 7. 04. Parzane.

Am 20. 12. 42:
1. Žlvković Draga, Hausfrau, geb. 28. 11. 01. Nisch,
2. Milenković Miodrag, Student, geb. 21. 9. 26. Belgrad,
3. Petrović Stojan, Lehrer, geb. 25. 11. 19. Gornje Gore,
4. Milošević Todor, Bauer, geb. 1889 Gornji Rin,
5. Petković Dragoljub, Gastwirt, 1898 Orana,
6. Radojčić Velja, Bauer, geb. 1889 Dobro Polje,
7. Savković Hranislav, Lehrer, geb. 2. 12. 71. Trnava,
8. Stefanović Jelica, Arbeiterin, geb. 27. 12. 19. Leskovac,
9. Sofrann Rosalija, Arbeiterin, geb. 28. 7. 07. Ivanov,
10. Stojanović Ćira, Bauer, geb. 1917 Donji Dušnik.

Am 25. 12. 42:
1. Hercog Djuro, Schüler, geb. 18. 12. 14. Kupres-Bugojno,
2. Janković Dragiša, Musikant, geb. 1915 Tomislavci,
3. Lazarević Ljutica, Kaufmann, geb. 9. 3. 13. Belgrad,
4. Uskoković Dragoljub, Mechaniker, geb. 15. 4. 16. Babičku,
5. Paunović Živojin, Maler aus Kruševac, geb. 1892,
6. Obradović Nikola, Sattler aus Kruševac, geb. 1883,
7. Aleksić Novica, Pensionär aus Kruševac, geb. 1889,
8. Popović Rista, Zollbeamter aus Kruševac, geb. 1886,
9. Nikolić Mihajlo, Kaufmann aus Kruševac, geb. 1897,
10. Valjarević Dušan, Pensionär aus Kruševac, geb. 1898.

Belgrad, den 29. Dezember 1942.

Der Kommandierende General und Befehlshaber in Serbien

119 Announcement by the Commanding General and Commander in Serbia (General of the Artillery Paul Bader) of the shooting of 30 hostages, 29 December 1942.

120   Members of the General Police [Ordnungspolizei] posing in front of a destroyed building in Lidice, June 1942.
On 10 June 1942 all men in the town were shot dead in retaliation for the assassination attempt on Reinhard Heydrich, the Deputy Reich Protector for Bohemia and Moravia. The town was blown up by the Morigl Engineers (Engineer Battallion 14 in Weißenfels).

not a mine remains that is not destroyed for years to come, that not a well remains that has not been poisoned. The enemy must find a completely burnt-out and destroyed land. Discuss these matters immediately with Stapf and give it your best shot.

Heil Hitler!
Yours,
signed: H. Himmler.

2.) Chief of the General Police [Ordnungspolizei]
3.) Chief of Security Police and Security Service
4.) SS Lieutenant General [Obergruppenführer] Berger
5.) Chief of the Units to Combat Bandits [Banden-Kampfverbände]

Sent copies for their information.

For [signed: signature]
SS Lieutenant Colonel

Text 94

Excerpts from the report by the commander of the 9th Company of the 433rd Infantry Regiment, First Lieutenant Hans-Dietrich Walther to the 704th Infantry Division (Commander Brigadier General Heinrich Borowski), concerning the shooting of Jews and Gypsies, 1 November 1941.

Jews and Gypsies have been shot as hostages here. A note by the head of the Foreign Ministry's section "Jewish question, Freemasons, and Expatriation", Franz Rademacher, says in

this context: "By order of the commander, 100 Serbs are to be shot for every German soldier killed. In the execution of this order the active Communist leaders of Serbian nationality – some fifty in number – are to be shot first, and then increasingly Jews as Communist agitators".

In accord with the SS office I picked up the selected Jews or Gypsies from the prison camp in Belgrade.
[...]
After arriving some 1 1/2 – 2 km from the chosen site [north of Pancevo-Jabuka] the prisoners got out and proceeded on foot while the truck was sent back immediately with its civilian drivers, to give them as little reason for suspicion as possible. Then I had the road closed to all traffic for reasons of security and secrecy.
The place of execution was secured by 3 machine-guns and 12 riflemen.
[...]
Most of the time is taken up by digging the trenches, while the shooting itself goes very quickly (100 men in 40 minutes).
The luggage and valuables were collected immediately and taken away in my truck to be turned over to the NSV [National Socialist Welfare].
It is easier to shoot the Jews than the Gypsies. One must admit that the Jews go to their deaths very calmly – they die very quietly – while the Gypsies cry and scream and keep moving around when they are already standing at the place of execution. Some of them even jumped into the trench before the first shots were fired and pretended to be dead.
In the beginning my soldiers were not much affected. On the second day, however, it became clear that some of them do not have the nerves to carry out shootings over a longer period of time. It is my personal impression that during the shooting itself one does not have any mental reservations. These only set in days later, in the evenings, when one has a chance to think it over in peace.

Text 95

The destruction of the town of Kalavrita as reflected in the Army Operations Staff's situation reports of 3 to 15 December 1943.

3.12.43
LXVIII A.K. [Army Commando]: [...] An operation against bandits in the Kalavrita area by the A.A. 116 has been initiated.

10.12.43

LXVIII A.K.: According to the testimony of two soldiers who escaped, 78 German soldiers of the 5th Rifle Regiment 749 (117th Rifle Division), which was wiped out on 18.10 near Kalavrita [Pelopones, 40 km southwest of Patras], were shot by bandits in the mountains southwest of Kalavrita. Reprisal measures are being carried out.

11.12.43

LXVIII A.K.: In the course of the operation near Kalavrita segments of the northern group have been assigned to carry out reprisals north of Kalavrita (daily report).

12.12.43

LXVIII A.K.: Continuation of Operation Kalavrita without contact with the enemy. Nine villages were destroyed and 142 male inhabitants shot as part of punitive measures.

13.12.43

LXVIII A.K.: Operation Kalavrita has been completed except for local reconnaissance 20 km southwest of Kalavrita and continuation of punitive measures.

15.12.43

LXVIII A.K.: [...]As part of continued reprisals in the Kalavrita area one more village and two monasteries have been destroyed. Among others Kalavrita has been destroyed. A total of over 500 men have been shot. Bodies of 70 German soldiers who had been shot were found.

Text 96

The "Guidelines for the Prosecution of Crimes against the Reich or the Occupation Forces in the Occupied Territories", the so-called "Night and Fog Decree", issued by Hitler as Commander-in Chief of the German Army on 7 December 1941.

2.) The Führer and Commander-in-Chief
         of the Army

Guidelines

for the prosecution of crimes against the Reich or the occupation forces in the occupied territories.
7 December 1941
Since the beginning of the Russian campaign, Communist elements and other anti-German cir-

cles have increased their attacks against the Reich and the occupation forces in the occupied territories. The extent and dangerousness of these subversive activities compel us to take the most severe measures against the perpetrators for reasons of deterrence. The following guidelines are to be followed for the time being:

I.

In the occupied territories, crimes committed by non-German civilians that are directed against the Reich or the occupation forces or that endanger their security or combat effectiveness are punishable by death.

II.

The crimes of Section I are only to be tried in the occupied territories if it is probable that death sentences will be issued against the perpetrators or at least against the main culprit and if the trial and the enforcement of the death penalty can be carried out with all possible dispatch.

III.

Perpetrators who are brought to Germany are only subject to military trial here if special military matters require it. If there are inquiries about these perpetrators, German and foreign agencies are to be told that they are under arrest, but that the state of the proceedings does not permit further information.

IV.

The commanders in the occupied territories and the supreme judicial authorities carry personal responsibility for the enforcement of this decree within their jurisdiction.

V.

The Chief of the Army High Command determines in which occupied territories this decree will be applied. He is authorised to comment, to issue enforcement regulations and to make additions. The Reich Minister of Justice will issue the enforcement guidelines for his domain.

On behalf of
the Chief of the Supreme Command
of the Army
Keitel.

2.6. Racism and Genocide

Racism was the centrepiece of the National Socialist world-view. This world-view was not a coherent theoretical construct, but at most a systematisation of the thoughts expressed by Hitler in *Mein Kampf*. These thoughts were nothing more than radicalised versions of fragments of nineteenth-century political ideologies. In the nineteenth century, racism served the legitimation of European imperialism as well as the maintenance of the hegemony and privileges of a white upper class in racially mixed societies. It did not, however, go so far as to deny those people deemed "racially inferior" the right to exist at all.

This was precisely the result of Hitler's brand of racism, which made hatred of Jews, converted from Christian anti-Judaism into racist anti-Semitism, into a pillar of his ideological structure. Hitler recognised only polar opposites: "the Aryan" representing "light" on the one side, and "the Jew" as the "most extreme contrast to the Aryan" on the other. The opposition between "superior" and "inferior" was transformed into one between "good" and "evil". In so doing, Hitler provided Germans with the "moral" justification for participating in the persecution of Jews. This juxtaposition also made it possible to move from persecution to extermination, and not to spare women and children, since the goal was not to kill individuals, but to wipe out the entire "Jewish race" as the personification of "evil".

The National Socialist leadership not only implanted in the German people a hatred for Jews, but also conveyed to them the conviction that they as "Aryans" were destined to rule the world. The consciousness of class conflict, still alive in the First World War, disappeared during the Second World War in favour of the conviction that in the occupied territories, even a private could strut around as a member of the "master race".

Both sides of National Socialist racism – genocide and the ideology of the "master race" – led not only to complete military disaster but beyond this to the greatest moral crisis ever faced by the German people. In other fascist states – Italy, Spain – genocide was not a political programme, nor did the population stand solidly behind its fascist leaders. Thus coming to terms with the fascist epoch was primarily a problem of domestic politics, which adherents and opponents of the system had to regulate amongst themselves. In Germany, in contrast, the extent of the crimes was so great that it cast a shadow over German history as a whole.

121   The headquarters of "euthanasia" crimes at Tiergarten-straße 4, 1940.
The building no longer exists today. A commemorative plaque has been embedded in the ground on the site, next to the Philharmonie.

The "euthanasia murders"

The National Socialists also directed racist ideology against their own people: those with "hereditary diseases" [Erbkranke] were to be prevented from reproducing, and "burdensome lives" [Ballastexistenzen] were to be "culled out" [ausmerzen]. Compulsory sterilisation was already introduced in 1933 and from 1938 on disabled people, beginning with children, were denied the right to live. Midwives were required to report children born with physical or mental disabilities. Parents were compelled to place them in the children's wards of homes and sanatoria, where they were then murdered. In October 1939 Hitler authorised "specially appointed doctors" to perform "mercy killings" on those "sick people who were, as far as it was humanly possible to tell, incurable". What was being regulated here, however, was not the mercy killing requested by a terminally ill patient – his or her will to live or longing to die was immaterial – but rather the immunity from prosecution of doctors who complied with the National Socialist mandate to kill. This action, erroneously and cynically referred to as "euthanasia", was carried out by an organisa-

tion created expressly for the purpose, which had its offices at Tiergartenstraße 4 ("Aktion T 4"). The patients were taken from hospitals and sanatoria to killing centres at Brandenburg, Bernburg, Grafeneck, Hadamar, Hartheim and Sonnenstein where they were usually murdered with poison gas. This procedure had been recommended by the Criminal Technical Institute of the Reich Criminal Police Office.

The murder of those patients deemed "unworthy of life" [lebensunwert] had to be officially discontinued on 24 August 1941 because of public protests. According to the perpetrators themselves, 70,273 persons had been killed by that point. But even after that date people continued to be murdered by starvation, pills or lethal injection.

"Euthanasia" was also practiced in the occupied territories, particularly in Poland and the Soviet Union. The justifications here were often brutally pragmatic: hospitals or institutions were required for the occupying forces, and they were evacuated by killing the inmates.

In all, more than 200,000 people fell victim to the "euthanasia" murders in Germany and the occupied territories.

Text 97

Letter from the Reich Governor [Reichsstatthalter], on behalf of Dr Friemert, to Bronislawa Biniatowska, concerning notification of the death of Hedwig Biniatowski [actually: Jadwiga Biniatowska], 9 July 1940.

The regional sanatorium [Landesheilanstalt] Tiegenhof (in Polish Dziekanka) mentioned in the letter-head was in German-annexed western Poland (Warthegau).

Reich Governor
Provincial [Gau] Self-
Administration
Wilhelmstr. 29
A.Z. Regional Sanatorium
Tiegenhof

Posen
Landeshaus
Post-office box 381
Telephone 0745-48

Bronislawa Biniakowska
Schamenstr. 8
Nackel

Re: Your letter of 10. 6. 40
Our investigations have shown that Hedwig Biniakowski, born on 11.10.21 at Nakel, about whom you enquired, was transferred to the

Regional Sanatorium at Kostem in December 1939 for organisational reasons.

In Kostem, however, she soon fell ill with influenza and her condition continued to worsen so that she died there on 25.1.1940 of pneumonia.

I enclose the medical death certificate.

On behalf of
Dr Friemert.

Text 98

Excerpts from the "USSR Incident Reports" [*Ereignismeldungen*] Nos. 156 and 173 of the Chief of Security Police and Security Service on shootings of mental patients, 16 January 1942 and 25 February 1942.

From Incident Report No. 156, 16.1.1942:

In the period between 24. and 30.11.41 Special Unit [*Einsatzkommando, EK*] 6 carried out 274 shootings. This number includes 19 political functionaries, 29 saboteurs and looters, and 226 Jews. In the period up to 12.11.41, EK 6 shot 800 out of a total of 1,160 mental patients in the insane asylum at Igrin near Dniepropetrovsk.

From Incident Report No. 173, 25.2.1942:

In recent weeks Special Unit 6 has shot 173 political refugees, 56 saboteurs, and 149 Jews. [...] In the period between 10.1. and 6.2.42, 17 professional criminals, 103 Communist functionaries, 16 partisans and ca. 350 Jews were executed by firing-squad. In addition 400 inmates of the insane asylum at Igrin and ca. 320 inmates of the insane asylum at Wasilkowska were eliminated.

Genocide against the Gypsies (Roma)

Even before 1933, life was not easy for Gypsies in a society that had little sympathy for cultural ways of life different from its own. After the National Socialists assumed power this problem became even more extreme, because the norms of the "German national community" permitted no deviation. Finally, Himmler's decree that the "Gypsy question" must be tackled in the context of "the nature of this race" set the course for extermination, since it was no longer a matter of compulsory social integration, but rather of "racial traits" which applied as much to assimilated Gypsies as to those still following a traditional way of life.

In their commentary to the "Nuremberg Laws", Wilhelm Stuckart and Hans Globke had already certified that the Gypsies, like the Jews, were of "alien blood". The "racial scientists" also did not allow themselves to be swayed by the "Aryan" origins to which Gypsies could point. Ninety per cent of the Gypsies living in Germany, i.e., mainly Sinti, were declared "Gypsies of mixed blood" [*Zigeunermischlinge*], and it was precisely this "mixed character" that was viewed as a threat to the racial substance of the German people. The extermination of the European Gypsies occurred in the shadow of the "final solution to the Jewish question": cars carrying Gyspies were "appended" to deportation trains, the Special Units in the Soviet Union and the German Army's firing squads in Serbia "dealt with the Gypsies at the same time". At the end of the war the Gypsies of Europe had more than a quarter of a million dead to mourn.

Although Otto Ohlendorf, Head of Department III in the Reich Security Main Office and of Special Group D in the Soviet Union, testified at the Nuremberg war crimes trials that the Gypsies had been "dealt with just like the Jews", in postwar Germany the genocide against the Roma was either not acknowledged or even denied altogether. Only in the last decade has a change occurred here.

Text 99

Excerpts from the circular Directive of 8 December 1938 by the *Reichsführer-SS* and Chief of German Police Heinrich Himmler, concerning the "Settlement of the Gypsy Question".

1. (1) The experiences collected thus far in combatting the Gypsy plague, and the knowledge gained from racial-biological research would make it seem advisable to keep in mind the nature of this race when tackling the settlement of the Gypsy Question.
[...]

(3) I therefore direct that all Gypsies, whether sedentary or not, as well as persons roaming in Gypsy fashion must be rounded up [*erfaßt*] by the Reich Criminal Police Office – Central Reich

122   Deportation of Gypsies, Hohenasperg, May 1940.

Administration for Combatting Gypsy Malefaction.
[...]

2. (1) Prior to submitting a report, all Gypsies, Gypsies of mixed blood and persons roaming in Gypsy fashion over the age of six must be registered with the Criminal Identification Department [*erkennungsdienstlich zu behandeln*].
[...]

3. (1) The ultimate determination as to whether someone is a Gypsy, a Gypsy of mixed blood, or another person roaming in Gypsy fashion will be made by the Reich Criminal Police Office based on the testimony of an expert.
(2) I therefore direct [...] that all Gypsies, Gypsies of mixed blood and persons roaming in Gypsy fashion be compelled to submit to a racial-biological examination required for the presentation of testimony by an expert, and to provide the necessary information about their heredity. The implementation of this directive is to be ensured by means of police coercion.
[...]

Text 100

Express letter of 29 January 1943 from the Reich Security Main Office to the Directors of the Criminal Police Offices, concerning the confinement of "Gypsies of Mixed Blood", "Romany Gypsies" and "Balkan Gypsies" to a concentration camp.

Berlin, 29 January 1943
Reich Security Main Office
VA 2 No. 59/3 g

Express Letter
[...]
Subject: Confinement of Gypsies of mixed blood, Romany Gypsies and Balkan Gypsies to a concentration camp
[...]
I. By order of the *Reichsführer-SS* dated 16 December 1942 [...] Gypsies of mixed blood, Romany Gypsies and members of Gypsy clans of non-German blood and Balkan origins are to be selected according to set guidelines, and to be

confined to a concentration camp in the course of an operation lasting only a few weeks. For the sake of brevity, this group of persons will be referred to henceforth as "Gypsy persons" [*zigeunerische Personen*].

Confinement will take place by families, regardless of the degree of mixed blood, in Concentration Camp (Gypsy Camp) Auschwitz.

[...]

III. 1. Attempts should be made to obtain consent for sterilisation from Gypsy persons above 12 years of age who are not yet sterile;

[...]

4. In case of refusal, the Reich Criminal Police Office, after having ascertained the reasons, will decide what steps are to be taken.

[...]

Text 101

Chronology of the deportation of Gypsies to Auschwitz in 1943-44.

1943
February
26.2.: The first transport of Gypsies from the German Reich on the basis of the *RSHA* Decree of 29.1.43 is carried out. Men, women and children are billetted in the unfinished camp section BIIe at Birkenau. It was henceforth called Gypsy Family Camp B II e.

March
1.3.: Second "Gypsy transport" of men, women, and children is billetted in the "Family Camp" at Birkenau.
3.3.: Third "Gypsy transport" of men, women, and children.
5.3.: Fourth "Gypsy transport" of 470 persons from the Reich territory: 219 men and boys (Z-392 – Z-610), 251 women and girls (Z-438 – Z-688).
Including this transport, 828 people, including 391 men and boys and 437 women and girls, had been brought to the camp thus far.
7.3.: Collective transport of Gypsies from the German Reich, Yugoslavia, Poland and Czechoslovakia: 387 male (Z-611 – Z-997) and 510 female inmates (Z-689 – Z-1198).
8.3.: "Gypsy transport" from Czechoslovakia and the German Reich: 590 male (Z-998 – Z-1587) and 584 female inmates (Z-1199 – Z-1782).
9.3.: 300 Gypsies from the Reich territory: 147 male (Z-1588 – Z-1734) and 153 female inmates (Z-1783 – Z-1935).

11.3.: "Gypsy transport" from Czechoslovakia: 351 men and boys (Z-1735 – Z-2085) and 413 women and girls (Z-1936 – Z-2349).
12.3.: "Gypsy transport" from the Reich territory: 113 men and boys (Z-1087 – Z-2199) and 130 women and girls (Z-2350 – Z-2479).
13.3.: "Gypsy transport" from the Reich territory: 640 men and boys (Z-2220 – Z-2839) and 713 women and girls (Z-2480 – Z-3192).
14.3.: "Gypsy transport" from the Reich territory: 461 men and boys (Z-2840 – Z-3330) and 505 women and girls (Z-3193 – Z-3697).
15.3.: "Gypsy transport" from the Reich territory: 215 males (Z-3301 – Z-3515) and 244 females (Z-3698 – Z-3941).
16.3.: "Gypsy transport" from the German Reich, Hungary and Poland: 565 males (Z-3516 – Z-3680) and 198 females (Z-3944 – Z-4141).
17.3.: "Gypsy transport" from Czechoslovakia, the German Reich, and Poland: 332 males (Z-3681 – Z-4012) and 366 females (Z-4142 – Z-4508).
18.3.: "Gypsy transport" from the Reich territory: 307 males (Z-4013 – Z-4319) and 340 females (Z-4509 – Z-4847).
19.3.: "Gypsy transport" from Czechoslovakia: 545 males (Z-4320 – Z-4864) and 529 females (Z-4848 – Z-5376).
23.3.: 1700 unregistered men, women and children are brought from Bialystok. Because of suspected typhus they die in the gas chambers.
24.3.: "Gypsy transport" from the Reich territory: 133 males (Z-4957 – Z-5089) and 128 females (Z-5519 – Z-5646).
27.3.: "Gypsy transport" from the Reich territory: 251 males (Z-5146 – Z-5396) and 263 females (Z-5700 – Z-5962).
28.3.: "Gypsy transport" from the Reich territory: 160 males (Z-5397 – Z-5458 and Z-5462 – 5559) and 192 females (Z-5963 – Z-6154).
31.3.: "Gypsy transport" from Vienna and Lakkenbach Camp: 182 males (Z-5612 – Z-5793) and 256 females (Z-6211 – Z-6466).
According to these figures, 5,910 men and boys and 6,151 women and girls were brought to the camp during this month. Including the unregistered Polish Gypsies of both sexes 13,763 people were admitted to the camp.

1944
[...]

April
15.4.: 884 inmates from Camp Section B II e of the Auschwitz II Concentration Camp are transferred to Buchenwald Concentration Camp.

16.4.: Transport from the German Reich and Poland: 407 male Gypsies (Z-9384 – Z-9790) and 445 female Gypsies (Z-10086 – Z-10530). 935 men and women were registered.

May and June
12.5.: From the St. Josefspflege children's home in Mulfingen: 39 boys (Z-9873 – Z-9892) and 19 girls (Z-10629 -Z-10647).
24.5.: 82 male Gypsies are transferred from Auschwitz to Flössenburg and 144 female Gypsies to Ravensbrück Concentration Camp.
219 male and female Gypsies from the Reich territory, Poland, Russia and Czechoslovakia were registered.

July and August
42 people were admitted in July.
2.8.: 1408 Gypsies of both sexes are transferred to Buchenwald Concentration Camp. 2,897 men, women and children are murdered in the gas chambers.

October
5.10.: 1,188 inmates from Buchenwald Concentration Camp, including 800 Gypsies, former inmates of Auschwitz, are transferred to Auschwitz II.
10.10.: 800 Gypsies die in the gas chambers of Crematorium V.
18.10.: 218 women are transferred from Buchenwald Concentration Camp.

Some 21,300 people are mentioned as registered on admission to the Gypsy Family Camp. In addition there were at least 352 births in the camp.

The Extermination of the European Jews

The persecution of the Jewish population in Germany began immediately after power was turned over to Hitler. Alongside assaults by the SA, the "boycott day" of 1 April 1933 was a major vehicle for testing the extent to which the population would tolerate or even support anti-Jewish measures. The 1st Ordinance supplementing the "Reich Citizenship Law" of 14 November 1935 defined who was to be considered a Jew. This created the legal basis for robbing Jews of their businesses ("Aryanisation") and systematically depriving them of citizenship rights. The anti-Jewish measures reached their pre-war climax in the pogrom of 9-10 November 1938.

All of these measures were intended, among other things, to bring about the emigration of Germany's Jewish population. The theft of Jewish property, however, made this increasingly difficult. When German Jews were forbidden to emigrate in October 1941, of over 500,000 Jews who had lived in Germany in 1933, only 163,969 still resided in the so-called *Altreich* (Germany with its 1937 borders). In that same month deportations to the east began. German policy was no longer to expel Jews, but rather to exterminate them ("final solution of the Jewish question") in all areas under German occupation and in the countries yet to be conquered. At the so-called "Wannsee Conference" of 20 January 1942, the Chief of the Reich Security Main Office, Reinhard Heydrich, calculated the number of Jews living in Europe as 11 million, thus indicating the size of the target of his murderous programme. At the time of the Wannsee Conference the murders had already begun, carried out by the Reich Security Main Office's Special Units in the Soviet Union. The extermination camp at Chelmno (Kulmhof) was founded in October-November 1941. In the course of 1942 extermination camps were established at Belzec, Sobibór and Treblinka. The staff of the *"T 4-Aktion"* were leading participants in the estab-

123   The murder of Jews at Winniza in the Ukraine, 1942.

lishment of these camps. The camps at Majdanek and Auschwitz-Birkenau, which were originally intended as a prisoner of war camp and a concentration camp, respectively, also became sites of mass gassing. A total of between five and six million Jews were murdered.

Text 102

Excerpts from a note by SS Lieutenant Colonel [*Obersturmbannführer*] Walther Rauff, Head of Division II D ("Technical matters") in the Reich Security Main Office, concerning "technical alterations to the special vehicles now in use and under construction", 5 June 1942.

D 3 a (9)	Berlin, 5 June 1942
No. 214/42 g. Rs.	Sole copy.
	Top Secret! [Stamp]

I. Note:

Subject: Technical alterations to the special vehicles now in use and under construction.

Since December 1941, for example, 97,000 have been processed with three vehicles, without any defects arising in the vehicles. [...]

Our experiences up until now make the following technical alterations appear advisable:

1.) In order to allow for a rapid flow of CO without overpressure, two open slits of 10 X 1 cm clear breadth should be made in the rear wall. [...]

2) The vehicles are usually loaded with 9–10 per m^2. The spacious Saurer special vehicles cannot be used for these purposes because, although there would be no overload, their cross-country mobility would be reduced. A reduction of the loading space appears necessary. [...] The abovementioned problem cannot be solved, as it has been up until now, by reducing the number of pieces per load. A reduction in the number of pieces would require a longer operating time, because the empty spaces would also have to be filled with CO. In contrast, with a smaller and completely filled loading space a considerably shorter operating time would suffice, because there would be no empty spaces.

In a discussion with the manufacturers, it was pointed out from this side that shortening the car of the truck would bring with it an unfavourable shift of weight. [...]

In fact, however, an involuntary redistribution of the weight does occur, in that the cargo gravitates towards the rear door during operation and always lies mainly there. In this way no additional stress on the front axle occurs.

6) The lighting fixtures should be better protected than previously against destruction. [...] When the rear door is closed and darkness thus ensues, the cargo always exerts a strong pressure towards the door. [...]This results from the cargo's gravitation towards the light when it becomes dark. This makes it difficult to latch the door. It was also noted that the ensuing noise, probably in connection with the uncanniness of the darkness, always begins when the doors close. It is thus advisable that the lighting be turned on before and during the first few minutes of operation. Lighting is also advantageous during night operations and the cleaning of the vehicle's interior.

Text 103

Excerpts from the autobiography of Rudolf Höss, commandant of Auschwitz, on the function of the murder of Soviet prisoners of war with Zyklon B as a model for the mass murder of the European Jews, 1947.

I was not properly conscious of the first gassing of human beings; perhaps the procedure as a whole made too much of an impression on me. I remember much better the gassing of 900 Russians soon afterwards in the old crematorium, since using Block 11 would have caused too much trouble. While they were still being unloaded several holes were simply knocked through the earth and cement ceiling of the morgue. The Russians had to undress in the outer room and they all went quite calmly into the morgue since they had been told they were to be deloused there. The whole transport walked right into the morgue. The door was locked and the gas poured in through the openings. How long the killing took I do not know. The hum could still be heard for quite a while, however. When it was thrown in some people cried "Gas" and a great roaring began and a rush to both doors. They withstood the pressure, however. – After several hours the room was opened and aired out. Then I saw the gassed corpses en masse for the first time. [...] But I must be frank, this gassing had a calming effect on me, since the mass extermination of the Jews was due to begin soon, and neither Eichmann nor myself knew yet what method of killing might be used on the expected masses. [...] Now we had discovered the gas and the procedure as well.

Text 104

Excerpt from the protocol of the conference ("Wannsee Conference") held on 20 January 1942 in Berlin-Wannsee where the organisational execution of the "Final Solution of the Jewish Question" was coordinated according to plan.

124   Deportation of Jews in Budapest, 1944.

II.
SS Lieutenant General Heydrich, Chief of Security Police and Security Service, opened the meeting by informing those present that the Reich Marshal had put him in charge of preparations for the final solution of the Jewish question, and noted that they had been invited to the conference in order to clarify fundamental issues. The Reich Marshal's request that a draft be submitted to him with regard to the organisational, functional, and material considerations in connection with the final solution of the European Jewish question requires that all central agencies directly concerned with these issues first meet together in order to coordinate their lines of action.
The authority for processing the final solution of the Jewish question is centralised in the hands of the *Reichsführer-SS*, head of German Police (Head of Security Police and Security Service), regardless of geographic boundaries.
[...]

III.
In lieu of emigration, the evacuation of the Jews to the east has emerged as an additional possible solution, now that the appropriate prior authorisation by the Führer has been obtained. But although these operations are to be regarded solely as temporary measures, practical experiences are already being gathered here and will be of major importance for the upcoming solution of the Jewish question. Roughly eleven million Jews will probably be involved in the solution of the European Jewish question. They are distributed as follows among the individual countries:

[...]
In the course of the final solution the Jews are to be sent in a suitable manner and under appropri-

ate direction to do labour in the east. Separated by sex, those Jews able to work will be led in large labour crews into these areas while building roads. In the process, large numbers will undoubtedly drop away through natural attrition. The final remainder that conceivably will still be left and that undoubtedly constitutes the sturdiest segment will have to be dealt with accordingly, as it represents a natural selection which, when left at liberty, must be seen as a germ cell of new Jewish development. (See the lessons history teaches).
In the course of the practical implementation of the final solution, Europe will be combed from west to east. Priority will have to be given to the area of the Reich, including the Protectorate of Bohemia and Moravia, if only because of housing shortages and other socio-political necessities.
The evacuated Jews will initially be brought without delay into so-called transit ghettos, and from there will be transported further east. [...]

3. The Chance for a New Beginning

3.1. The Occupation

At the Yalta Conference in February 1945 the "Big Three" – the United States, the Soviet Union and Great Britain – had decided on the joint administration of Germany, which was to be divided into zones of occupation after the "unconditional surrender". Berlin, which would not belong to any of the zones and which was to be administered jointly by the victorious powers, was chosen as the seat of the Allied Control Council. The fact that Berlin was conquered by Soviet troops, however, meant that for two and a half months, before the Quadripartite Administration – now including France as the fourth victorious power – was installed in mid-July, the city was under the sole authority of the Soviets.

On 27 April, during the battle for Berlin, the City Commandant General Nikolai Bersarin assumed, with his Order No. 1, the "entire administrative and political authority" in Berlin. After an initial phase of uncontrolled violence against the civilian population the City Commandant managed relatively quickly to create somewhat "orderly conditions" and to ensure that the city was supplied with the most important foodstuffs. By mid-May not only had district administrations been established, but also a Berlin municipal authority [Magistrat]. Clearing work was organised and cultural initiatives encouraged. With the beginning of denazification and the registration of political parties, fundamental political decisions were made which would set precedents for further developments. On 5 June the four Commanders-in-Chief announced their joint assumption of supreme governmental authority in Germany. At the same time they confirmed their intention of establishing an Inter-Allied Administration of the Reich capital, although the first Western Allied troops did not reach Berlin until early July. On 12 July the American and British City Commandants officially took over their sectors (while the French sector was only created on 12 August because of disagreements over its boundaries). The four City Commandants met twenty-two times during the year at the Allied Commandatura, with the chairmanship rotating monthly. They issued over 300 orders and regulations.

Practical politics was dominated by efforts to feed the population, by denazification measures, reeducation programmes, reconstruction and industrial dismantlement, and social and cultural policy initiatives. The Allied Commandatura adopted all regulations issued up until 11 July and established the principle of unanimity for all further decision-making. On controversial questions, not least regarding personnel policy, the individual City Commandants introduced the desired regulations unilaterally in their own sectors.

The Allied Control Council for Germany held its first meeting on 30 July and established itself in the period that followed in the building of the Superior Court of Justice [Kammergericht] at Kleistpark. The agreements reached by the victorious powers during the "Berlin Conference", which met from 17 July to 2 August in Potsdam, were fundamental to its work. During the second half of 1945 the will to shape the post-war order in Berlin jointly still predominated, but the conflicts of interests could no longer be overlooked, so that the borders between the sectors soon assumed more than merely formal significance.

125   The first City Commandant of Berlin, General Nikolai E. Bersarin, leaving his headquarters in Luisenstraße (later: Hermann-Matern-Straße) in the Mitte district, May 1945.
The troops under the command of Bersarin were the first to reach Berlin. It was for this reason that Bersarin (1903-1945) was appointed City Commandant of Berlin on 27 April 1945, even before the fighting had ended. He threw himself into his work with great personal commitment, particularly to ensure that the Berlin population had adequate provisions, and he was therefore held in high esteem in Berlin.
On 16 June he went on a motorcycle tour of inspection. At the intersection of Alt-Friedrichsfelde and Schloßstraße he collided with a Soviet military lorry and was killed instantly.

BEFEHL

des Chefs der Besatzung der Stadt Berlin

_____April 1945   Nr. 1.   *Stadt BERLIN*

Heute bin ich zum Chef der Besatzung und zum Stadtkommandanten von Berlin ernannt worden.

Die gesamte administrative und politische Macht geht laut Bevollmächtigung des Kommandos der Roten Armee in meine Hände über.

In jedem Stadtbezirk werden gemäß der früher existierenden administrativen Einteilung militärische Bezirks- und Revierkommandanturen eingesetzt.

Ich befehle:

1. Die Bevölkerung der Stadt hat volle Ordnung zu bewahren und an ihren Wohnsitzen zu verbleiben.

2. Die Nationalsozialistische Deutsche Arbeiterpartei und alle ihr unterstellten Organisationen (Hitlerjugend, N.S. Frauenschaft, N.S. Studentenbund usw.) sind aufzulösen. Ihre Tätigkeit wird hiermit verboten.

Das gesamte führende Personal aller Dienststellen der N.S.D.A.P., Gestapo, Gendarmerie, des Sicherheitsdienstes, der Gefängnisse und aller übrigen staatlichen Dienststellen hat sich binnen 48 Stunden nach Veröffentlichung dieses Befehls in den militärischen Bezirks- und Revierkommandanturen zwecks Registrierung zu melden.

Binnen 72 Stunden haben sich ebenfalls alle in der Stadt Berlin verbliebenen Angehörigen der deutschen Wehrmacht, der SS und der SA zwecks Registrierung zu melden.

Wer sich zu der festgesetzten Frist nicht meldet oder wer sich der Verbergung solcher Personen schuldig macht, wird gemäß den Gesetzen der Kriegszeit zu strenger Verantwortung gezogen.

3. Die Beamten und Angestellten der Bezirksdienststellen haben sich zu mir zwecks Bericht über den Zustand ihrer Dienststellen und Entgegennahme von Anweisungen über die weitere Tätigkeit dieser Dienststellen zu melden.

4. Alle kommunalen Betriebe wie Kraft- und Wasserwerke, Kanalisation, städtische Verkehrsmittel (Untergrund- und Hochbahn, Straßenbahn und Trolleybus);

alle Heilanstalten;

alle Lebensmittelgeschäfte und Bäckereien haben ihre Arbeit zur Versorgung der Bevölkerung wieder aufzunehmen.

Arbeiter und Angestellte der obengenannten Betriebe haben an ihren Arbeitsstätten zu bleiben und ihre Pflichten weiterzuerfüllen.

5. Angestellte der staatlichen Verpflegungslager sowie Privateigentümer von Lebensmittellagern haben binnen 24 Stunden nach Veröffentlichung dieses Befehls alle vorhandenen Lebensmittelvorräte bei dem militärischen Bezirkskommandanten zwecks Registrierung anzugeben und sie nur mit Erlaubnis der militärischen Bezirkskommandanten herauszugeben.

Bis Sonderanweisungen ergehen, erfolgt die Verabfolgung von Lebensmittel in den Lebensmittelgeschäften gemäß den früher existierenden Normen und Lebensmittelkarten. Lebensmittel sind nicht mehr als für 5—7 Tage auszureichen. Für Ausgabe von Lebensmitteln über die existierenden Normen oder für Ausgabe von Lebensmitteln auf Karten von Personen, die in der Stadt nicht mehr anwesend sind, werden die daran schuldigen dienstlichen Personen zu strenger Verantwortung herangezogen.

6. Inhaber von Bankhäusern und Bankdirektoren haben alle Finanzgeschäfte zeitweilig einzustellen. Alle Safes sind sofort zu versiegeln. Man hat sich bei den militärischen Kommandanturen sofort mit einem Bericht über den Zustand des Bankwesens zu melden.

Allen Bankbeamten ist kategorisch verboten, jegliche Werte zu entnehmen. Wer sich der Übertretung dieses Gebotes schuldig macht, wird nach den Gesetzen der Kriegszeit strengstens bestraft.

Neben den im Umlauf befindlichen Reichszahlungsmitteln werden obligatorisch die Okkupationsmarken der Alliierten Militärbehörde in Umlauf gesetzt.

7. Alle Personen, die Feuerwaffen und blanke Waffen, Munition, Sprengstoff, Radioempfänger oder Radiosender, Fotoapparate, Kraftfahrzeuge, Krafträder, Treib- und Schmierstoff besitzen, haben oben Erwähntes

binnen 72 Stunden nach Veröffentlichung dieses Befehls auf den militärischen Bezirkskommandanturen abzuliefern.

Für Nichtablieferung aller oben erwähnten Gegenstände in der festgesetzten Zeit werden die Schuldigen gemäß den Gesetzen der Kriegszeit streng bestraft.

Die Inhaber von Druckereien, von Schreibmaschinen und anderen Vervielfältigungsapparaten sind verpflichtet, sich bei den militärischen Bezirks- und Revierkommandanten zwecks Registrierung zu melden. Es ist kategorisch verboten, jegliche Dokumente ohne Erlaubnis der militärischen Kommandanten zu drucken, zu vervielfältigen, auszuhängen oder in der Stadt in Umlauf zu setzen.

Alle Druckereien werden versiegelt. Einlaß erfolgt nur auf Erlaubnis des militärischen Kommandanten.

8. Der Bevölkerung der Stadt ist verboten:

a) zwischen 22.00 und 08.00 morgens Berliner Zeit die Häuser zu verlassen, auf den Straßen und Höfen zu erscheinen, sich in unbewohnten Räumen aufzuhalten und dort irgendwelche Arbeit zu verrichten.

b) nichtverdunkelte Räumlichkeiten zu erleuchten.

c) ohne Erlaubnis der militärischen Kommandanten irgendwelche Personen, darunter auch Angehörige der Roten Armee und der Alliierten Truppen, in den Bestand der Familie zu Wohnungs- und Übernachtungszwecken aufzunehmen.

d) Eigenmächtiges Wegnehmen der Dienststellen und Privatpersonen zurückgelassener Habe und Lebensmittel.

Einwohner, die die erwähnten Verbote verletzen, werden gemäß den Gesetzen der Kriegszeit zu strenger Verantwortung herangezogen.

9. a) Der Betrieb von Vergnügungsstätten (Kino, Theater, Zirkus, Stadion),

b) Gottesdienste in den Kirchen,

c) der Betrieb von Restaurants und Gaststätten ist bis 21.00 Uhr Berliner Zeit erlaubt.

Für die Ausnutzung öffentlicher Betriebe für die Roten Armee feindseligen Zwecken, für die Störung der Ordnung und Ruhe in der Stadt —, wird die Verwaltung dieser Betriebe zu strenger Verantwortung gemäß den Gesetzen der Kriegszeit herangezogen.

10. Die Bevölkerung der Stadt wird gewarnt, daß sie für feindseliges Verhalten gegenüber Angehörigen der Roten Armee und Alliierter Truppen die Verantwortung gemäß den Gesetzen der Kriegszeit trägt.

Im Falle von Attentaten auf Angehörige der Roten Armee oder der Alliierten Truppen oder für Verübung anderer Diversionsakte gegenüber dem Personalbestand, dem Kriegsmaterial oder Kriegsgut von Verbänden der Roten Armee und der Alliierten Truppen werden die Schuldigen dem militärischen Standgericht überliefert.

11. Verbände der Roten Armee und einzelne Militärangehörige, die in Berlin eintreffen, sind verpflichtet, sich in den von den militärischen Bezirks- und Revierkommandanten angewiesenen Unterkünften Quartier zu nehmen.

Angehörigen der Roten Armee ist ohne Erlaubnis der militärischen Kommandanten die eigenmächtige Aussiedlung oder Umsiedlung der Einwohner, Entnahme von Gütern und Werten bei Einwohnern der Stadteinwohnern verboten.

CHEF DER BESATZUNG UND STADTKOMMANDANT VON BERLIN
OBERBEFEHLSHABER DER N-ten ARMEE
GENERALOBERST N. BERSARIN

STABSCHEF DER BESATZUNG
GENERALMAJOR KUSCHTSCHOW

126   Order No. 1 of 27 April 1945 by the Berlin City Commandant General Nikolai Bersarin.

With Order No. 1 Bersarin took over the "entire administrative and political authority" in occupied Berlin.

127   Red Army trucks loaded with potatoes are being unloaded at a depot in Friedenau, May 1945.

128   Brigadier General Lyne inspecting a parade on the occasion of the entry of the British troops into Berlin on 4 July 1945.

Text 105

Journal entry for 14 May 1945 by an unknown Berlin woman, concerning the delivery of flour by the Red Army.

Members of the Red Army transported flour (and coal) to the bakeries with Army trucks. People formed long queues to buy the first freshly baked bread.

The sound of an engine wrenched me out of my first sleep last night. There were voices and horns outside. I stumbled to the window. Below there was actually a Russian lorry full of flour. The baker already has coal, so he can bake, he has something for the cards and numbers. I heard him cheering and saw him throw his arms around the neck of the Russian driver, who was beaming as well. They do enjoy playing Father Christmas.

129   Street signs in Müllerstraße in Wedding, 1945.

Text 106

Journal entries by Karla Höcker on the requisitioning of houses by the British occupation troops on 4 July and 1 August 1945.

4 July
[…]
It has happened. When we returned home yesterday evening from a rally of the Cultural Federation for Democratic Renewal at Radio House, two MPs were standing by the front door. It was a good thing that I had already spoken to Arnold – just in case something like this happened. The whirlwind of packing, carrying, and organising goes by as in a dream. One feels quite empty inside, quite numb. Sleep is unimaginable. […]
British officer, intelligent, superior, speaking very good German, chairs the meeting. Next to him a very young Colonel, stolid, blond, earnest, with the typical Anglo-Saxon upper lip. Both have lists in front of them, and read out the conditions under which we must vacate the buildings. We may not take any furniture with us, no bedsteads, wireless sets, lamps, carpets, books, musical notes; the deadline: we must give up our keys tomorrow at 10 a.m. And we may not return to the house, not even as an exception. The English are polite, firm and completely impersonal. Executive organs, as the officer says. And he adds: "The officers of the British Army are not hooligans. You will get your flats back in perfect con-

dition when we move out". When. That's something, anyway.
[…]
1 August
In Charlottenburg the requisitioning of entire blocks of houses and streets continues. Kaiserdamm, Fritschestraße, Leistikowstraße. Hundreds, perhaps thousands of people are suddenly without furniture, beds, stoves. Nobody asks where they will go, who will take them in, how they will continue to live. But strangely enough it "works" somehow. One doesn't hear of anyone camping out. And yet these sudden seizures are unsettling and create a new kind of insecurity; we already knew the other, the Russian, a bit. This is more exact, more bureaucratic, but also not exactly pleasant.

Text 107

Journal entry for 2 June 1945 by an unknown Berlin woman on sewing the flags of the four Allies.

On 5 June 1945 the Commanders-in-Chief of the Allied occupation troops, Eisenhower, Montgomery, de Lattre de Tassigny and Zhukov met in Ber-

130 The headquarters of the Allied Control Council in the former Superior Court of Justice [*Kammergericht*] at Kleistpark in Schöneberg, 1945.

In July 1945 Berlin became the seat of the Allied Control Council for Germany. It was responsible for the Quadripartite Administration of all four zones of occupation. At the same time it also oversaw the Quadripartite Administration of Berlin, which was entrusted to the Allied Commandatura. This was composed of the four City Commandants of Berlin, each of whom was solely responsible for his sector, and installed military governments there. The four Allies also maintained a few mutual institutions such as the Allied prison for war criminals in Spandau and the headquarters of the Allied Air Directorate at Tempelhof.

131 Trilingual signpost in Nürnberger Straße in the American Sector, 1945.

The division of Berlin into four sectors brought with it the first indications of a drawing of borders within the city. The multilingual sector signposts were a visible symbol of this. Berliners were still able to cross the otherwise almost unrecognizable borders between sectors. The regulations, however, were determined by the occupying powers of the respective sectors.

lin to sign the "Declaration Regarding the Defeat of Germany and the Assumption of Supreme Authority by the Allied Powers". For this occasion an order was issued to decorate the city with the flags of all four Allies.

At noon I lay in the sun on the balcony of the attic flat. I could see directly into the window of the flat across the way. A woman was treading away at her sewing machine quilting red and blue stripes together. Then she cut circles out of a white rag and pinked the edges into stars. Stars and stripes. It is supposed to be an American flag. On the stairs Frau Grindige asked me how many stars there are on the American flag. I didn't know whether it was 48 or 49, and told her to consult the widow's lexicon. It is a laborious flag for German women sewing by hand, even the colours make a lot of work, the pattern even more so. The Russian flag is so simple in comparison: all one needs is an old swastika flag, which you can find in any house that wasn't bombed; you remove the black-and-white swastika and sew the yellow hammer and sickle and star onto the red. I saw touchingly crooked little hammers and bent sickles. The tricolour is easiest, the French were victors too, after all: simply blue, white and red, three stripes sewn together vertically and there you are. For the red most women

BEFEHL

der Interalliierten Militärkommandantur
der Stadt berlin

11. Juli 1945   *Nr. 1*   *Berlin*

Die Interalliierte Militärkommandantur hat die Kontrolle über die Verwaltung der Stadt Berlin am 11. Juli 1945 übernommen.

Alle früher vom Chef der Garnison und Militärkommandanten der Roten Armee der Stadt Berlin und von den unter alliierter Kontrolle stehenden deutschen Behörden ausgegebenen Befehle und Anordnungen, die die Ordnung und Haltung der Bevölkerung der Stadt Berlin regulieren, sowie die Verantwortung der Bevölkerung für die Verletzung der Befehle und Anordnungen und für gesetzwidrige Handlungen gegen die alliierten Okkupationstruppen betreffend, bleiben bis auf besondere Verfügung in Kraft.

Die Militärkommandanten der Stadt Berlin

UdSSR	USA.	Großbritannien:
Generaloberst	Generalmajor	Generalmajor
GORBATOW	PARKS	LYNE

132 Order No. 1 of the Inter-Allied Military Commandatura for Berlin, 11 July 1945.

After 11 July the Soviet occupying power was no longer solely responsible for the administration of Berlin. It had to share authority with the Americans and the British and, from 12 August on, the French as well. In their first order the Military Commandants decreed that all orders and regulations that had been issued by the Soviet occupying power and the German authorities would remain in force. New orders for the whole of Berlin could only be decided unanimously. This ensured that the joint administration of Berlin, which all desired, would be subject to mutual blockages.

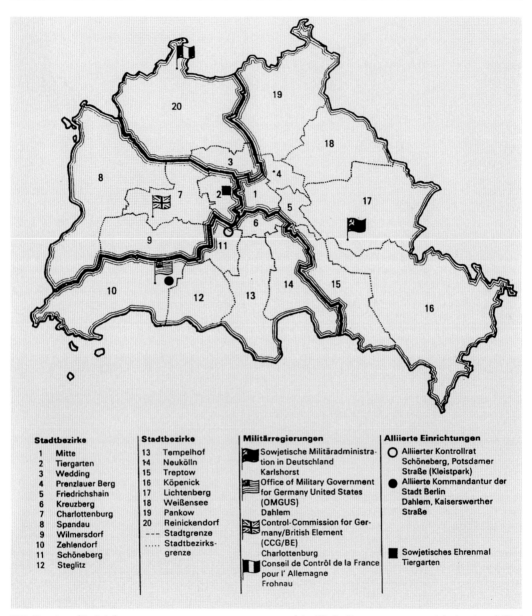

Stadtbezirke		Stadtbezirke		Militärregierungen	Alliierte Einrichtungen
1	Mitte	13	Tempelhof	Sowjetische Militäradministra-tion in Deutschland Karlshorst	Alliierter Kontrollrat Schöneberg, Potsdamer Straße (Kleistpark)
2	Tiergarten	14	Neukölln		
3	Wedding	15	Treptow		
4	Prenzlauer Berg	16	Köpenick	Office of Military Government for Germany United States (OMGUS) Dahlem	Alliierte Kommandantur der Stadt Berlin Dahlem, Kaiserswerther Straße
5	Friedrichshain	17	Lichtenberg		
6	Kreuzberg	18	Weißensee		
7	Charlottenburg	19	Pankow		
8	Spandau	20	Reinickendorf	Control-Commission for Ger-many/British Element (CCG/BE) Charlottenburg	
9	Wilmersdorf	---	Stadtgrenze		
10	Zehlendorf	.....	Stadtbezirks-grenze		Sowjetisches Ehrenmal Tiergarten
11	Schöneberg			Conseil de Contrôl de la France pour l' Allemagne Frohnau	
12	Steglitz				

133 Overview of Berlin's four sectors.
The map shows the division of Berlin into sectors, the headquar-

ters of the Allied military governments and the location of Allied military institutions in the various sectors.

use ticking or remnants of Nazi flags. It is easy to find scraps of bedsheets for the white. Here, too, the problem is blue. I saw people cutting up children's clothing and tableclothes for it. The widow sacrificed an old yellow blouse for the hammer, sickle and Soviet star. The British Union Jack was also pieced together according to her lexicon, the only problem is that it doesn't flutter, but projects from the flagpole stiff as a board – stiff from several metres of wire sewn onto the background of blue apron material in order to hold the red diagonal and cross-stripes. Such a thing is only possible here. An order was issued – by whom, I don't know – to fly the flags of the four victors. And lo and behold, German house-wives produced these flags out of next-to-nothing.

Text 108

French military government decree concerning the establishment of the French Sector, 12 August 1945.

The districts of Reinickendorf and Wedding were transferred from the British sector to create the French sector. The French City Commandant de Beauchèsne adopted all decrees issued by the Soviet and British City Commandants.

French Military Government
Greater Berlin

Decree

In agreement with the Allies, I assume the duties of Military Commandant of the districts of Reinickendorf and Wedding as of 12 August 1945.
In full awareness of my duties I shall employ the requisite force as well as the necessary understanding.
I shall pursue the following three objectives:
the maintenance of the strictest order;
the exercise of the most complete fairness;
the provision of the greatest possible and most indispensable assistance to the population.

I am convinced that the population will facilitate the fulfillment of my duties. It knows that France is generous. But it must also remember how France has suffered.
France cannot forget the 175,000 hostages shot by the Germans on our soil, nor the villages set on fire, nor the citizens who were slaughtered or burnt alive, nor the 200,000 deportees who died as victims in concentration camps after suffering the most terrible torments. True to its greatness and its traditions of generosity, France does not desire revenge after the victory. It is France's right, however, to demand of the German population that it show, through strict discipline and cooperation, that it has parted once and for all from the Nazi crimes and methods whose collaborators, or at least whose silent observers, they were for so many years.
All decrees and announcements issued by the Russian and British Commandants remain in force.

Berlin, 12 August 1945.

The Commanding General
of the French Military Government
of Greater Berlin
signed: de BEAUCHESNE

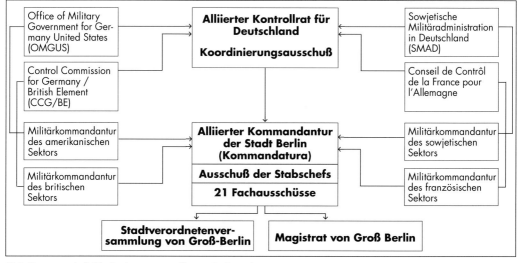

134 Overview of all Allied administrative offices in Berlin and their interrelationships.

135   Men and women of the British Army outside the Reich
Chancellery, which they were to be shown by Soviet soldiers in
July 1945.

136   A view of the conference room during the "Berlin Conference" at Cäcilienhof in Potsdam on 17 July 1945.
The conference with the three heads of state of the USA, the
Soviet Union and Great Britain – Truman, Stalin and Churchill
(later: Attlee) opened on 17 July 1945. It ended on 2 August
1945 with the signing of the political and economic "Principles
to govern the treatment of Germany in the initial control
period", the so-called Potsdam Agreement.

137   Allied officers jointly inspecting a parade on the occasion
of the unveiling of the Soviet war memorial in the Tiergarten,
11 November 1945.

138   British and American soldiers dancing at an excursion
café after the removal of the prohibition on "fraternisation",
18 July 1945.

3.2.   The Liberated and the Stranded

When the Red Army marched into Berlin, they found a large number of men and women whom one might refer to as "compulsory Berliners", since they had been brought to and held in the city against their will. They were prisoners of war from many nations who had been used particularly in industry during the final phase of the war. They were also forced labourers, primarily from Poland and the Soviet Union, who were intended to keep armaments and other production sectors important for the war effort afloat. The addresses of 666 forced labourer camps in Berlin have been traced. Finally, there were the concentration camp inmates, over 90% of them foreigners, who did forced labour in Berlin branch camps, including defusing blind shells. For all of these people, the Soviet victory at the end of fighting on 2 May undoubtedly meant liberation. This was also true of Soviet prisoners of war and forced labourers, although in the Soviet Union they would soon be confronted with the unfounded accusation of having collaborated with the "Third Reich". The term "Displaced Persons" (DP's) was coined in 1945 for the people who had been expelled or abducted from their homelands as a result of the war and German rule in Europe. Not only the occupying powers, but also international aid organisations, above all the UNRRA (United Nations Relief and Rehabilitation Administration), which acted in the name of the newly founded United Nations, organised provisions for them and a return to their home countries. Where repatriation was simple it was accomplished quickly, so that a stay in the camps only served the preparation and organisation of transport. The situation was more complicated for those Eastern Europeans, in particular, who did not wish to return to Poland or the Soviet Union, but for whom not enough host countries could be found. In the course of 1945 (and later as well) growing numbers filled the DP camps, which had been set up mainly in the American and British sectors. It was especially difficult for Jewish survivors of the National Socialist camps who could not or did not want to return to their former homes. They were joined, beginning in 1945, by Jews from Poland who were fleeing to the west to escape anti-Jewish attitudes and excesses. They, too, were housed in the DP camps, some of which were run by Berlin's Jewish Community.

Quite another group of involuntary temporary Berliners were those people who had fled before the advancing Red Army or had been forced to leave their homes by the expulsion of Germans from the territories east of the Oder and Neisse rivers. It was forbidden to move to Berlin, a prohibition that was renewed several times during the year, but also one that was circumvented on a massive scale. It was said that 500,000 refugees were arriving in Berlin every month. To be sure, their stay in one of the 59 transit camps was usually brief, but even simply moving millions of people through the city meant that some 50,000 had to be housed and fed at any given time.

139 French prisoners of war and political prisoners of various nationalities after their liberation by Soviet soldiers, west of Berlin, probably on 8 May 1945.

140 French prisoners of war and female political prisoners in their prison uniforms after being liberated, west of Berlin, probably on 8 May 1945.

141 Members of the British military liberated by the Red Army
from a German prisoner of war camp near Berlin, 1945.

142 Russian women after their liberation from a camp near
Berlin and Soviet soldiers on 20 April 1945.

Text 109

Arrivals and Departures of DP's at the Zehlendorf Camp, November 1945.

Report on Displaced Persons and Organisational Measures

November 1945

Displaced Persons

a.) In the month of November 5,251 displaced persons were admitted to the DP camp in Zehlendorf; 5,143 left the camp. On 30 November there were 519 persons at the camp, including 109 from the Baltic states. This group of 109 persons has been refused admission to the British camp at Hesslingen; thus it was agreed with the USFET that they would be accepted. They will be transferred to Frankfurt by train.

b.) It was also agreed that one hundred U.S. citizens who are currently living at the Zehlendorf DP camp would be sent to Frankfurt by train as soon as the U.S. Consulate in Berlin has verified the U.S. citizenship of these people.

c.) A milk bar has been opened in the DP camp for children up to the age of fourteen, which is open in the mornings and afternoons.

d.) List of the displaced persons who were repatriated in November:

Nationality	Arrivals	Departures
Belgian	196	166
Chinese	18	18
Danish	15	16
Dutch	415	516
French	699	605
Luxembourgeois	13	11
Norwegian	4	10
Polish	–	9
South American	28	33
Spanish	2	1
Swedish	–	5
Swiss	491	587
Stateless and Persecutees	3,296	3,140
USA	25	–
Sum	5,252	5,143

Remaining at the camp: 519
Total number of departures from August to October: 10,224

143 A mother liberated from a concentration camp with her children in Berlin, summer 1945.

Text 110

DP camps in Berlin, 1945.

– Potsdamer Chaussee, "Wiesengrund" (Zehlendorf district). The camp was established on 8 July with a capacity of 2,000 persons, but was already turned into a transit camp for Allied and former prisoners of war on 19 July.

– Potsdamer Chaussee 87, "Düppel Center" (Zehlendorf district). After November this camp, which looked after ca. 3,400 people, increasingly took in Polish Jews; the U.S. Army turned it over to the UNRRA in January 1946.

– Teltower Damm 97-92, (Zehlendorf district, near the present site of the Kennedy School), opened on 5 August. The camp founded by the U.S. Army housed 650 persons, 12% of whom were Jewish.

– Eichborndamm 140-148 (Reinickendorf district). Originally established on 1 December by Berlin's Jewish Community, it was run after 1946 by the aid organisation UNRRA but continued to be administered by the Jewish Community.

– Iranische Straße 3 (Wedding district). Also established by the Jewish community and turned over to the UNRRA in 1946.

– Oranienburger Straße 31 (Mitte district). Established and administered by the Jewish Community.

– Rykestraße 53 (Prenzlauer Berg district). Also established and administered by the Jewish Community.

Camps are also mentioned in Ruhleben and Tempelhof, but with no more precise location given.

Text 111

Report of 20 November 1945 by the Municipal Police [*Schutzpolizei*] on the occupancy rates at refugee camps in the American sector (referred to here as a "zone").

In July 1945 there were 48 refugee camps in Berlin. By order of the Soviet Provisions Commandant, Colonel Kroll, the refugees received soup and 100 g of bread. They were then required to leave Berlin within twenty-four hours. Because many of them were incapable of moving on, not least for reasons of illness, the Allies and the municipal authorities had to create additional capacities for the provision of health care and food.

Berlin, 20 November 1945

The command of the Municipal Police reports, as was requested by telephone at 1900 hours, the refugee camps in the American zone.

			Occupancy	
1.) Kreuzberg	Fichtestr. 4–12 bunker		1100	pers.
2.) Zehlendorf	Leuchtenburg Barracks, Leuchtenburgstr.	ca 400		"
3.) Schöneberg	Priesterweg/ Sachsendamm		500	"
	Friedenau: Fregestr. 13/14		35	"
4.) Steglitz	Unter d. Eichen 93		170	"
	Albrechtstr. 14a		100	"
	Paulsenschule in Flemmingstr.		100	"
	Lankwitz bunker		1000	"
5.) Tempelhof	Lichtenrade Barracks, Steinstr.		600	"
	Roonstr.		400	"
	Bayerischestr.		500	"
	Marienfelde Barracks, Buckower Chaussee 9		1000	"
	Mariendorf Barracks Askania Barracks		500	"
6.) Neukölln	Rudow/ Köpenickerstr.		700	"
	Buckow-Ost, Johannisthaler Chaussee		1000	"

144 Appeal by the Mayor of Zehlendorf for donations of clothing for children's homes and refugee camps, 8 October 1945.

145 A refugee train in Berlin, 1945.

146   Entrance to the former air-raid shelter in Fichtestraße
(Kreuzberg district), no date.
Between 1945 and 1948 the former bunker housed a U.S. military prison (for convicted American soldiers) and a refugee
camp.

3.3.   Everyday Life in the Ruins

For the great majority of Berliners, the post-war period began with a terrifying end, with the experience of catastrophe. The final weeks of the war and the first days of occupation made the idea that something resembling "normal life" might soon return appear absurd. After leaving their cellars and timidly looking around the neighbourhood, taking their first steps into a now-foreign world, however, people's vital spirits returned, and the struggle for survival under post-war conditions began.

This period – in Berlin more than elsewhere – belonged to women. They did what they had already been doing for some time before the end of the war, and would continue to do for a long time afterwards: they tried, with remarkable success, to secure an existence for their families. This was particularly true of those families without husbands and fathers, but frequently also for those with men at home who could no longer fulfill their traditional roles as protector and breadwinner. Although there was scarcely a woman to be found in the upper echelons of the new administration and political parties, everyday life in the city was largely dominated by women. It was women who set up provisional living quarters, who fetched water from the public pumps, who collected wood and other fuel, who made clothing out of uniforms and flags, who dragged or pushed the hand-carts and prams that were the chief means of transportation, through the landscapes of debris. As *Trümmerfrauen*, literally, "rubble women", they made an essential contribution to clearing work and the reconstruction of the city. Under extreme conditions, they retained the will to live that was indispensable for an individual and social new beginning.

To be sure, from mid-May on the first ration-cards were distributed, but the food supply remained anything but adequate. A black market developed, which was combatted but never really controlled by the authorities, particularly since women and children were major participants. The "barter centres" officially set up in September attempted with some success – almost three-quarters of a million people had visited these centres by the end of the year – to meet the continually growing need for exchange, which was born of hardship. Hoarding trips into the nearby countryside became an everyday occurrence, like the many legal and illegal attempts to acquire firewood. Hardship criminality rose rapidly: alongside black market dealings, thefts of coal, firewood, and food from shops and gardens were the most common offences. The hardship was so great that over 650,000 people received public relief in the autumn of 1945. Money lost its value and cigarettes became the new leading currency.

Daily life among the rubble was not only hardship and misery, however. The little joys of everyday life and holidays gradually returned, from walks and swimming to the cinema and dancing, from the first sporting events and little outings to concerts and theatre performances. Despite all the burdens still to be borne one thing was clear: survival had been worth it.

147 War graves at Nollendorfplatz in Schöneberg, no date.

Text 112

Journal entry for 14 May 1945 by an unknown Berlin woman.

On my way to the hydrant I passed many graves. Almost every front garden has such a silent billet. Sometimes there is a German steel helmet, sometimes the standard Russian wooden column glaring bright red with the white Soviet stars. They must have dragged whole truckloads of these monuments with them.

Text 113

Journal entry for 2 May 1945 by Karla Höcker.

We are moving back upstairs. I board up the windows blown out when the rocket launcher hit. Suddenly we hear that they are distributing food at Rollenhagen's. Geri and I go over, find the shop door open, a Russian soldier standing in front, beside him a civilian with a blue, red and white badge. Food? Nichevo! But the same thing

148 Flats with vegetables growing on the makeshift balcony in
the ruins of a house, 1946.

149 Makeshift flat in Berlin, 1945.

150 Two Berlin women transporting a coffin by rack-wagon, 1945.

is supposed to be going on at Scholz's. People press in through broken shop windows; there is no Russian here distributing anything. While we stand around undecided, something awful happens. The mob – but it is the local mob – pounces on the flour, semolina, margarine and noodles, tearing open and overturning drawers; hands rummaging around, greedily collecting sugar to stuff it into the jars they have brought along. It scatters by the pound, falling to the floor, dirty boots tramp over it. Other people push down to the cellar, where they discover crates of tomato paste and other good things. People are seized by a frenzy of covetousness, the solid citizens are losing control.

In Lindenallee there are Russian soldiers. Some have requisitioned bicycles, they are making their first attempts, clumsy as cavemen. But they seem to be enjoying themselves immensely. In Nußbaumallee a gigantic crater in a garden, a grenade hit, the garage broken open. Many houses in this area have new damage and shell holes; broken branches lie in the street, which is strewn with shell-splinters, bullets, and pieces of uniforms. A dead Red Army soldier at the corner of Nußbaum- and Kastanienallee. His face, smeared with blood, looks made-up. Strange

how in reality things are often laid on a bit too thick.

Text 114

Journal entries by the seventeen-year-old Lieselotte G., 30 April to 10 May 1945.

30.4. I was at the top of the cellar stairs with Frau Berendt when the bomb hit. The Russians are here. They are completely drunk. Rapes at night. Not me. But Mother. Some people 5-20 times.

1.5. The Russians coming and going. All the clocks are gone. The horses are lying on our beds in the courtyard. The cellars have been broken into. We have fled to Stubenrauchstr. 33.

2.5. The first night of peace. From Hell to Heaven. We cried when we discovered the lilacs blooming in the courtyard.

All wireless sets must be turned in.

3.5. Still in Stubenrauchstr. Can't go to the window in case a Russian sees me. They say there are rapes everywhere.

4.5. In Derfflingerstr., no news of Papa.

151 Berliners using hand-carts and prams as a means of transport, 1945.

5.5. Back to Kaiserallee. Chaos!

6.5. Our house was hit 21 times! Cleared out and packed all day. Night assault. I crawled under the bed for fear the Russians were coming. But the house was only rattling so because of the shelling.

7.5. Shovelled the street clear. Fetched numbers for bread, tidied up and cleaned.

8.5. Shovelled the street. Queued for bread. News that Papa is alive.

9.5. Armistice. There's milk for Margit.

10.5. Tidied up.

Text 115

Journal entry for 13 May 1945 by Margret Boveri.

It is astonishing how fast everything happens. The removal of heaps of debris from the streets, organised by the citizens themselves, many of them also conscripted for much more extensive clearing work; the public utilities taken in hand by their clerks and workers, who became skilled at repair during the bombing raids. In Friedenau some streets already have water and electricity; four trams are supposedly already serving segments of lines; on our circular railway we hear steam locomotives whistling at night; there has already been water in our cellar twice for an hour at a time. In Friedenau the people are also getting special rations because Friedenau surrendered without a fight.

Text 116

Excerpt from a study by Hilde Thurnwald concerning youthful black marketeers [*Schwarzhändler*] and racketeers [*Schieber*], 1948.

In this context one must once again point to the black market, which attracts not only schoolchildren but often teachers as well. Occasionally it brings teachers and pupils together and undermines the class's respect for the teacher's character. It is well-known that the black market plays a significant role in school life among children of all ages, above all at boys' schools.

[...]

152 Queuing at a bus stop in Kaiserdamm, 1945.

153 Ferry across the Landwehrkanal at the wrecked Möckern
Bridge, 1945.

154 Berlin *Trümmerfrauen* ("rubble women") pushing a truck with debris, 1945.

These young people, disinclined to regular work or serious effort, mainly the well-known "youthful racketeers", mostly 18- to 20-year old boys, can be found in certain cafés in certain districts of Berlin, sitting around from morning til night, usually with their girls, and selling cigarettes, alcohol and other stimulants.

Many of these youths carry on their business in agreement with their families or in concert with their fathers, mothers and siblings.

Text 117

Journal entry for 6 September 1945 by Karla Höcker.

Growing one's own vegetables and potatoes was a means of supplementing meagre food rations. To be sure, not everyone was willing to go to the effort, and "field theft" was a frequently reported offence in 1945.

Went to the garden in the evening to water, dead tired. But we want to harvest our vegetables, tomatoes, potatoes. I came into the garden from Lindenallee, as I always do now, and felt straight away that something wasn't right. I leaned my bicycle against the chestnut tree, and then I realised. Our little potato field, that had stood so nicely, had been ransacked and plundered with indescribable brutality. Tiny bulbs, doll potatoes were strewn all around, scarcely a stock was left standing; it was a bit like child murder. I was devastated. All the effort it had cost us to find seed-potatoes! They would have yielded two hundred pounds, salvation for the winter.

I gather the marble-sized potatoes. Swarms of mosquitoes buzz around me, otherwise it is dead quiet. In the dark through Lindenallee, past our old flat. And my desk-lamp is burning, my wireless is playing – in my room! I cried uncontrollably. It was silly, of course, I realised it right away. But the incident with the potatoes was just too much for me.

155 Berlin *Trümmerfrau* ("rubble woman") cleaning bricks, 1946.

The "rubble women" of Berlin came to symbolise clearing work in the first weeks and months after the end of the war. Over 50,000 "rubble women" worked in Berlin clearing away the debris of destroyed houses, freeing the streets for traffic and recovering old bricks as building material for the reconstruction of the city.

The "rubble women" often performed the heaviest labour for very low wages. They at least got better ration-cards and thus did not have to depend on the "starvation cards".

156 Berliner making a successful deal with a British soldier, 1945. She carefully counts the cigarettes she has received in exchange.

157 British Military Police taking away black marketeers, among them Soviet soldiers, after a raid in 1945.

158 Women queuing to buy food with ration-cards in 1945.

159 A view of the deforested Tiergarten after the great "wood action", no date.

160 Returned prisoners of war conversing with Berlin women
in 1945.
During the summer and autumn of 1945 the first Berliners
returned from prisoner of war camps. They had difficulty adjust-
ing to post-war Berlin.

161   Children returning home with sacks of hoarded goods
and firewood in 1945.

3.4. Denazification and Anti-Fascism

The Allies agreed that the end of the "Third Reich" must be accompanied by the punishment of those guilty of the crimes committed both inside and outside Germany, and by a thorough "denazification" of society. This came as no surprise to the Germans. The arrests and dismissals began immediately, at the beginning of May, and in early July the municipal authority [*Magistrat*] presented the first report on its denazification measures in the personnel field: by that time 11,677 people had been dismissed from the municipal administration, 7,631 from the postal and telecommunications service, 1,102 from the Higher Fiscal Board, and 903 from BEWAG, the electric power-supply company. NSDAP functionaries and members were enlisted for special labour details. "Nazi property" had to be reported and was then confiscated. In the private sector as well 1,400 businesses belonging to "active Nazis" were closed. The introduction of standardised questionnaires and special denazification committees made the procedures tighter but also more formalised, such that the category "fellow traveller" assumed growing significance.

The internment of National Socialist functionaries played an important role not only during the initial weeks, and there was a very high death rate in the Soviet zone's internment camps (later called "special camps"). Public space, too, required denazification, from the swastikas all over the city to street names, postage stamps and official seals. A "general cleansing" of Berlin street names was begun in the summer of 1945, and by December 677 "politically outmoded" street names had been replaced, often by their pre-Nazi appellations.

On 18 October 1945 the "International Military Tribunal for the Trial of the Major War Criminals" met for the first time in the Allied Control Council building. The "Nuremberg trials" opened in Berlin with the presentation of the bill of indictment, and then continued on 20 November 1945 in Nuremberg.

On 3 June 1945 the central committee "Victims of Fascism" [*Opfer des Faschismus, OdF*] was set up within the Berlin municipal authority. It was responsible in particular for the social needs of people who had been persecuted under the Nazi regime. Since the committee distinguished between "victims" and "anti-fascist fighters", and only felt responsible for the latter (because the number of victims would have been too great in any case), conflicts soon arose over who would be recognized as an "OdF". It was some time, for example, before assistance was offered to persecuted Jews who had not belonged to a resistance group. As of March 1946, only some 6,000 persons had received an "OdF card". The public high point of the central committee's activities was the "Commemorative Rally for the Victims of Fascist Terror" which attracted ca. 70,000 people to Neukölln on 9 September.

The schools were a central arena for measures to denazify Berlin society. All National Socialists were dismissed and teachers' assistants and new teachers (many of them women) hired to replace them. In September there were already over 4,000 teachers' assistants and new trainee teachers. At the same time the old books were withdrawn, new ones produced and new guidelines established in order to ensure children a democratic education.

162   A sergeant of the British Army at the entrance to the former Reich Chancellery, no date.

Text 118

Allied Law No. 5, concerning the dissolution of the NSDAP and other National Socialist organisations, 12 July 1945.

Control Area of the Supreme Commander, AEP
Greater Berlin

Law No. 5

Dissolution of the National Socialist German Workers' Party (NSDAP)

In order to put an end to the rule of lawlessness, terror and inhumanity established by the NSDAP within the occupied territory, it is hereby determined that:

1. The National Socialist German Workers' Party and the agencies, organisations and institutes listed below will be dissolved and declared unlawful to the full extent of their activities within the occupied territory. Any activity on the part of the party, the following agencies, organisations and institutes, with the exceptions made in Para 5, is prohibited:

1. *Partei-Kanzlei* (Party Chancellery),
2. *Kanzlei des Führers der NSDAP* (Chancellery of the Führer of the NSDAP),
3. NSDAP organisations abroad,
4. *Volksbund für das Deutschtum im Ausland* (National Association for Germanism Abroad),
5. *Volksdeutsche Mittelstelle* (Main Office for Ethnic Germans),
6. *Parteiamtliche Prüfungskommission zum Schutze des NS-Schrifttums* (Party Review Board for the Protection of NS Writings),
7. *Reichsorganisationsleiter der NSDAP* (NSDAP Director of Reich Organisations),
8. *Reichsschatzmeister der NSDAP* (NSDAP Reich Treasurer),
9. *Beauftragte des Führers für die Ueberwachung der gesamten geistigen und weltanschaulichen Schulung und Erziehung der NSDAP* (Führer's Commissioner for the Surveillance of all NSDAP Intellectual and Ideological Indoctrination and Training),
10. *Reichspropagandaleiter der NSDAP* (NSDAP Reich Propaganda Director),
11. *Reichsleiter für die Presse und Zentralverlag der NSDAP* (*Eher-Verlag*), (Reich Director for the Press and the Central Publishing House of the NSDAP),
12. *Reichspressechef der NSDAP* (NSDAP Reich Press Director),
13. *Reichsamt für das Landvolk* (Reich Office for the Rural Population),
14. *Hauptamt für Volksgesundheit* (Central Office of Public Health),
15. *Hauptamt für Erzieher* (Central Office for Educators),
16. *Hauptamt für Kommunalpolitik* (Central Office for Municipal Policy),
17. *Hauptamt für Beamte* (Central Office for Civil Servants),
18. *Hauptamt für Technik* (Central Office for Technology),
19. *Hauptamt für Kriegsopfer* (Central Office for Victims of War),
20. *Beauftragte der NSDAP für alle Volksumfragen* (NSDAP Commissioner for Surveys of the Population),
21. *Rassenpolitisches Amt der NSDAP* (NSDAP Office of Racial Policy),

22. *Amt für Sippenforschung* (Office of Genealogical Research),
23. *Kolonialpolitisches Amt der NSDAP* (NSDAP Office of Colonial Policy),
24. *Außenpolitisches Amt der NSDAP* (NSDAP Office of Foreign Policy),
25. NSDAP parliamentary group,
26. *NS-Frauenschaft* (NS Women's Organisation),
27. *Deutsches Frauenwerk* (German Women's Association),
28. *Reichsfrauenführung* (Reich Women's Leadership),
29. *NSD-Aerztebund* (Medical Association),
30. *NS-Bund Deutscher Technik* (German Technology Association),
31. *NS-Lehrbund* (Teaching Association)
32. *Reichsbund der Deutschen Beamten* (Reich Association of German Civil Servants),
33. *Reichskolonialbund* (Reich Colonial Association),
34. *NS-Schwesternschaft* (Nurses' Association),
35. *Reichsstudentenführung* (Reich Student Leadership),
36. *NSD-Studentenbund* (NS Students' Association),
37. *Deutsche Studentenschaft* (German Students Association),
38. *NS-Altherrenbund der Deutschen Studenten* (Old Boys' Association of German Students),
39. *NSD-Dozentenbund* (Association of University Teachers),
40. *NS-Rechtswahrerbund* (NS Association of Protectors of the Law),
41. *Reichsbund Deutsche Familie* (Reich German Family Association),
42. *Deutsche Arbeitsfront* (German Labour Front),
43. *NS-Reichsbund für Leibesübungen* (Reich Association for Physical Training),
44. *Reichskriegerbund* (Reich Soldier's Association),
45. *NS-Kriegsopferversorgung* (*NSKOV*) (War Victims' Relief),
46. *Winterhilfswerk des Deutschen Volkes* (German People's Winter Aid),
47. *Reichskulturkammer* (Reich Chamber of Culture),
48. *Deutscher Gemeindetag* (German Federation of Municipalities),
49. *Geheime Staatspolizei* (Secret State Police),
50. *Deutsche Jägerschaft* (German Hunters' Association)

51. *Sachverständigenbeirat für Bevölkerungs- und Rassenpolitik* (Expert Advisory Board for Population and Racial Policy),
52. *Reichsausschuß zum Schutze des Deutschen Blutes* (Reich Committee for the Protection of German Blood).

2. The quasi-military organisations listed below, their recruiting offices, training centres and the warehouses belonging to them are to be dissolved at once. Regulations regarding personnel and equipment will be issued by the military government. Until receipt of these regulations all career officers and troops will remain at their posts. Further recruitment is prohibited.

1. SA (*Sturmabteilung*), including the *SA Wehrmannschaften*,
2. SS (*Schutzstaffeln*), including the *Waffen SS* (Combat SS),
3. NSKK (*NS-Kraftfahrer-Korps*) (NS Motor Corps),
4. NSFK (*NS-Fliegerkorps*) (NS Flyers' Corps),
5. HJ (*Hitler-Jugend*) (Hitler Youth), including its various sub-organisations,
6. RAD (*Reichsarbeitsdienst*) (Reich Labour Service),
7. OT (*Organisation Todt*),
8. TN (*Technische Nothilfe*) (Technical Emergency Aid).

3. All offices of *Volkswohlfahrt* [the National Socialist welfare organisation], in the occupied territory will be closed. Welfare activities will be taken over by the Lord Mayor, pending further instructions from the military government.

4. Any activity on the part of organisations dissolved or closed by the military government, or by their officers or members, and any actions intended in any way to facilitate or lead to the continuation or reestablishment of such activities, are prohibited.

5. All monies and assets, all property, all equipment, account books and papers of any organisation named in this law are to be preserved intact and delivered or transferred according to the regulations issued by the military government. Until delivery or transfer has occurred all property, account books and papers are to be available for inspection. Officers and other persons to whom such objects have been entrusted, as well as administrative officers are to remain at their posts until further notice; they are

answerable to the military government and must see that all necessary measures are taken to ensure that the monies and assets, property, equipment, account books and papers will be preserved unharmed, and that all regulations of the military government regarding the freezing and supervision of assets will be observed.

6. Any violation of the stipulations of this law will be punished by a court of the military government with the legally allowed sentence it deems appropriate, including the death penalty.

7. This law comes into effect on the day of its promulgation.

On behalf of the Military Government.

Text 119

Notification by the municipal authority [*Magistrat*], Department of Trade, on the "Removal of Fascist Elements from Trade" [*Bereinigung des Handels von faschistischen Elementen*], July 1945.

Removal of Fascist Elements from Trade.

[...]
It is recommended to the district mayors that:
1. closed shops whose owners have fled be confiscated and entrusted to reliable merchants;
2. shops whose owners were active members of the NSDAP, SA or SS not be supplied with rationed essential commodities;
3. shopkeepers who did not belong to the NSDAP but who propagated fascist or militarist ideas be warned and, if necessary, have their shops closed;
4. if requirements call for the continued running of shops mentioned under paragraphs 1 and 3, a new owner is to be officially appointed. In this case absolute suitability and reliability is essential.

The municipal authority, Department of Trade, is to be provided with a list of people who have been deprived of their businesses.

Berlin, 22 May 1945.

The municipal authority [*Magistrat*] of the city of Berlin
Department of Trade and Crafts
Orlopp

Text 120

Excerpt from the Memorandum of 6 July 1945 concerning dismissals of former members of the NSDAP and other National Socialist organisations from the Berlin municipal administration.

At the end of July 25,000 administrative employees had been dismissed. When they registered at the Unemployment Office they received an hourly wage of 72 pfennigs as "reconstruction and conscripted labourers" [*Aufbau- und Einsatzarbeiter*] and the lowest level of ration-card V.
This memorandum is a copy made by the Research Group for Post-War History on behalf of the Berlin Senator for National Education in 1953.

Memorandum

on the meeting of the Heads of Personnel Departments in the Offices of the District Mayors on 6 July 1945 in the Berlin municipal building [*Stadthaus*].
The meeting began at 4 p.m. and ended around 5.45 p.m.
Chairman: Town Councillor Arthur Pieck

Subject: The enforcement of the two orders issued by Marshal Zhukov.
Order No. 1: Dismissal of Nazis.

Herr Pieck opened the meeting by reading out the reports from the individual districts on dismissals of Party members. Since 1.5.45, when the municipal administration was established, it has dismissed 11,677 Party members, in the postal and telecommunications service 7,631, the Higher Fiscal Board [*Oberfinanzpräsidium*] 1,102, and *Bewag* 903 Party members, however these figures are not exhaustive, but only intended to give a general picture.

It is absolutely certain that the Marshal's order is to be followed with the utmost severity and the dismissals to be issued uncompromisingly. This is, however, especially difficult in the health and building sectors. All available specialists in these fields absolutely must be brought in. In order to avoid the gaps (particularly in health care) which arise as a result of immediate dismissals, and which cannot be allowed because of the potentially greater harm to the city in the momentary situation, it is permissable to apply for rehabilitation. Such applications must, however, be submit-

MG / PS / G / 9a
(Rev. 15 May 45)

MILITARY GOVERNMENT OF GERMANY

Fragebogen

WARNING: Read the entire Fragebogen carefully before you start to fill it out. The English language will prevail if discrepancies exist between it and the German translation. Answers must be typewritten or printed clearly in block letters. Every question must be answered precisely and conscientiously and no space is to be left blank. If a question is to be answered by either "yes" or "no", print the word "yes" or "no" in the appropriate space. If the question is inapplicable, so indicate by some appropriate word or phrase such as "none" or "not applicable". Add supplementary sheets if there is not enough space in the questionaire. Omissions or false or incomplete statements are offenses against Military Government and will result in prosecution and punishment.

WARNUNG: Vor Beantwortung ist der gesamte Fragebogen sorgfältig durchzulesen. In Zweifelsfällen ist die englische Fassung maßgebend. Die Antworten müssen mit der Schreibmaschine oder in klaren Blockbuchstaben geschrieben werden. Jede Frage ist genau und gewissenhaft zu beantworten und keine Frage darf unbeantwortet gelassen werden. Das Wort „ja" oder „nein" ist an der jeweilig vorgesehenen Stelle unbedingt einzusetzen. Falls die Frage durch „Ja" oder „Nein" nicht zu beantworten ist, so ist eine entsprechende Antwort, wie z. B. „keine" oder „nicht betreffend" zu geben. In Ermangelung von ausreichendem Platz in dem Fragebogen können Bogen angeheftet werden. Auslassungen sowie falsche oder unvollständige Angaben stellen Vergehen gegen die Verordnungen der Militärregierung dar und werden dementsprechend geahndet.

A. PERSONAL / A. Persönliche Angaben

1. List position for which you are under consideration (include agence or firm). — 2. Name (Surname). (Fore Names). — 3. Other names which you have used or by which you have been known. — 4. Date of birth. — 5. Place of birth. — 6. Height. — 7. Weight. — 8. Color of hair. — 9. Color of eyes. — 10. Scars, marks or deformities. — 11. Present address (City, street and house number). — 12. Permanent residence (City, street and house number). — 13. Identity card type and number. — 14. Wehrpass No. — 15. Passport No. — 16. Citizenship. — 17. If a naturalized citizen, give date and place of naturalization. — 18. List any titles of nobility ever held by you or your wife or by the parents or grandparents of either of you. — 19. Religion. — 20. With what church are you affiliated? — 21. Have you ever severed your connection with any church, officially or unofficially? — 22. If so, give particulars and reason. — 23. What religious preference did you give in the census of 1939? — 24. List any crimes of which you have been convicted, giving dates, locations and nature of the crimes.

1. Für Sie in Frage kommende Stellung: ....

2. Name ....   3. Andere von Ihnen benutzte Namen
   Zu-(Familien-)name   Vor-(Tauf-)name

   oder solche, unter welchen Sie bekannt sind. ....

4. Geburtsdatum ....   5. Geburtsort ....

6. Größe ....   7. Gewicht ....   8. Haarfarbe ....   9. Farbe der Augen ....

10. Narben, Geburtsmale oder Entstellungen ....

11. Gegenwärtige Anschrift ....
                                                              (Stadt, Straße und Hausnummer)

12. Ständiger Wohnsitz ....
                                                              (Stadt, Straße und Hausnummer)

13. Art der Ausweiskarte ....   Nr. ....   14. Wehrpaß-Nr. ....   15. Reisepaß-Nr. ....

16. Staatsangehörigkeit ....   17. Falls naturalisierter Bürger, geben Sie Datum und Einbürgerungsort an.

18. Aufzählung aller Ihrerseits oder seitens Ihrer Ehefrau oder Ihrer beiden Großeltern innegehabten Adelstitel.

19. Religion ....   20. Welcher Kirche gehören Sie an? ....   21. Haben Sie je offiziell oder inoffiziell

Ihre Verbindung mit einer Kirche aufgelöst? ....   22. Falls ja, geben Sie Einzelheiten und Gründe an. ....

                                                              23. Welche Religionsangehörigkeit

haben Sie bei der Volkszählung 1939 angegeben? ....   24. Führen Sie alle Vergehen, Uebertretungen oder Verbrechen

an, für welche Sie je verurteilt worden sind, mit Angaben des Daturms, des Orts und der Art. ....

B. SECONDARY AND HIGHER EDUCATION / B. Grundschul- und höhere Bildung

Name & Type of School (If a special Nazi school or military academy, so specify) Name und Art der Schule (Im Fall einer besonderen NS oder Militärakademie geben Sie dies an)	Location Ort	Dates of Attendance Wann besucht?	Certificate Diploma or Degree Zeugnis, Diplom o. akademischer Grad	Did Abitur permit University matriculation? Berechtigt Abitur oder Reifezeugnis z. Universitätsimmatrikulation?	Date Datum

25. List any German University Student Corps to which you have ever belonged. — 26. List (giving location and dates) any Napola, Adolph Hitler School, Nazi Leaders College or military academy in which you have ever been a teacher. — 27. Have your children ever attended any of such schools? Which ones, where and when? — 28. List (giving location and dates) any school in which you have ever been a Vertrauenslehrer (formerly Jugendwalter).

25. Welchen deutschen Universitäts-Studentenburschenschaften haben Sie je angehört? ....
26. In welchen Napola, Adolf-Hitler-, NS-Führerschulen oder Militärakademien waren Sie Lehrer? Anzugeben mit genauer
    Orts- und Zeitbestimmung. ....
27. Haben Ihre Kinder eine der obengenannten Schulen besucht? ....   Welche, wo und wann? ....

28. Führen Sie (mit Orts- und Zeitbestimmung) alle Schulen an, in welchen Sie je Vertrauenslehrer (vormalig Jugendwalter)
    waren. ....

C. PROFESSIONAL OR TRADE EXAMINATIONS / C. Berufs- oder Handwerksprüfungen

Name of Examination Name der Prüfung	Place Taken Ort	Result Resultat	Date Datum

163   Title page of a questionnaire issued by the U.S. military government in Germany to check NS memberships, May 1945 (issued in Berlin in the summer of 1945).

40. Indicate on the following chart whether or not you were a member of and any offices have held in the organizations listed below. Use lines 96 to 98 to specify any other associations, society, fraternity, union, sydicate, chamber, institute, group, corporation, club or other organization of any kind, whether social, political, professional, educational, cultural, industrial, commercial or honorary, with which you have ever been connected or associated. — Column 1: Insert either "yes" or "no" on each line to indicate whether or not you have ever been a member of the organization listed. If you were a candidate, disregard the columns and write in the word "candidate" followed by the date of your application for membership. — Column 2: Insert date on which you joined. — Column 3: Insert date your membership ceased if you are no longer a member. Insert the word "Date" if you are still a member. — Column 4: Insert your membership number in the organization. — Column 5: Insert the highest office, rank or other post of authority which you have held at any time. If you have never held an office, rank or post of authority, insert the word "none" in Columns 5 and 6. — Column 6: Insert date of your appointment to the office, rank or post of authority listed in Column 5.

40. In der folgenden Liste ist anzuführen, ob Sie Mitglied einer der angeführten Organisationen waren und welche Aemter Sie darin bekleideten. Andere Gesellschaften, Handelsgesellschaften, Burschenschaften, Verbindungen, Gewerkschaften, Genossenschaften, Kammern, Instituten, Gruppen, Körperschaften, Vereine, Verbände, Klubs, Logen oder andere Organisationen beliebiger Art, seien sie gesellschaftlicher, politischer, beruflicher, sportlicher, bildender, kultureller, industrieller, kommerzieller oder ehrenamtlicher Art, mit welchen Sie je in Verbindung standen oder welchen Sie angeschlossen waren, sind auf Zeile 96–98 anzugeben.

1. Spalte: "Ja" oder "nein" sind hier einzusetzen zwecks Angabe Ihrer jemaligen Mitgliedschaft in der angeführten Organisation. Falls Sie Anwärter auf Mitgliedschaft oder unterstützendes Mitglied oder im „Opferring" waren, ist, unter Nichtberücksichtigung der Spalten, das Wort „Anwärter" oder „unterstützendes Mitglied" oder „Opferring" sowie das Datum Ihrer Anmeldung oder die Dauer Ihrer Mitgliedschaft als unterstützendes Mitglied oder im Opferring einzusetzen.
2. Spalte: Eintrittsdatum.
3. Spalte: Austrittsdatum, falls nicht mehr Mitglied, anderenfalls ist das Wort „gegenwärtig" einzusetzen.
4. Spalte: Mitgliedsnummer.
5. Spalte: Höchstes Amt, höchster Rang oder eine anderweitig einflußreiche, von Ihnen bekleidete Stellung. Nichtzutreffendenfalls ist das Wort „keine" in Spalte 5 und 6 einzusetzen.
6. Spalte: Antrittsdatum für Amt, Rang oder einflußreiche Stellung laut Spalte 5.

	1 Yes or No ja oder nein	2 From von	3 To bis	4 Number Nummer	5 Highest Office or rank held Höchstes Amt oder höchster Rang	6 Date Appointed Antrittsdatum
41. NSDAP						
42. Allgemeine SS						
43. Waffen-SS						
44. Sicherheitsdienst der SS						
45. SA						
46. HJ einschl. BdM						
47. NSDStB						
48. NSDoB						
49. NSFrauenschaft						
50. NSKK						
51. NSFK						
52. Reichsb. der deutschen Beamten						
53. DAF						
54. KdF						
55. NSV						
56. NS-Reichsb. deutsch. Schwestern						
57. NSKOV						
58. NS-Bund Deutscher Technik						
59. NS-Aerztebund						
60. NS-Lehrerbund						
61. NS-Rechtswahrerbund						
62. Deutsches Frauenwerk						
63. Reichsbund deutscher Familie						
64. NS-Reichsb. für Leibesübungen						
65. NS-Altherrenbund						
66. Deutsche Studentenschaft						
67. Deutscher Gemeindetag						
68. NS-Reichskriegerbund						
69. Reichsdozentenschaft						
70. Reichskulturkammer						
71. Reichsschrifttumskammer						
72. Reichspressekammer						
73. Reichsrundfunkkammer						
74. Reichstheaterkammer						
75. Reichsmusikkammer						
76. Reichskammer d. bildend. Künste						
77. Reichsfilmkammer						
78. Amerika-Institut						
79. Deutsche Akademie München						
80. Deutsches Auslandsinstitut						
81. Deutsche Christen-Bewegung						
82. Deutsche Glaubensbewegung						
83. Deutscher Fichte-Bund						

164 Section of a questionnaire issued by the U.S. military government in Germany concerning membership in organisations of the "Third Reich", May 1945.

165 Members of a Berlin denazification board during a meeting, 1946.

ted to the Marshal himself. It may thus happen that a party member returns as a temporary conscripted worker at a wage of 72 pfennigs an hour. The party member remains at his assigned post until an anti-fascist has been properly trained. If, however, party members should try to avoid dismissal by arguing that their membership lasted only a few months, this is no grounds for rehabilitation, and they will be dismissed just like everybody else. These rehirings, like dismissals, must be processed through the Unemployment Office.

All party members, without exception, must be removed from the schools.

Text 121

Memorandum of 7 July 1945 from the Department of Financial Affairs and Taxation of Berlin's Higher Fiscal Board [*Oberfinanzpräsidium*], concerning the difficulty of dismissing all NSDAP members in their department.

Exceptions to the dismissal of former Nazi Party members were made if the persons in question were deemed "indispensable" for the administration. This memorandum is a copy made by the

Research Group for Post-War History on behalf of the Berlin Senator for National Education in 1953.

Copy

Department of Financial Affairs and Taxation
Higher Fiscal Board
Berlin, 7 July 1945,
Kurfürstendamm 193–194

To the Department of Personnel Issues and Administration, here

The dismissal of all Party members confronts the administration with nearly insoluble problems. The higher civil servants are the backbone of the administrative department. As internal auditors, assessment officers and senior cashiers they underwent years of training to prepare for their profession and, in most cases, over years of professional experience, acquired an extensive expertise in tax law, bookkeeping and accountancy, as well as an indispensable knowledge of the field. These personnel cannot be replaced in the foreseeable future even by members of the commercial professions, bank clerks etc. The percentage of former Party members is particularly high among their ranks, as the following figures illustrate:

	NSDAP members
Former civil servants of the	
higher level	60%
senior level	65%
clerical level	46%
lower level	37%
Former salaried employees	34%
Workers	13%

Text 122

A so-called *"Persilschein"*, 10 July 1945.

From June on, those affected by the "Removal of Fascist Elements from Trade" [*Bereinigung des Handels von faschistischen Elementen*] could appeal to the board of arbitration set up by the municipal authority. Appellants brought forward testimonies of good character from family members, neighbours or colleagues, so-called "Persilscheine", named after the detergent. The boards, made up of representatives of political parties and women's committees, could not keep up with the mass of appeals: at the end of 1945 the board of arbitration had issued 1,500 verdicts, but 2,000 cases remained to be heard.

Emma v. Wedel
Berlin-Wilmersdorf
Markobrunnerstrasse 18 I

The Honourable Lord Mayor
Dear Sir,
Herr Rudolf Lutze of Fasanenstrasse 48. *Gth*, a former Party member has turned to the Office of the Mayor of Wilmersdorf in Albrecht-Achillesstr. with the request that he may once again be able to work in the catering profession. I hear that this request has been passed on to the Lord Mayor. I feel that I too must put in a good word for Herr Lutze.
I have known Herr Lutze for almost 25 years, and I also know why he joined the Party: he was the manager of a restaurant in Rankestr., which was founded by a Jewish gentleman. Most of the customers were Jewish, and they encouraged him to join the Party. Because Herr Lutze had a large number of Jewish friends he believed firmly that he could protect them if he joined the Party. He could not know that matters would turn out very differently. As the enclosed affidavits (copies) demonstrate, he remained true to his beliefs and behaved in an exemplary manner. I followed his career continuously until I was sent to a concentration camp in 1942, and can offer only the most positive testimony to his character.

When I ask today that he be released from the disadvantages arising from his Party membership, I do so because I know that we are speaking of the fate of a decent man who was never politically active and who vehemently disapproved of the brutalities of the Nazi regime.

Emma v. Wedel
Wilmersdorf
Markobrunnerstrasse 18 I

Text 123

Memorandum of 29 September 1945 from the U.S. Military Government to the Allied Commandatura, concerning the dismissal of Prof. Ferdinand Sauerbruch as Director of the Department of Health in the Berlin municipal authority [*Magistrat*].

The well-known physician, who was never a member of any NS organisation, was able to remain Director of Surgery at the *Charité* Hospital.

U.S. Headquarters Berlin [...]
and
Headquarters of the First Army Air Corps
Berlin, Germany

APO 755, U.S. Army
29 September 1945

Re: Dismissal of Dr. Ernst F. Sauerbruch

To: Allied Commandatura, Berlin

1. We herewith request the consent of the Commandatura to the dismissal of Dr. Ernst F. Sauerbruch from his present position as Director of the Central Public Health Office for Berlin.

2. According to the U.S. Armed Forces in the European Theatre, this man falls under the category of people subject to automatic arrest. During the Nazi regime he prospered and enjoyed a high position, by means of which his reputation and background directly and indirectly served the prestige of the Nazi Party. The following facts, among others, are to be considered:

   a. Director of the *Charité* Hospital
   b. Rank of General (Brigadier of the Army Medical Corps [*Generalarzt*] and Chief Army Surgeon)

c. Holder of the honorific title *Staatsrat* [Privy Councillor], which was bestowed on him in 1934 under the Nazi regime.

d. Annual income during the Nazi period of 200 – 300,000 marks.

3. We are of the opinion at this time that this physician does not represent a threat to the security of the troops, but consider it necessary that, according to U.S. Army policy, and in light of the excellent work done particularly by the Russian Army in removing Nazis and other persons who were connected to the Nazis, this physician not be retained in a prominent position.

James M. Gavin
Brigadier General, U.S.Army
Commanding General

Text 124

Personal statement of 1 November 1945 by Ferdinand Sauerbruch to the U.S. military government in Berlin, concerning his dismissal as Director of the Department of Health in the Berlin municipal authority.

1 November 1945

Gentlemen,

On 12 October the Allgemeine Zeitung announced the dismissal of Professor Sauerbruch as Director of Public Health. Five days later he received official confirmation from the municipal authority [*Magistrat*] along with the grounds for this order. One can of course resign oneself to the fact itself, but not to the grounds named. [...]

I have always declared my opposition to the National Socialist notion of the physician and humanity, verbally as well as in writing, and have tried to convey to medical students higher concepts of our responsibility to the sick and needy. [...]

Because there were no medals, I was offered the title of Privy Councillor [*Staatsrat*]. I accepted this honour as a recognition of my medical work and achievements while refusing to enter the Party and emphasising that I must retain my personal and above all my academic freedom. [...]

The second accusation made against me is my position as a so-called Army doctor. Firstly, I would like to make clear that I was not an Army

Opfer des Faschismus

sind die Frauen und Männer, die trotz Naziterrors für die Ideen des Fortschritts und der Gerechtigkeit grausamste Martern über sich ergehen ließen.

Die besten Kräfte des deutschen Volkes litten und starben für uns. Sie blieben nicht untätig, sondern fanden Wege

für den Kampf um die Freiheit.

Nicht durch die Drohungen der Naziverbrecher ließen sie sich abschrecken. Sie wußten, wie gefährlich ihr Handeln war, aber sie setzten trotzdem ihr Leben ein, sie waren

Kämpfer gegen den Faschismus

166 Handbill concerning the victims of fascism, dated 15 July 1945.

167 Front page of the *Berliner Zeitung* for 19 October 1945, on the first meeting of the International Military Tribunal.
Before it met in Nuremberg, the International Military Tribunal opened on 18 October 1945 in the former building of the Superior Court of Justice [*Kammergericht*] in Potsdamer Straße (Schöneberg district).

168 Bestowing decorations on the victims of fascism at the
great Berlin commemorative rally on 9 September 1945.

doctor, but a consulting surgeon to the Army in
the IIIrd military district with the rank of Brigadier
of the Army Medical Corps [*Generalarzt*]. [...]

Let me also mention that my entire circle of friends
was anti-National Socialist. In this context I would
like to mention General Beck, Minister Popitz,
Lieutenant General Olbricht, the former Consul
General in America Kiep, Ambassador v. Hassel,
the former Undersecretary Planck, Captain Jes-
sen, Count Stauffenberg, the great chemist Will-
stedter and Professor Bonhoeffer, men most of
whom were victims of the 20th of July. [...]

[signed:] Sauerbruch

Text 125

**Excerpt from a circular concerning aid
measures sent by the central committee
"Victims of Fascism" on 28 June 1945 to
all district sub-committees and printed in
the *Berliner Zeitung* for 30 June 1945.**

The victims of fascism are millions of people,
including all those who lost their homes, their
flats, their possessions. The victims of fascism are
men forced to become soldiers and to join the
ranks of Hitler's battalions, they are all those who
had to give up their lives for Hitler's criminal war.
Victims of fascism are the Jews persecuted and

169 Participants wearing concentration camp uniforms at the
commemorative rally for the victims of fascism held at Werner-
Seelenbinder-Stadium (Neukölln district) on 9 September 1945.

170 March to the commemorative ceremony for the victims of
fascism, 9 September 1945.

WER WEISS WO ?

WEDDINGER!
Wir suchen 100.000 KINDER
verschiedener Nationalität die von
den Nazi'S aus FRANKREICH
verschleppt wurden.

Mitteilung erbitten:
Der Bezirksausschuss „Opfer des Faschismus"
Wedding, Müllerstr. 146-147, Zi. 360, TEL. 46 05 26

Das Jugendamt Wedding
Müllerstr. 146-147
Zimmer 331
Tel 46 18 52

171   Poster of the Wedding district committee of "Victims of Fascism" seeking information on the whereabouts of children abducted from France by the Nazis, 1945.

murdered as victims of fascist racial madness, they are the Jehovah's Witnesses and "employment contract offenders" [*Arbeitsvertragsünder*]. But we cannot stretch the term "victims of fascism" so far. They all endured and suffered difficult things, but they did not fight! They will and must be helped within the structures of general relief.

Only those men and women, whatever their religious and political convictions, who under Hitler's dictatorship fought heroically for the liberty of the German people and thus faced severe persecution and abuse, who were expelled from the country, who sacrificed their health and property and languished for many years in prisons and concentration camps, can be included in the special measures of the Berlin municipal authority [*Magistrat*].

Text 126

Order from the Allied Commandatura to the Lord Mayor of Berlin concerning preferential treatment for victims of fascism, 17 October 1945.

Copy

KOMMANDANTURA INTERALLIED DE
BERLIN
ETAT-MAJOR

17 October 1945   BX/O (45) 167

Order to the Lord Mayor

Re: Preferential Treatment for Victims of Fascism

The ALLIED KOMMANDATURA OF BERLIN orders the following:

1. You will undertake all necessary administrative measures to ensure that
a) all requests and petitions coming to you from recognised victims of fascism will receive the most favourable treatment,
b) all requests and petitions for preferential treatment regarding clothing, housing, medical attention, food, work, and in general, all petitions for assistance will be studied and treated as carefully as possible. Decisions on these requests must be made fairly and promptly.
2) This order becomes effective immediately.
3) Confirm receipt of this letter indicating date and number.
On behalf of the ALLIED KOMMANDANTURA OF BERLIN

P. DUSSERIS
Chef d'Escadron
Chef d'Etat-Major
(Stamp) (Signature)

Text 127

"Current Organisational Announcements" of the "Victims of Fascism", district committee Wedding, 1945.

Current Announcements:

Subject: *SS-Scharführer* Bouchsein, Oranienburg
All former political prisoners from Oranienburg Concentration Camp who are in a position to give incriminating testimony against the above-named, who is under arrest, are requested to convey their information immediately to the district committee.

Subject: Christian Lutrop, born 15.7.96
The abovenamed was, according to his own statements, camp leader for the Organisation

Todt in Graz and there also had inmates of the Nettenheim Concentration Camp (sub-camp of Dachau) in his charge.

It is assumed that he is a war criminal.

All former inmates of the abovementioned camp are requested to inform the district committee if they can give incriminating testimony.

Subject: All former inmates of Sachsenhausen

Albert Bauer, born on 19.5.00 at Plauen. The abovenamed was block elder [*Blockältester*] of Isolation Block 58 and chief of the prisoners' police.

He was responsible for numerous cases of abuse and also was particularly cruel to foreign prisoners. Bauer is currently under arrest.

All former inmates are requested to convey their statements about Bauer to the district committee.

[...]

Subject: Commemorative portfolio

We already indicated in our previous circular 2/46 that we need pictures of people who were executed and murdered, along with biographical information. Please do not keep us waiting much longer. We will have negatives of the photos made immediately so that the families can have the pictures back as quickly as possible.

Subject: Library for the "Victims of Fascism"

Our first call for donations of books for the library we intend to establish has already had a certain success.

We have already received some 60 books.

172 Teaching assistants in Pankow attend school themselves when not teaching, no date.

173 A Jewish teacher who has returned to Berlin, standing in front of a school with his daughter in 1945.

We therefore ask each comrade once again to help us put together a good library.
[...]

Text 128

From a report in the newspaper *Berlin am Abend* concerning the reopening of the schools in Schöneberg, 17 July 1945.

The newspaper *Berlin am Abend* was published in only a few numbers.

Reopening of the Schools

The Schöneberg district has 12 elementary schools. The first of them could already be reopened on 26 May. Instruction resumed in the remaining 11 on 29 May. In all, 4,600 children are enrolled in the elementary schools, taught by 167 teachers in 155 classes. The shortage of elementary school teachers has been alleviated by the hiring of teaching assistants, which has thus far caused neither personal nor scholastic problems. In the district of Schöneberg two middle schools have also reopened, three secondary schools, one school for backward children and four vocational schools as well as the Pestalozzi-Fröbel House, the Lette House, the School of Civil

Engineering and the State School of the Arts. The secondary schools have a staff of thirty-six instructing 600 pupils in 22 classes. Instruction at the School of Civil Engineering (Kurfürstenstr.) and the State School of the Arts (Grunewaldstr.) resumed on 2 July.

Text 129

Marshal Zhukov's order of 16 September 1945, concerning the turning over of National Socialist and military literature.

The Elimination of Nazi Literature

Decree by the Chief Director of the Soviet Military Administration

In order to facilitate the rapid eradication of Nazi ideas and militarism, as expressed in their wide dissemination in the publication of various kinds of literature during the years of fascist rule, the Chief Director of the Soviet Military Administration in Germany, Marshal of the Soviet Union G. Zhukov

orders:

1. All owners of private libraries, bookshops and publishing houses are to turn over to the District Commandatura by 1 October 1945:
   a) all books, brochures, periodicals, albums and other literature containing fascist propaganda, racial theory, literature concerning the violent capture of foreign countries, and all kinds of literature directed against the Soviet Union and other allied nations,
   b) all military literature, including textbooks and teaching materials for military academies, also scholarly and technical literature connected with the military.

2. All former state and municipal libraries, university directors and directors of other institutions of higher education, scholarly research institutes, presidents of academies, as well as associates of scientific and technical organisations to eliminate from the libraries under their authority, by means of special commissions under the chairmanship of the institute director, all fascist military literature, as mentioned in §1 with the accompanying card catalogues, and to turn them over to the representative of the military commander's office.

174 Returning Nazi schoolbooks, no date.

3.5. Administration and Politics

During the conquest of the city some small groups had formed spontaneously to participate in the creation of an anti-fascist order "from below". Receiving no support from the
occupying power, however, they disappeared again after only a few days. The administration was established "from above", in the name and under the responsibility of the
Soviet City Commandant.

By mid-May the public was presented with a Berlin municipal authority [Magistrat]
headed by the architect and engineer Dr Arthur Werner, a political unknown. Alongside moderate and conservative professionals – including some prominent men such as
Professors Sauerbruch and Scharoun – most members of the municipal authority were
communists. The municipal authority was installed by and bound to the orders and
directives of the City Commandant and later of the Allied Commandatura. The district
authorities [Bezirksämter] were instituted as the municipal authority's executive organs;
in September the municipal authority's right to install and dismiss district mayors and
councillors was confirmed. The judicial system, whose reorganisation was begun on 18
May in the form of administrative or district courts, was also temporarily incorporated
into the municipal administration.

It was clear that the administration faced massive, nearly insoluble tasks. An experienced machinery was lacking, since the former NSDAP members had to be dismissed.
On 31 May the municipal authority dissolved all civil service contracts according to a
directive from the City Commandant, so that all public servants became either salaried
employees or wage workers. Nonetheless, the practical tasks were tackled with great
energy and with remarkable success. This was true of the work of clearing rubble and
securing buildings, the reestablishment of water, electricity, gas, rail and bus services,
and of the acquisition and distribution of food. The reorganisation of a municipal police
force, which was essential under the circumstances, also made rapid progress.

Surprisingly enough, on 10 June, only a month after the end of the "Third Reich", the
Soviet Military Administration for Germany (SMAD) was already permitting the establishment and activities of "anti-fascist" political parties. Thus the Communist Party
(KPD), Social Democratic Party (SPD), Liberal Democratic Party (LDPD) and Christian
Democratic Union (CDU) were all founded within a very short space of time. The KPD
was the first, since it had already known that permission was pending. The moderate
parties took several weeks to get approval. The strong tendencies towards a unified
socialist party were blocked by the KPD before it changed course in autumn and – supported by the SMAD – pushed for a quick fusion of SPD and KPD. Among the SPD,
however, the mood in favour of a unity party was declining since autumn. Still, despite
increasing political tensions, 1945 was characterised by practically-oriented cooperation among the parties.

On 13 June a "Preparatory Trades Union Committee for Greater Berlin" was constitut-
ed, and published an appeal to found an organisationally and ideologically unified
trade union. The formation of the union proceeded quickly but was soon impaired by

the attempt to emphasise communist interests to the exclusion of others. Social Democratic trade unionists came under increasing pressure as early as late 1945.

Bekanntmachung
über die Bildung einer Berliner Städtischen Selbstverwaltung

Am 11., 12. und 13. Mai dieses Jahres fanden Versammlungen von Vertretern verschiedener öffentlicher Gruppen der Stadt Berlin statt, bei denen die Fragen über die Lebensmittelversorgung der Bevölkerung der Wiederherstellung der Kommunalwirtschaft und der schnellsten Einrichtung normalen Lebens in der Stadt aufgeworfen wurden.

Auf diesen Versammlungen wurde beschlossen, eine Städtische Selbstverwaltung von Berlin aufzustellen, in deren Bestand folgende Personen aufgenommen wurden:

1. Doktor Arthur WERNER, Architekt und Ingenieur für Elektrotechnik und Maschinenbau.
2. Karl SCHULZ, ehem. Hochschulrektor.
3. Karl MARON, Schlosser, Sozialpolitiker.
4. Doktor HERMES, bedeutender Fachmann in Fragen der Landwirtschaft und der Lebensmittelversorgung.
5. Paul SCHWENK, ehem. Mitglied des Preußischen Landtages, großer Fachmann in Fragen der Kommunalwirtschaft.
6. KRAFT, Ingenieur, bedeutender Fachmann in Fragen der städtischen Wirtschaft.
7. Arthur PIECK, aktiver Funktionär der Gewerkschaftsbewegung.
8. SCHIERACK, Ingenieur.
9. Professor SAUERBRUCH, Chirurg.
10. Otto LORINZ, Lehrer.
11. KEELER, Nachrichteningenieur.
12. Otto GESCHKE, ehem. Mitglied des Reichstages.
13. Josef ORLOP, Eigentümer eines Lebensmittelgeschafts, ehem. Abgeordneter Kandidat des Preußischen Landtages.
14. BUCHHOLZ, Pfarrer.
15. Edmund NORDWIG, Finanzfachmann u. a.

Die Aufstellung der führenden Mitarbeiter der Berliner Städtischen Selbstverwaltung wurde am 14. Mai dieses Jahres dem sowjetischen Militärkommando vorgelegt und erhielt dessen Beistimmung.

Die Berliner Selbstverwaltung ist im alten Gebäude am Alexanderplatz untergebracht und hat ihre Arbeit aufgenommen.

175 Announcement of the establishment of the municipal authority [*Magistrat*] on 14 May, published in the *Tägliche Rundschau* newspaper on 17 May 1945. Other members of the municipal authority were appointed on 19 May: Hans Jendretzky (Labour Affairs), Walter Jirak (Municipal Works), Hermann Landwehr (Economics), Prof. Hans Scharoun (Construction and Housing) and Otto Winzer (National Education [*Volksbildung*]).

176 The Lord Mayor Dr Arthur Werner (standing), the Soviet City Commandant General Nikolai Bersarin (left), Town Councillor for Labour Affairs Hans Jendretzky (background) and Mayor Karl Maron (right) at the constituent meeting of the first Berlin municipal authority [*Magistrat*] on 20 May 1945.

177 The municipal authority [*Magistrat*] in session, 1945.

Text 130

Wolfgang Leonhard's recollections of the dissolution of the anti-fascist committees, 1961.

Leonhard had come to Berlin in April 1945 with the "Ulbricht Group".

"In the past few days various offices, committees and organisations calling themselves anti-fascist committees, anti-Nazi groups, socialist bureaux, national committees or some such have been founded", explained Walter Ulbricht at one of the usual meetings.
I had also often encountered these offices while travelling through Berlin. I was convinced that Ulbricht would assign us the task of contacting them in order to support their work. "We have heard" – Ulbricht never said from whom or how – "that these offices have been started by Nazis. They are thus front organisations whose objective is to disturb the development towards democracy. We must do everything in our power to dissolve them".
[...]

A few days later the "deed" had been done. The committee was dissolved. The majority of its members withdrew into private life, disappointed. I met a few of them later. They worked in the administration and did their jobs dutifully, but one no longer sensed any fire, enthusiasm or initiative in them. The fate of the Charlottenburg committee is only one example. At the same period dozens of similar committees and initiatives, which had been founded from below, were dissolved.

Text 131

Arthur Werner's recollections of the circumstances surrounding his appointment to the office of Lord Mayor.

One day shortly after the entry of the Red Army I saw a gentleman standing by the garden-fence who called out to me:
"I'm looking for Dr Werner!"
When I said: "You're in the right place, here he is", he first made sure that I was who I said I was. Then he mentioned the name of one of my

178 The temporary Schöneberg Town Hall at Hauptstraße 19, May or June 1945.

former students and conveyed his greetings. We sat down in the garden and my guest asked me about my past and invited me to go with him to see a former member of the Reichstag.

[...] With him, too, the conversation began with my past, at the end of which the member of parliament said: "Now I would like to introduce you to the City Commandant of Berlin, General Bersarin". [...] After the introductions, and after I had answered many questions, the General said: "I intend to appoint you Lord Mayor".

[...]

"Come here tomorrow at twelve noon. I shall confirm you and the entire Berlin municiple authority."

Text 132

Resolution of the Berlin municipal authority concerning expense allowances for upper-level municipal servants, 16 July 1945.

Resolution: The following monthly expense allowance will be paid to the

Lord Mayor	1,000 RM
the Mayors	750 RM
Town Councillors	500 RM

It will be paid for the months of May, June and July. The Town Councillors' deputies will receive a monthly expense allowance of 250 RM, beginning with the day of their confirmation.

Text 133

Order of 25 May 1945 by General Bersarin concerning the organisation of the police and judiciary.

Order
by the Military Commandant of the
City of Berlin,
Bersarin, 25.5.45

In the interest of a speedy restoration of normal life to the population of the city of Berlin, in the interest of the fight against crime and disturbances to public order, the regulation of traffic on the streets and the protection of the structure of self-administration of the city of Berlin, the self-administration of the city has the permission of

the command of the Red Army to organise the municipal police force, the courts and the public prosecutor's office. These bodies were already established on 20 May of this year and have begun their regular work.

I order:

1. The Chief of Police for the City of Berlin, Colonel Markgraf, to dress the municipal police force in the uniforms that were in use before 1933 within the period between 25 May and 1 June of this year, and to post an adequate number of police in the city.
2. The civilian population of Berlin to follow the orders of the police, the courts and the public prosecutor's office as representatives of the municipal authority and to offer them every assistance.
3. The members of the Red Army of the Berlin garrison not to impede the police, the courts and the public prosecutor's office in the performance of their duties.

Garrison Chief and City Commandant of Berlin
General BERSARIN
Chief of the Garrison Staff of the City of Berlin
Brigadier General KUSHCHOV

Text 134

Announcement of 30 August 1945 from the Area Steward [*Obmann*] for the administrative district of Charlottenburg to all House Stewards.

House, street and block stewards were part of the administration. They distributed ration-cards, set up labour conscription, ferreted out Nazis and cleared out their flats, for example for returning concentration camp inmates. The stewards were confirmed (but not nominated) by the people who lived in their houses. The stewards initially performed these kinds of services for the district City Commandants and later for the district authorities. Their methods of denazification were sometimes criticised as excessively harsh, and they were compared to the Nazi *Blockwart*, the Party wardens who had been responsible for blocks of flats.

To all House Stewards!

1. The [former Nazi] Party members of our area are to assemble on Sunday 2.9.45 at 7.30

179 One of the first Berlin policemen in plain clothes with a Russian-German armband, May or June 1945.

180 One of the first Berlin policemen, provisionally uniformed with a Russian-German armband, May or June 1945.

a.m. at Fritsche Straße 74 at the corner of Wall Straße and will be taken to the Unemployment Office at 8 o'clock. Those with medical certificates and attestations will be registered there and exempted.

2. The administrative district Mitte needs to know whether the House Stewards are members of the SPD, KPD, Christ-Dem., Lib. Dem. parties or of no party.

3. The Unemployment Office requests a list of all male youths aged between 14 and 21, divided by name, address and age.

Please deliver the requested information to the office at Fritsche Str. 74 at the corner of Wall Str.

Area Steward
signed: Gösche

Text 135

Instructions for House Stewards, 29 August 1945.

Charlottenburg-Mitte, District Court [*Amtsgericht*].

1) The House Steward must act in an impartial and anti-fascist manner.

2) The House Steward is forbidden to communicate directly with the authorities, and all matters are to be regulated via the Area Steward.

3) The House Steward must possess a list of all house tenants, divided into [former Nazi] party members and non-members, and also including where each person is employed. The list is to be kept current.

4) All assignments of new tenants must be approved by the House, Street and Area Steward.

Der Magistrat der Stadt Berlin
Abt. für Finanz- und Steuerwesen
Oberfinanzpräsidium

16. Juli 1945

Berlin W 15, den 14. Juli 1945
Kurfürstendamm 193/194
Zimmer 280

Zeitgesch. Sammlung
7679

S 1230 - St IV Bt/Breker und Andere

1. FA Zehlendorf

Betrifft: Meldung der Steuerrückstände von führenden Personen und von Nutznießern des Nazi-Systems auf Grund der Rdvfg. vom 6. Juni 1945 - O 2150 - 5/45 - St IV Bt -

Wir bitten Sie, uns über den Stand der Beitreibung der Rückstände auf dem Laufenden zu halten, die nach Ihrer Sammelmeldung bei den nachstehend genannten Steuerpflichtigen bestehen.

Lfd.Nr.	N a m e	Steuernummer	Gesamtrückstand
2	Breker	1/641	252.797.--- RM
3	v. Treuenfeld	2/167	7.215,-- RM
4	Muhs	2/193	854,50 RM
6	v. Renteln	2/407	14.348,20 RM
11	Liebeneiner	2/869	14.148,98 RM
14	Piepenburg	3/728	751.426,-- RM
18	v. Behr	4/64	68.039,15 RM
20	Kleinmann	4/226	2.068,50 RM
21	Göring	4/142	51.616,25 RM
22	Jodl	4/463	1.530,-- RM
23	Dönitz	4/534	2.068,-- RM
25	Daluege	5/586	2.659,75 RM
26	Mueller	5/424	1.821,-- RM
27	Börger	5/593	3.626,-- RM
42	Götz	12/70	12.331,55 RM
43	Poll	13/161	10.008,-- RM
48	Kupfer	14/921	2.540,-- RM
53	Bürkner	15/39	33.057,25 RM
55	Durstmann	17a/365	294.397,20 RM
58	Bohle	17b/469	3.709,55 RM
61	Dr. Lutz	18/522	3.943,35 RM
62	Schwarz van Berk	18/589	2.314,-- RM
63	Melzer	18/658	22.227,15 RM
66	Pfundtner	19/328	4.195,-- RM
73	v. Siemens	21/244	21.288,-- RM
78	Schickedanz	23/40	4.896,-- RM
79	Sagebiel	23/119	2.231,50 RM
83	Stuckart	23/555	2.443,-- RM
86	Esser	24/241	984.-- RM
87	Sündermann	25/658	777,-- RM
89	v. Siemens	25/40	57.289,-- RM
90	Horcher	25/638	251.491,-- RM
93	Görlitzer	101/119	822,50 RM
97	Scherping	102/286	1.881,75 RM
98	Küper	104/730	2.358,-- RM
111	Schneller	115/145	2.220,-- RM
113	Stolle	115/317	1.600,-- RM
115	Meinberg	108/259	19.370,-- RM

Eg

181   Letter of 14 July 1945 from the Higher Fiscal Board [*Oberfinanzpräsidium*] to the Zehlendorf Revenue Office, concerning tax arrears.

182 The Tempelhof District Authority [*Bezirksamt*] and the U.S. Military Court in September 1945.

5) All conflicts between tenants are to be arbitrated by the House Steward. In serious cases the Area Steward will be brought in. Disagreements between the tenants and the House Steward are to be reported to the Area Steward immediately.

6) The House Steward bears full responsibility for the house bulletin board (blackboard), i.e., for the posting of new regulations and the removal of outdated announcements.

7) Regulations issued by the Area Stewards are to be filed carefully by date so that they may be consulted at any time.

8) The foundation of successful cooperation between the House Steward and the tenants is mutual trust and a comradely tone.

9) The House Steward bears full responsibilty for maintaining the cleanliness of the house, courtyard, and street at all times.

10) All flats that are vacant, become vacant or are not filled to capacity are to be reported immediately to the Area Steward.

11) The House Steward is responsible for seeing to it that ration-cards are distributed in exact accord with the guidelines of the Ration-Card Issue Office.

Text 136

Appeal of 15 June 1945 by the "Preparatory Trades Union Committee" for Greater Berlin.

The appeal called for the creation of independent and democratic unions. The new Trades Union Federation was intended to overcome the ideological splintering of unions that had existed during the Weimar Republic. Signatories included Jakob Kaiser from the former Christian unions as well as Ernst Lemmer from the former liberal Hirsch-Duncker unions. The Social Democrats (Bernhard Göring, Hermann Schlimme and Otto Brass) and Communists (Hans Jendretzky, Roman Chwalek and Paul Walter) were to have parity of representation on the Committee. To be sure, from the very beginning parity was not assured, since Otto Brass was already a member of the KPD.

At the same time, the organisation of trade unions by industry was to make the large number of earlier craft unions superfluous.

Neue Richter werden vereidigt

Bei der feierlichen Eröffnung des Bezirksverwaltungsgerichts im britischen Sektor von Berlin wurden die Richter von Major Rae vereidigt

GENERAL NARES ERÖFFNETE VERWALTUNGSGERICHT

Gegen Missbrauch von Amtsbefugnissen

Am Mittwoch erfolgte im Hause des früheren Reichsverwaltungsgerichts, Hardenbergstr. 31, in Anwesenheit von Generalmajor Nares, Kommandant des britischen Sektors von Berlin, die Eröffnung des neuen Bezirksverwaltungsgerichts.

Nach der Vereidigung des Präsidenten Dr. Franz Scholz und der fünf ihm beigegebenen Richter hielt Generalmajor Nares die Eröffnungsansprache. Er wies darauf hin, dass es immer wieder Beamte geben werde, die ihre Befugnis missbrauchten. In diesen Fällen sei es Aufgabe der Verwaltungsgerichte, den Bürger Gerechtigkeit finden zu lassen. Die Militärregierung habe die besten Männer, die zu finden waren, hier zu Richtern bestellt.

Vertrauen wiederherstellen

Präsident Dr. Scholz dankte dem General im Namen der ernannten Richter für das in sie gesetzte Vertrauen. Sie alle würden sich bemühen, das Vertrauen in die deutsche Rechtspflege wiederherstellen zu helfen.

Fanatismus muss verschwinden

Der Fanatismus, der das deutsche Recht in den letzten zwölf Jahren so schwer erschüttert habe, müsse für alle Zeiten verschwinden.

Es werde in Zukunft wieder Recht gesprochen werden ohne Ansehen der Person, der Rasse oder der Religion, getreu dem vor der Militärregierung abgelegten Eid.

Unter den geladenen Gästen befanden sich Oberbürgermeister Dr. Werner, der Präsident des Kammergerichtes, Prof. Dr. Kanger, und seine beiden Vertreter. Ferner waren die Amtsgerichtsdirektoren und Bezirksbürgermeister des britischen Sektors von Berlin erschienen.

Strassenjagd durch Düsseldorf

Jugendliche Einbrecher festgenommen

Bei der Verfolgung einer Bande jugendlicher Einbrecher in Düsseldorf kam es zu einer Strassenjagd durch das Zentrum der Stadt.

Stadtviertel abgeriegelt

150 deutsche Polizeibeamte und 30 britische Militärpolizisten hatten das Hellweg-Viertel abgeriegelt, wo sie 18 Jugendliche festnahmen. In einem Haus fanden sie noch vier bewaffnete Jugendliche, die flüchteten.

Jagd über drei Kilometer

Bei der Verfolgung feuerten die britischen Militärpolizisten auf die Flüchtenden und verletzten einen von ihnen am Bein. Dieser und ein anderer konnten schnell, ein dritter erst nach einer Jagd über drei Kilometer gestellt werden. Der Vierte entkam, obwohl man annimmt, dass er verwundet ist.

Kriminalpolizisten angeschossen

183 A newspaper story in *Der Berliner* for 20 December 1945 concerning the swearing-in by Major Rae of German judges at the District Administrative Court at Hardenbergstraße 31 in the British Sector in November 1945.

The swearing-in occurred in the presence of the Commandant of the British Sector, Brigadier General Nares, the Lord Mayor Dr Werner and the President of the Superior Court of Justice Dr Kanger in the building of the former Reich Administrative Court.

184 Otto Grotewohl and Wilhelm Pieck on 12 August 1945. The handshake between Otto Grotewohl and Wilhelm Pieck in August 1945 was intended to document the close cooperation between the two newly-founded labour parties KPD and SPD, which had been resolved in June.

APPEAL
of the Preparatory Trades Union Committee for Greater Berlin

The measures necessary to secure provisions for the population and to restore normal life have been taken. The order of the Supreme Commander of the Soviet military administration has given workers and employees the right to organise free unions.

The time to organise once again in unions, long-awaited by workers and employees, has finally come.

The undersigned have formed a committee to rebuild independent, democratic unions for

185 Wilhelm Pieck's KPD membership card, September 1945. The membership card, issued in September 1945 with the membership number 1 gives an indication of the new attitude towards the reestablished SPD: it notes that Pieck joined the SPD in 1895. His occupation is given as "Party worker".
Pieck had been a member of the Head Office (later the Central Committee) of the KPD since its founding in 1918. He emigrated to Moscow in 1933 via Paris, returning to Berlin on 1 July 1945. He was Chairman of the Central Committee of the reestablished KPD.

186 Otto Grotewohl's SPD membership card, July 1945. His membership card, number 2,006, carries a sticker noting that Grotewohl had "remained loyal" to the SPD between 1933 and 1945. His occupation is listed as "Departmental Head" (until autumn 1945 in the Schöneberg district authority [Bezirksamt]). The former SPD Reichstag deputy for Braunschweig Otto Grotewohl was incarcerated for a short period after 1933 and survived the war in Berlin. From June 1945 on he was one of the recognised spokesmen of the SPD Central Committee [Zentralausschuß] which had been founded in Berlin.

Greater Berlin. We are convinced that we are expressing the will of the working people of Berlin when we declare:

The new independent trade unions, which will bring together all earlier tendencies, must become a combat unit working towards the complete destruction of fascism and the creation of new democratic rights for workers and employees.

Their chief task is to assist in the rebirth of our people and the healing of the wounds inflicted upon the world by Hitler's accursed war. The work of the German trade unions should ensure the rekindling of the world's trust. They should help to create a democratic Germany, one that seeks to live in peace and amity with other peoples. Through honest hard work to reconstruct and compensate for that which was destroyed in other countries they desire to contribute to regaining the trust of other peoples.

The Committee will set out the trade union principles and bring them into conformity with the international trade union committee. We propose to the workers and employees of Berlin that they tell us their opinions on the following initial tasks of the independent trade unions:

1. Determined struggle against Nazi ideology and the poison of German militarism. Thus all posts in the municipal administration and works must be cleansed of active fascist elements.

187   Otto Grotewohl (SPD), Andreas Hermes (CDU), Wilhelm
Pieck (KPD) and, on the right, Waldemar Koch (LDPD), together
with the Lord Major Dr Arthur Werner, Juli 1945.

2. The deployment of all available manpower to secure provisions for the population and reconstruct Berlin through hard work. The speediest possible reestablishment of public utilities and workshops, energy and transport services in Greater Berlin.

3. Representation of workers and employees within the framework of the regulations of the occupation authorities through the negotiation of wage agreements and the organisation of industrial safety and of the mobilisation of labour. Cooperation in the rebuilding of the economy and national insurance, while securing for workers and employees the right to democratic co-determination.

4. Educating working people in the spirit of anti-fascism, democratic progress and for the recognition of their social situation. Engendering a sense of connection with workers in other countries and strengthening friendship with other peoples.

Workers and Employees!

Nazi tyranny is dead! It is now up to us, despite all the difficulties, to turn our hand to reconstruction. Once again, as in 1918, the fate of our homeland is in our hands. We must not fail this time.

Let us prove to the world that working people united, having learned from the past, conscious of their finest trade union traditions, are determined to be a bulwark against fascism, and that they are determined to do one's utmost for the creation of a democratic Germany and for a peaceful companionship with other peoples.

Berlin, 15 June 1945

The Preparatory Trades Union Committee for Greater Berlin

Otto Braß	Hermann Schlimme
Bernhard Göring	Paul Walter
Roman Chwalek	Jakob Kaiser
Ernst Lemmer	Hans Jendretzky

Vereinbarung

des Zentralkomitees der Kommunistischen und des Zentralausschusses der Sozialdemokratischen Partei Deutschlands

Am 19. Juni fand in Berlin die erste gemeinsame Sitzung der Vertreter der Sozialdemokratischen und der Kommunistischen Partei Deutschlands statt. Als Vertreter des Zentralausschusses der Sozialdemokratischen Partei waren die Genossen Erich Gniffke, Otto Grotewohl, Gustav Dahrendorf, Helmut Lehmann und Otto Meier, vom Zentralkomitee der Kommunistischen Partei die Genossen Walter Ulbricht, Anton Ackermann, Ottomar Geschke, Hans Jendretzki und Otto Winzer anwesend.

Die Aussprache war von dem festen Willen zur aufrichtigen Zusammenarbeit beider Parteien getragen. Sie verlief im Geiste gegenseitigen Vertrauens. Unter Achtung der demokratischen Grundsätze wurden folgende Vereinbarungen getroffen: Es wird ein

Gemeinsamer Arbeitsausschuß

bestehend aus je fünf Vertretern der beiden Zentralstellen gebildet. Dieser Ausschuß, der ein Ausdruck der Aktionseinheit der Kommunistischen und der Sozialdemokratischen Partei Deutschlands ist, stellt sich folgende Aufgaben:

1. Enge Zusammenarbeit bei der Durchführung der gemeinsam beschlossenen dringlichen Aktionsaufgaben zur Liquidierung der Ueberreste des Nazismus und zum Wiederaufbau des Landes auf sicherer Grundlage. Als Voraussetzung hierfür wird der Aufbau einer antifaschistischen, demokratisch-parlamentarischen Republik betrachtet, die die Fehler und Schwächen der Vergangenheit vermeidet und dem schaffenden Volke alle demokratischen Rechte und Freiheiten sichert.

2. Es sind alle notwendigen Schritte zu unternehmen, um mit allen anderen antifaschistischen demokratischen Parteien Vereinbarungen über die Bildung e i n e s f e s t e n B l o c k e s zu treffen.

3. Gemeinsame Vertretung der Interessen des schaffenden Volkes in Stadt und Land.

4. Durchführung gemeinsamer Veranstaltungen beider Parteien.

5. Gemeinsame Beratungen zur Klärung ideologischer Fragen.

Die Vertreter beider Parteien drücken ihren festen Willen aus, alles zu tun, um auf dem Wege guter Zusammenarbeit in allen Fragen des antifaschistischen Kampfes und des Wiederaufbaues die V o r a u s s e t z u n g e n f ü r d i e p o l i t i s c h e E i n h e i t d e s w e r k t ä t i g e n V o l k e s zu schaffen.

Der gemeinsame Arbeitsausschuß des Zentralausschusses der Sozialdemokratischen und des Zentralkomitees der Kommunistischen Partei Deutschlands empfiehlt den Organisationen beider Parteien, in allen Bezirken, Kreisen und Orten zusammenzutreten, ebenfalls gemeinsame Arbeitsausschüsse zu schaffen und in gleicher Weise zusammenzuarbeiten, wie das im zentralen Maßstab geschieht.

Berlin, den 19. Juni 1945.

Walter Ulbricht, Anton Ackermann, Ottomar Geschke, Hans Jendretzki, Otto Winzer, Erich Gniffke, Otto Grotewohl, Gustav Dahrendorf, Helmut Lehmann, Otto Meier.

188 Agreement of 19 June 1945 between the Central Committees of the KPD and the SPD.
The KPD understood this agreement more as a defensive measure against the further-reaching wishes of the Social Democrats, regarding it above all as part of a close cooperation with all four political parties in Berlin, in which the KPD would exercise substantial influence.

3.6. The Newspaper City Berlin

Ever since the Wilhelmine period, Berlin had had a national and international reputation as a leading "newspaper city". In 1890 there were no fewer than 60 daily papers, twelve of which even appeared twice daily. Immediately after the "seizure of power" the Nazi regime began systematically to destroy the diversity of opinion that had also characterised Berlin during the Weimar Republic. Through prohibitions, economic and political pressure, mergers, and (increasingly after 1937) closures, the number of newspapers was steadily reduced until only five remained in February 1945: the main Nazi party organ *Völkischer Beobachter*, *Angriff*, which had been founded by Goebbels, the *Berliner Morgenpost*, the *Deutsche Allgemeine Zeitung* and the *12-Uhr Blatt* (each of which was only four, and in the end two pages long). Between 22 and 27 April all newspapers suspended publication. Only *Der Panzerbär*, the "Combat Paper for the Defenders of Greater Berlin", continued to appear until 29 April.

When the *Panzerbär* ceased publication, the city was without a newspaper for 15 days – for the first time in 300 years. Posters and Army loudspeakers informed the population of the surrender and the first orders issued by the Soviet occupying power. After overcoming severe technical problems the Soviet authorities were able on 15 May to publish the first number of the *Tägliche Rundschau*, which at first bore the subtitle "Front newspaper for the German population". It was followed on 21 May by the *Berliner Zeitung*, which was soon declared the official organ of the newly created Berlin municipal authority. Both newspapers were distributed at no cost for several weeks.

This situation changed when the *Deutsche Volkszeitung*, the organ of the KPD, appeared for the first time on 13 June, two days after the party was reestablished. Other party newspapers only followed some time later: *Das Volk*, the SPD paper, debuted on 22 July, and the CDU's *Neue Zeit* on 22 July, while the Liberal Democrats did not bring out *Der Morgen* until 3 August. With some delay, after they had taken over their sectors, the Western Allies also published their own newspapers: *Der Berliner* (British) on 2 August, the *Allgemeine Zeitung* (American) on 8 August and the *Kurier* (-French) on 12 November. The first independent German newspaper, *Der Tagesspiegel*, appeared on 27 September and the U.S. military administration took this occasion to stop publication of the *Allgemeine Zeitung*, making the former the first daily paper with a "Western" licence. On 9 October Berlin's newspaper landscape was expanded by the publication of the FDGB (German trades union council) organ *Die freie Gewerkschaft* and on 7 December by the tabloid *Nacht-Expreß*.

Thus there were twelve newspapers as well as five magazines existing in Berlin until the end of 1945: the *Neue Berliner Illustrierte*, the women's magazine *sie*, the youth magazine *Horizont*, the satirical magazine *Ulenspiegel* and *Aufbau*, which was published by the *Kulturbund*. Under the circumstances, political controversies or open polemics were scarcely possible. For the time being, all newspapers were expected to keep to a more or less matter-of-fact and sober reporting of events, oriented towards the population's hunger for information.

189 Printing the first number of the *Berliner Zeitung* on 20 May 1945.

On 15 May Rudolf Herrnstadt, for many years Warsaw correspondent of the *Berliner Tageblatt*, and Fritz Erpenbeck, formerly a dramaturge for Erwin Piscator, returned from exile in Moscow. Upon arriving in Berlin Herrnstadt and Erpenbeck immediately jumped in a jeep and drove to Kreuznacher Straße in Wilmersdorf to speak to Helmut Kindler. Until the beginning of the war, Kindler had been an editor at the *Deutscher Verlag* in Tempelhof, and as a soldier in 1943 he had been arrested by the Gestapo. He had succeeded in reaching Berlin in February where he was hiding out in Kreuznacher Straße together with Gerhard Grindel.

Herrnstadt, Erpenbeck, Kindler and Grindel drove together in the jeep to Soviet headquarters in Friedrichsfelde, and a few days later from there to the printing shop at Urbanstr. 71 (Kreuzberg district). They put together an editorial staff for the *Berliner Zeitung*, which included Colonel Kirsanov and Rudolf Herrnstadt as editors-in-chief, and Gerhard Grindel, Helmut Kindler and the Soviet First Lieutenant Feldmann as the Berlin staff. Egon Bahr came in as a young editor.

190 Selling newspapers in the summer of 1945.
In Berlin, no newspapers appeared for 15 days. On 15 May 1945 the Soviet Army published the first paper, the *Tägliche Rundschau*.

191 Distributing the first issue of the Soviet-licensed newspaper
Berliner Zeitung on 21 May 1945.

192 Berlin newspapers, after the end of the war, 1945.

LINOLSCHNITT VON FRANZ HAACKEN

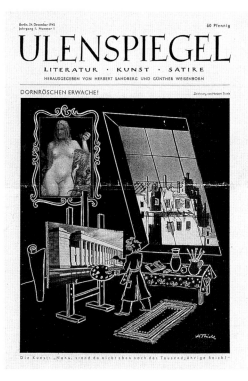

193 Front pages of Berlin magazines, after the end of the war, 1945.

3.7. Culture, the Universities, and Churches

Only a few weeks after Germany's surrender the first public cultural events were held in Berlin. This corresponded to the policy of the Soviet cultural officers who supported such initiatives out of a conviction that a culture based on open, humanistic traditions had an important role to play in building an anti-fascist democratic society. On 15 May, 15 cinemas were already showing Soviet feature films, news-reels and documentaries; later it was mainly feature films from the Western Allies. On 13 May the first public concert, played by the Berlin Chamber Orchestra, took place in the *Bürgersaal* of Schöneberg Town Hall. On 18 May the Orchestra of the German Opera House followed in the studio of the Radio House in Masurenallee, and on 26 May the Berlin Philharmonic under the direction of Leo Borchard played its first concert in the Titania-Palast in Steglitz.

On 19 May Berlin theatre people (Gustav Gründgens and Paul Wegener, among others) met at the invitation of the Soviet City Commandant to discuss the preconditions for reopening the city's theatres. On 27 May the first theatrical production took place at the Renaissance-Theater, and on 15 June the Municipal Opera opened with an evening of ballet in the makeshift auditorium of the ruined Theater des Westens. While the theatre returned to a rather classical programme, programmatically featuring Lessing's *Nathan the Wise*, the orchestras made a particular effort to perform the music of composers outlawed during the Nazi period.

After protracted preparations under the leadership of the writer Johannes R. Becher, who had returned from Moscow, the Cultural Federation for the Democratic Renewal of Germany (*Kulturbund zur demokratischen Erneuerung Deutschlands*) was founded. Under Becher's presidency the *Kulturbund*'s chair included artists such as Carl Hofer, Paul Wegener, and Bernhard Kellermann and politicians devoted to cultural policy such as Ferdinand Friedensburg (CDU), Gustav Dahrendorf (SPD), and Otto Winzer (KPD). Its objective was the "rebirth of the German spirit guided by an assertive democratic world-view". In the beginning, both the organisation's non-partisanship and the support of the occupying powers seemed assured.

The reopening of Berlin's institutions of higher education required more groundwork, so that the Berlin University and the School of Fine Arts (*Hochschule der Künste*) only resumed operation in the winter semester of 1945-46 and the Technical College (now the Technical University) only in April 1946. Not only did the rubble need to be cleared away and the professors denazified, but at least a provisional plan had to be developed for higher education in a democratic society.

Since relations between the Christian churches and National Socialism had been characterised by growing tensions in the regime's later years, the churches were regarded as having a relatively clean record, despite early approval of the "Third Reich". In the transitional period their significance thus extended well beyond pastoral activities. Immediately after the surrender survivors of Nazi terror created a new Jewish Community. The first religious service was held on 11 May at the Jewish Cemetary in Weissensee.

194 Colonel Sergei Tulpanov, Director of the Soviet Information
Department, and Major Alexander Dimshits, on the occasion of
the handing-over of the first shooting permit to *Deutsche Film
AG (DEFA)* at Babelsberg on 17 May 1946.
As cultural officers of the Soviet Military Administration for Germany (SMAD) both played an important rôle with the reconstruction of the cultural life in Berlin

195   The Berlin Philharmonic Orchestra, piano concert with Walter Gieseking, under the direction of Leo Borchard's successor Sergiu Celibadache, 1945.

Text 137

The leading Soviet cultural officer Sergei Tulpanov recalls the new beginning of cultural policy in Germany.

We knew that the time we were supposed to be shaping was one that was long past in the Soviet Union, i.e., in Germany we were living through a period similar to developments in the Soviet Union in the 1920s: a period of storm and stress.

Text 138

The historian Wolfgang Schivelbusch on the "typical" SMAD cultural officer.

The typical SMAD cultural officer was of Jewish descent, born between 1900 and 1910 in Petersburg, and had experienced the Revolution as a boy and the NEP years as a young man. He studied at one of the old educational institutions in Petersburg, which were under Lunacharskii's protection. And at the end of the 1920s he was just about to enter cultural life as a member of the intelligentsia when the cultural revolution thwarted any such plans. The Director of the SMAD Cultural Department Alexander Dimshits and his boyhood friend Grigori Weispapier – editor of the *Tägliche Rundschau* in 1945 – were pure incarnations of this type. Their parents' homes would have been considered incomplete without an extensive literary-scholarly library and a Steinway grand piano in the drawing-room. Different languages were spoken on different days of the week: German, French, English. The sons visited the German *Reformschule*, the traditional elite school of the Petersburg educated bourgeoisie.

Text 139

Inge Deutschkron, who survived the last years of the Nazi regime in hiding, recalls the period after the liberation.

The thought of leaving Berlin was not an easy one. In that first year after the war Berlin was a lively cultural centre. Theatres, operas, cabarets,

196 The improvised box-office of the *Schiller-Theater* at Bismarckstraße 110, set up in a former air-raid shelter, 1945.

pal theatre. Alongside these there arose everywhere little cabarets [*Kleinkunstbühnen*] whose growth, sometimes wild, sometimes stunted, initiated public discussions and also the necessary licensing measures. What was behind all this was the fact that a large number of unemployed artists in Berlin were eager to work and make a living again. The Berlin theatre's healthy will to live, met by an equally healthy appetite for theatre on the part of the Berlin audience, was also behind it.

Text 141

Letter of 12 October 1945 from Friedrich Wolf to Else Wolf.

Over the past ten days I have been reworking *Der Arme Konrad* as a radio play for *Berliner Rundfunk* and am directing it myself; I have already had six general rehearsals and many single ones, including one that lasted all night from 10 to 6 the next morning. [...]
Performance on 18.X. from 7.15 to 9 p.m.; later it will be repeated on another frequency over Leipzig. I am getting 2,500 M for the work. The most important thing is that I'm enjoying myself immensely, since the actors, musicians and choir are all terribly enthusiastic about the piece and their work; just imagine, many of them, after rehearsing in the theater from 10 a.m. to 2 p.m., then taking half an hour for lunch, then performing in the theatre from 3 to 5 p.m., come here at 10 p.m., having cycled through the dark and not very comfortable or safe Berlin to this remote radio station in order to work through the night. This artistic obsession makes up for all the sergeantish and parvenu nonsense springing up all around me, which I now don't have to see.

exhibitions opened and, to some extent out of the blue, offered new perspectives, experiments and ideas. It was as if creative energies that had been held back for years had suddenly broken loose. We met writers, painters, actors whose works the Nazis had banned and who had been persecuted. We devoured the once-forbidden literature. We took every opportunity to celebrate, danced the night away and rejoiced at a light-heartedness we had never known before.

Text 140

Paul Rilla on theatre in Berlin, 23 August 1945.

Regular theatre work
On the situation in Berlin

In the first weeks after the collapse of Hitlerism theatres were already operating again. Actors' collectives came together, and set themselves up in makeshift halls. In the suburban districts former cinemas were converted into theatres, which were often intended as a sort of regional munici-

Text 142

Henry C. Alter in a U.S. half-weekly report on film in Berlin, 18 August 1945.

At the moment there are 52 operable movie theatres in the American Sector, 48 of which are actually in operation; 8 of them show American pictures, 6 are at the disposal of the Special Service, which means that 34 movie theatres are supplied by Soyusintorgkino mainly with Russian films. Around 10% of the Russian films are documentaries such as "Berlin", "Vienna", "San Fran-

197 *Deutsche Staatsoper*, Friedrichstraße (the *Admiralspalast*
before the war) in September 1946.

198   *Berliner Rundfunk* begins anew at Radio House, Masurenallee (Charlottenburg district), 1945.

cisco" etc., which we also agree should be
shown to the Germans. The rest are Russian feature films, usually without subtitles, and they are
usually so poorly attended that the movie theatre
owners cannot even cover costs.

This situation is extremely unhealthy. It is therefore
recommended that programs be devised that give
our distributors control over the entire American
Sector and the supplying of all movie theatres.

199   Poster for the "Exhibition of New Art" [*Ausstellung Junger
Kunst*] at the *Galerie Gerd Rosen*, Kurfürstendamm 215, in
1945.
With the exhibition advertised in Heinz Trökes' poster, the *Galerie Gerd Rosen* opened on 3 August 1945 as the first private
art gallery in post-war Berlin. The gallery, which was set up by
Gerd Rosen and Heinz Tröke, was attached to an antiquarian
bookshop. The first exhibition showed works by Trökes, Jürgen
Eggert and Wladimir Lindenberg as well as works from private
collections by Barlach, Chagall, Klee, Kokoschka and the painters of "Die Brücke".

200 People queuing outside the Cosima Cinema in Friedenau
to see Charlie Chaplin's *Gold Rush* in the autumn of 1945.

201 Students with cardboard for making temporary repairs on
destroyed windows at Berlin University, Unter den Linden,
1945.

Text 143

The guiding principles of the *Kulturbund*, passed at the founding meeting in the *Kulturbund* offices at Schlüterstraße 45 (Charlottenburg district) on 8 August 1945.

The "Cultural Federation for the Democratic Renewal of Germany" brought together representatives of intellectual and cultural life. They included Johannes R. Becher, Gustav v. Wangenheim, Paul Wegener and Friedrich Friedensburg. Through lectures and exhibitions, communists and political moderates worked together to revive the buried heritage of German humanism.

The Guiding Principles of the Cultural Federation for the Democratic Renewal of Germany

1.
Destruction of Nazi ideology in all areas of life and knowledge. Struggle against the intellectual fathers of Nazi crimes and war crimes. Struggle against all reactionary militaristic attitudes. To purge public life and keep it free of these influences.

2.
Formation of a unified national front of German intellectual workers. Creation of a steadfast unity between intellectuals and the people. In the conviction that our people can survive and have the power to change: rebirth of the German spirit guided by an assertive democratic world-view.

3.
An examination of the total historical development of our people, and in this context a survey of the positive and negative forces as they affected all areas of our intellectual life.

4.
The rediscovery and encouragement of our people's liberal, humanist, truly national traditions.

5.
The incorporation of the intellectual achievements of other peoples into the cultural rebuilding of Germany. Paving the way for communication with the upholders of culture of other nations. Regaining the world's trust and respect.

6.
The dissemination of truth. Regaining objective standards and values.

7.
The struggle for the moral recuperation of the people, particularly influence over the intellectual care and training of youth and university students. Vigorous encouragement of the coming generation and the recognition of extraordinary achievements through scholarships and prizes.

8.
Cooperation with all democratically-minded ideological, religious and church movements and groups.

Text 144

From a report in the *Berliner Zeitung* on an event at the *Hebbel-Theater* entitled "-Auto-da-fe, burned books, living literature" [*Scheiterhaufen, verbrannte Bücher – lebendige Dichtung*], 18 September 1945.

It was a fine idea of the *Hebbel-Theater's* to bring back to life, through a performance, those works of our nation's authors that were thrown on the funeral pyre by the Nazi bibliophobes. All those books that fell victim to the most shameful auto-da-fe of all times were assembled in a great pile on the stage, and while Goebbels' rantings in the *Völkische Beobachter* were read out, images were projected over the scene which forcibly struck once again the consciences of all those who had borne the barbarous act in silence.

Then the actors grabbed books out of the pile and began to read passages of prose and poetry from all those well-known authors to whom, on the occasion of this performance, we already paid detailed homage in our Sunday edition. Names like Thomas Mann, Franz Werfel, Bert Brecht, Stefan Zweig, Kurt Tucholsky, Klabund and others, which resonate internationally, were mentioned, as well as more obscure and embattled works, and in each case it was up to the audience to determine whether their words still speak to us today.

Günther Weisenborn, the house dramaturge, himself one of the outlawed, spoke about "Poets and Arsonists", particularly stressing the intellectual origins of the war. The flames of the pyre at Opernplatz, he emphasised, had spread to all of Europe, and the ashes of that criminal act today cover all of Germany. But the more ruins surround us, the more intellectual greatness we must display.

202 One of the first meetings of the *Kulturbund* at Schlüterstraße 45, in 1945.
On the narrow side of the table, from the back: Johannes R. Becher; to his right: Karl Heinz Martin; behind him: Dr Ferdinand Friedensburg; from right to left: Paul Wegener, Prof. Johannes Stroux, Prof. Max Vasmer; behind him: Klaus Gysi.

Text 145

Minutes of the Pastors' Assembly [*Pfarrerkonvent*] of the Berlin district [*Kirchenkreis*] of Kölln Stadt on 25 May 1945.

Pastors' Assembly of the district of Kölln Stadt on 25 May 1945 at the home of the Superintendent.

Sup[erintendent] Tamaschke opened the meeting at 10.30 a.m. with a reading from Isaiah 45 and a prayer, remembered the passing of Pastor Schmidt von Thomas and offered the assembly's condolences to Pastor Hollweg on the passing away of his wife.

The Superintendent reported on the reorganisation of the Consistory, and its first activities, including collections for the reconstruction of Berlin's churches, which are to be taken on Trinity Sunday during intercessions for the new church leadership.

There is no further information about the municipal synod [*Stadtsynode*].

Collections, with the exception of that mentioned above, should be transferred by the banks.

The Superintendent gives an overview of the condition of church buildings in the district of Kölln, of those spaces that are still usable, and of the ecclesiastical staff in the congregations.

In the north of the city there have been attempts to place a church kindergarten in municipal hands.

The Superintendent gives a detailed account of a meeting of representatives of all denominationson on 7 May at the headquarters of the Russian District Commandant of Kreuzberg, and of a special service for exaudi in passion at the request of the Commandant.

203   Pastor Martin Niemöller preaching in Dahlem on 28 October 1945.
Martin Niemöller (1892-1984), the son of a pastor, only began his theological studies at the age of 27, and took up a ministry at St Anne's Church in Dahlem in 1931. He founded the "Pastor's Emergency Federation" [Pfarrernotbund] in August 1933 to oppose the National Socialist orientation of the "German Christians". Niemöller was forbidden to preach, but disobeyed and was arrested by the Gestapo in 1937. He was liberated from a concentration camp by U.S. troops in 1945.

There follows a discussion of identification cards for pastors and church functionaries so that they may walk the streets freely. Nothing has been accomplished so far.

The danger of losing cemeteries to the city is mentioned. Pastor Radicke recommends that we register the cemeteries as firms with the Unemployment Office. The municipal burial offices are referring too any burials.

In answer to enquiries it is noted that typewriters may be used.

The district office of the Inner Mission at Schleiermacherstr. 12 requests church space, stationary supplies and a new allocation of workers.

In Thabor a pastor's flat is vacant, which Br[other] Kirste will take. Party members may no longer participate in the meetings of the parish councils. Queries and discussion concerning housing problems, particularly of evacuees, telephones etc. Br[other] Richter is looking for an organ-builder. The meeting closed at 1 p.m. with a prayer by Br[other] Antony.

3.8.   Dismantlement and Reconstruction

Berlin's economic development after the war was shaped on the one hand by various efforts to restore the city's infrastructure and production capacities, and on the other by the dismantling of industrial plant. The Allies had already agreed during the war that Germany would be required to pay material compensation - particularly in the form of a transfer of industrial plant and withdrawals from running production - for the war damage they had caused in many countries. Since Berlin was not simply the capital, but also the largest German industrial site, it was particularly affected by the policy of deindustrialisation.

Even before the Western Allies took over their sectors, the Soviets had already begun dismantling and removing manufacturing plants, especially in the western part of the city. The dismantling continued after the arrival of the Western Allies, lasting until 1949 in West Berlin and until 1953 in East Berlin. It was most dramatic in the large-scale enterprises of the electrical industry (Siemens, AEG, Osram, etc.) and in machine build-ing factories. Other branches of industry, such as chemical plants (Schering), were also affected. By the end of 1945, losses to the city's industrial capacity as a result of dis-mantlement amounted to 53% in the west and 25% in the east.

The reconstruction of the city began with the clearing of debris and efforts to restore the city's transport and supply systems. All men between the ages of 15 and 65 and all women between 15 and 60 were conscripted for labour; they were required to report to the responsible District Authority in order to contribute to "systematic reconstruction". Because of their different occupational qualifications every fifth to sixth woman, but only every tenth man, was set to work clearing rubble.

After the total collapse of the city's transport system, service already resumed on the first small segments of underground railway lines and trams in May. By the end of the year the greater part of the underground network was back in operation. In May and June 1945 electricity and gas returned bit by bit, but energy remained strictly rationed, even after regular deliveries of coal from the Ruhr to Berlin began in the summer. The rebuilding of Berlin's industries proved extraordinarily difficult; although only some 25% of 1936 capacities had been lost through wartime destruction and evacuations of equipment, the losses as a result of dismantling were far greater. In addition there were the problems of raw materials and the disruption of traditional economic networks. Nevertheless, larger as well as smaller plants were at least partially rebuilt.

The Allied decision that not only food but also raw materials and equipment for the Ber-lin sectors were to be brought in from their respective zones of occupation set the stage, as early the summer of 1945, for an increased separation of the city's individual sectors.

204 *BEWAG* (Berlin's electric power-supply company),
machine-shop of the Power Station West before dismantlement,
no date.

205 *BEWAG* (Berlin's electric power-supply company),
machine-shop of the Power Station West after dismantlement,
30 November 1945.

Text 146

Dismantlement list for the main laboratory at Schering, 7 June 1945.

On 28 May 1945 a 300-man Soviet commando occupied the Schering works and began dismantling the equipment. The entire action lasted four weeks. On 16 June, i.e., during the dismantling, a circular was sent to all department heads at Schering: "Subject: Compensation questions: in order, where appropriate, to be able to register our requests for compensation at short notice, we must be in a position to present the necessary supporting documents to the responsibile authorities as soon as possible. We therefore request that you submit to us by 23 June a complete list of all company property turned over to the occupying authorities in the course of dismantling and requisitioning etc." It is questionable whether the dismantlement lists reflect the true extent of dismantling; the extent of dismantling at Schering was certainly less than at Berlin's electrical and machine-building firms.

Berlin, 7.6.45
Dr Ey/rch
The Dismantlement of the Main Laboratory

Crate No.	Packers	Contents
1	Schmidt, Budig	coarse scales
2	Seiffert, Bartsch	pan-scale
3	Barm, Avend, Seiffert H.	analytical scales
4	Randwere, Hrynyschin	"
5	Schmidt, Budig	scales
6	Schulze, Conrad	microscope
7	Daniels, Conrad, Schulze	large centrifuge, among other things, stand in crate 13
8	Daniels, Conrad	4 stirring motors
9	Conrad, Daniels, Schulze	Pfeiffer pump
10	" " "	resistances, motors
11	Schmidt, Budig	scales
12	Bartsch, Bibau, Seiffert	"
13	Conrad, Schultze	centrifuge stand for crate 7
14	" "	drying oven

206 Dismantled tracks at Potsdamer Bahnhof, 1945.

Crate No.	Packers	Contents
15	Schmidt, Budig	porcelain suction-filters
16	Dr Winzer	small centrifuge with table, 2 binoculars, resistances
17	Schmidt, Budig	suction-filters
18	Winzer, Dr Schotte	4 microscopes
19	Bibau, Seiffert	porcelain
20	Grieger, Kurz	"
21	Seiffert, Michulitz, Hoppe	glass
22–24	" " "	"
25–26	Kurz, Krüger	porcelain

Crate No.	Packers	Contents
27	Bibau, Frau Schilke	glass
28–29	Seifert, Frl Kirschbaum, Gross	porcelain
30	Frl Otto, Knoll	"
31	Kratzel, Schulze	glass flasks
32	Dr Hrynyschin, Kratzel, Schultze	drying oven, quartz lamp
33	Döring, Mühlefeld	glass
34	Kratzel, Wittmann	porcelain
35–36	" "	glass
37	Kurz, Krüger	porcelain
38	Seiffert, Gross	"

207 Press for making bricks out of crushed brick, 1945.

208 Women repairing the tracks of the Berlin underground,
on 24 September 1945.

209 Lagerplatz für aus Trümmern gewonnene Ziegelsteine,
Möckernstraße (Bezirk Kreuzberg), Dezember 1945.

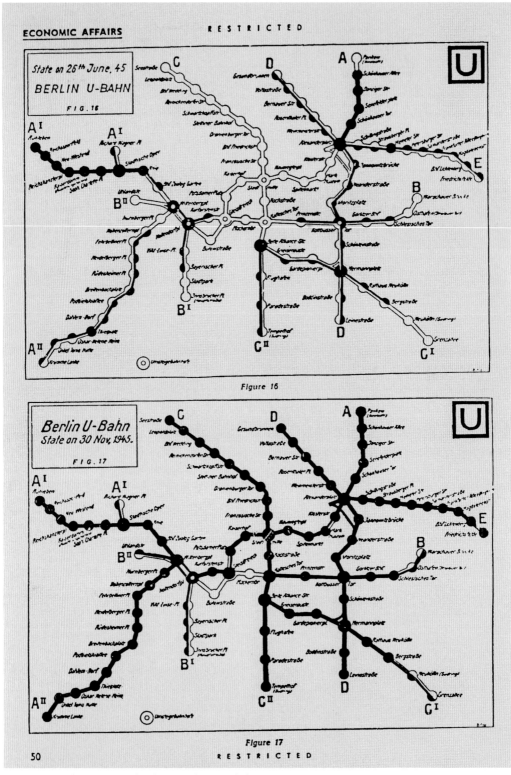

Figure 16

Figure 17

210 Overview of the segments of underground lines on which
service had resumed, 26 June and 30 November 1945.

211 Repairing the overhead contact line of a tram, 1945.

212 Service resumes on tram line 77 in Berlin-Wilmersdorf on 22 September 1945.

213 Resumption of production in the Tegel Municipal Works (formerly Borsig) in 1945.

214 Karl Maron (on the left), the First Vice-Mayor, and Municipal Architect Hans Scharoun in Parochialstraße (Mitte district), in 1945 or 1946.

"Of the three most important blueprints for the city two were named after suburban districts: the 'Zehlendorf Plan' and the 'Hermsdorf Plan'. The third, the 'Collective Plan' developed by the municipal authority's planning group under the leadership of Hans Scharoun, took the intentions of the other two plans to their logical conclusion: the transformation of Greater Berlin into a more dispersed and greener garden city. [...] 'What remained', Scharoun remarked in 1946, 'after bomb attacks and the final battle had accomplished a mechanical dispersal [...] allows us to shape it into a city landscape. Thus it is possible to divide the immense and immeasurable into moderate parts that can be taken in at a glance, and to place these parts in relation to each other, just as forest, meadow, mountain and lake work together in a beautiful landscape.'" (W. Schivelbusch, Vor dem Vorhang, 1995). The grand blueprints were only completed in 1946.

215 An iron-foundry in Herzbergstraße in Neukölln resumes production in 1946.

1945/1 · ERSTES OKTOBERHEFT · PREIS 20 PF.

NEUE Berliner Illustrierte

Foto: Hans H. Hartmann

Oberbürgermeister Dr. Werner besuchte Klingenberg

das mächtige, Berlin mit Strom-versorgende Kraftwerk, dessen Schlote jetzt wieder rauchen. In der benach-
barten Siedlung unterhält er sich mit einer Arbeiterin, die mitgeholfen hat und ihm stolz ihr Jüngstes zeigt.

216 Front page of the *Neue Berliner Illustrierte* with a photograph of the Lord Mayor Dr Werner in front of the Klingenberg
Power Plant in October 1945.

Appendix

List of Archives and Collections used

Akademie der Künste, Berlin
Amerika-Gedenkbibliothek, Berlin
Archiv für Kunst und Geschichte, Berlin
Archiv für Zeitgeschichte Hans Gräfer, Berlin
Archiwum Panstwowe Muzeum w Oswiecimie, Warsaw
Berlin Museum, Berlin
BEWAG-Archiv, Berlin
Bildarchiv Pisarek, Berlin
Bildarchiv Preußischer Kulturbesitz, Berlin
Bilddokumentation Berliner Verlag, Berlin
Bilderdienst Süddeutscher Verlag, Munich
Bundesarchiv, Koblenz
Bundesarchiv, Abt. Potsdam, Potsdam
Bundesarchiv, Berlin Document Center, Berlin
Bundesarchiv, Filmarchiv, Berlin
Bundesarchiv/Militärarchiv, Freiburg
Bundesarchiv, Stiftung Archiv der Parteien und Massenorganisationen der DDR, Berlin
Bundesarchiv, Zwischenarchiv Dahlwitz-Hoppegarten, Berlin
Central Museum of the Armed Forces, Moscow
Central Museum of the October Revolution, Moscow
Deutsches Historisches Museum, Berlin
Evangelisches Zentralarchiv, Berlin
Franz-Neumann-Archiv, Berlin
Hauptstaatsarchiv Düsseldorf, Düsseldorf
Hulton Deutsch Collection, London
Imperial War Museum, London
Institut für Internationale Pädagogische Forschung, Berlin
Jugendmuseum Schöneberg, Berlin
Keystone Pressedienst, Hamburg
Yevgeny Khaldeiij, Moscow
Landesarchiv Berlin, Berlin
Landesbildstelle Berlin, Berlin
Morus Verlag, Berlin
Museum Karlshorst, Berlin
Museum für Verkehr und Technik, Berlin
Novosti Press Agency, Moscow
Politisches Archiv des Auswärtigen Amtes, Bonn
Popperfoto, Northhampton
Sächsische Landesbibliothek / Deutsche Fotothek, Dresden
Sammlung Friedrich, Berlin
Schering AG, Berlin
Schulmuseum, Berlin
Senatsverwaltung für Bau- und Wohnungswesen, Berlin
Siemens Forum, Berlin
Stadtarchiv Hadamar, Hadamar
Stadtbücherei Schöneberg, Berlin
State Historical Museum, Moscow
Stiftung Neue Synagoge / Centrum Judaicum, Berlin
Stiftung Topographie des Terrors, Berlin
St. Thomas Gemeinde, Berlin
Suhrkamp Verlag, Frankfurt a. M.
Ullstein Bilderdienst, Berlin
United Nations Archives, New York
Zentralrat deutscher Sinti und Roma, Heidelberg

Materials in Private Collections:
Hellmut Bock, Berlin
Dr Ekhard Haack, Berlin
Andreas Hallen, Berlin
Dr Siegfried Heimann, Berlin
Karl Kunath, Berlin

Bibliography

Altner, Helmut. *Totentanz Berlin. Tagebuch eines Achtzehnjährigen.* (Offenbach, 1947).

Aly, Götz, ed. *Aktion T 4 1939–1945. Die „Euthanasie"-Zentrale in der Tiergartenstraße 4.* (Berlin, 1987).

Benz, Wolfgang, ed. *Dimension des Völkermords. Die Zahl der jüdischen Opfer des Nationalsozialismus.* (Munich, 1991).

Berliner Geschichtswerkstatt, ed. *Der Wedding hart an der Grenze. Weiterleben in Berlin nach dem Krieg.* (Berlin, 1987).

Borée, Karl Friedrich. *Frühling 1945. Chronik einer Berliner Familie.* (Darmstadt, 1954).

Boveri, Margret. *Tage des Überlebens.* (Berlin, 1968).

Buchheim, Hans, et. al. *Anatomie des SS-Staates.* 2 vols. (Munich, 1967).

Bundesminister der Justiz, ed. *Im Namen des Deutschen Volkes. Justiz und Nationalsozialismus.* (Cologne, 1989).

Chamberlin, Brewster S. *Kultur auf Trümmern. Berliner Berichte der amerikanischen Information Control Section Juli-Dezember 1945.* (Stuttgart, 1979).

Das Deutsche Reich und der Zweite Weltkrieg. 6 vols. Ed. Militärgeschichtliches Forschungsamt. (Stuttgart, 1979–1990).

Das erste Jahr – Berlin im Neuaufbau. Ein Rechenschaftsbericht des Magistrats der Stadt Berlin. (Berlin, 1946).

Demps, Laurenz. "Die Luftangriffe auf Berlin. Ein dokumentarischer Bericht". Parts I–III. *Jahrbuch des Märkischen Museums,* IV, 1978, pp. 27–68; VIII, 1982, pp. 7–44; IX, 1983, pp. 19–48.

Demps, Laurenz. *Die Wilhelmstraße. Eine Topographie preußisch-deutscher Macht.* (Berlin, 1994).

Deutschkron, Inge. *Ich trug den gelben Stern.* (Cologne, 1978).

Eine Frau in Berlin. Tagebuchaufzeichnungen. (Geneva, 1959).

Europa unterm Hakenkreuz. Die Okkupationspolitik des deutschen Faschismus (1938–1945). Eight-volume edition of documents. (Berlin, 1988–1995).

Findahl, Theo. *Letzter Akt / Berlin 1939–1945.* (Hamburg, 1946).

Fisher, David and Anthony Read. *Der Fall von Berlin.* (Berlin, 1995).

Girbig, Werner. *... im Anflug auf die Reichshauptstadt. Die Dokumentation der Bombenangriffe auf deutsche Städte – stellvertretend für alle deutschen Städte.* (Stuttgart, 1973).

Gosztony, Peter, ed. *Der Kampf um Berlin 1945 in Augenzeugenberichten.* (Munich, 1985).

Groehler, Olaf. *Berlin im Bombervisier. Von London aus gesehen 1940–45.* (Berlin, 1982).

Haase, Norbert. *Das Reichskriegsgericht und der Widerstand gegen die nationalsozialistische Herrschaft.* (Berlin, 1993).

Hilberg, Raul. *The Destruction of the European Jews.* 3 vols. Revised und definitive edition. (New York – London 1985).

Höcker, Karla. *Beschreibung eines Jahres. Berliner Notizen 1945.* (Berlin, 1984).

Hurwitz, Harold. *Demokratie und Antikommunismus in Berlin nach 1945.* 3 vols. (Cologne, 1983–84).

Italiander, Rolf, Arnold Bauer and Herbert Krafft. *Berlin. Stunde Null 1945.* (Düsseldorf, 1979).

Kardorff, Ursula von. *Berliner Aufzeichnungen. Aus den Jahren 1942–1945.* (Munich, 1962).

Keiderling, Gerhard. *„Gruppe Ulbricht" in Berlin. April bis Juni 1945.* (Berlin, 1993).

Kenrick, Donald and Grattan Puxon. *Sinti und Roma – die Vernichtung eines Volkes im NS-Staat.* (Göttingen, 1981).

Kmiecik, Edward. *Berliner Victoria 24.04. – 2.05.1945. Polnische Soldaten am Brandenburger Tor.* (Warsaw, 1972).

Kuby, Erich. *Die Russen in Berlin 1945.* (Munich, 1965).

Lakowski, Richard. *Seelow 1945. Die Entscheidungsschlacht an der Oder.* (Berlin, 1994).

Leonhard, Wolfgang. *Die Revolution entläßt ihre Kinder.* (Frankfurt a. M., 1961).

LeTissier, Tony. *Der Kampf um Berlin 1945. Von den Seelower Höhen zur Reichskanzlei.* (Frankfurt a. M., 1991).

Mühlen, Bengt von zur, ed. *Der Todeskampf der Reichshauptstadt.* (Kleinmachnow, 1994).

Müller, Rolf-Dieter and Gerd R. Ueberschär. *Kriegsende 1945. Die Zerstörung des Deutschen Reiches.* (Frankfurt a. M., 1994).

Ranke, Winfried et. al. *Kultur, Pajoks und Care-Pakete. Eine Berliner Chronik 1945–1949.* (Berlin, 1990).

Reichhardt, Hans. *„raus aus den Trümmern"* (exhibition catalogue). *Vom Beginn des Wiederaufbaus in Berlin 1945.* 2nd ed. (Berlin, 1988).

Ribbe, Wolfgang, ed. *Geschichte Berlins. Von der Märzrevolution bis zur Gegenwart.* 2 vols. (Munich, 1987).

Schäfer, Hans Dieter. *Berlin im zweiten Weltkrieg. Der Untergang der Reichshauptstadt in Augenzeugenberichten.* (Munich, 1985).

Scheel, Klaus, ed. *Die Befreiung Berlins 1945. Eine Dokumentation.* (Berlin, 1985).

Schivelbusch, Wolfgang. *Vor dem Vorhang. Geist, Kunst, Politik in Berlin 1945–1948.* (Munich, 1995).

Schlegelmilch, Arthur. *Hauptstadt in Zonendeutschland. Entstehung der Berliner Nachkriegsdemokratie 1945–1949.* (Berlin, 1993).

Studnitz, Hans Georg von. *Als Berlin brannte. Diarium der Jahre 1943–1945.* (Stuttgart, 1963).

Volkmann, Hans-Erich, ed. *Ende des Dritten Reiches – Ende des Zweiten Weltkriegs. Eine perspektivische Rückschau,* im Auftrag des Militärgeschichtlichen Forschungsamtes. (Munich, 1995).

Vollnhals, Clemens, ed. *Entnazifizierung. Politische Säuberung und Rehabilitierung in den vier Besatzungszonen 1945–1949.* (Munich, 1991).

Abbreviations

Abn.	Abnahme [decrease]
Abt.	Abteilung [department]
AEG	Allgemeine Elektricitäts-Gesellschaft
A.G. (AG)	Aktiengesellschaft [public limited company]
AK	Armeekorps [Army Corps]
AOK	Armeeoberkommando [Army High Command]
A.RH.	Am Rhein
B-17	Boeing – 17 »Flying Fortress«
BDM	Bund Deutscher Mädel [League of German Girls]
BEWAG	Berliner Städtische Elektrizitäts Werke A.G. [Berlin Municipal Electrical Works]
Bln.	Berlin
BVG	Berliner Verkehrs-Aktiengesellschaft (BVG) [Berlin Transport]
CBS	Central Broadcasting Service
CCG/BE	Control Commission for Germany / British Element
CDU	Christlich-Demokratische Union [Christian Democratic Union]
CO	Carbon monoxide
D	Defendant
DAF	Deutsche Arbeitsfront [German Labour Front]
Div.	Division
DNVP	Deutschnationale Volkspartei [German National People's Party]
DP	Displaced Person
Dr	Doctor
ehem.	ehemalig [former, formerly]
EK	Einsatzkommando [Special Unit]
FDJ	Freie Deutsche Jugend [Free German Youth]
F.H.Qu.	Führerhauptquartier [Führer's Headquarters]
Fig.	Figur [figure]
Flak	Flugabwehrkanone [anti-aircraft gun]
g	Gramm [gram(me)]
GDR	German Democratic Republic
geb.	geboren [born]
geh.	geheim [Secret]
Gestapo	Geheime Staatspolizei [Secret State Police]
gKdos.	geheime Kommandosache [Command Secret]
GmbH	Gesellschaft mit beschränkter Haftung [private limited company]
g.Rs.	geheime Reichssache [Top Secret]
Gth	Gartenhaus [side-wing of block of flats]
He 111	Heinkel 111
H.Gr.	Heeresgruppe [Army Group]
HJ	Hitler-Jugend [Hitler Youth]
I.G. Farben	Interessengemeinschaft Farbenindustrie A.G.
Il-2	Iljuschin-2 »Sturmovik«
KLV	Kinderlandverschickung [Children's rural evacuation]
KPD	Kommunistische Partei Deutschlands [German Communist Party]
KPdSU	Kommunistische Partei der Sowjetunion [Communist Party of the USSR]
KZ (K.Z.)	Konzentrationslager [concentration camp]
LDPD	Liberaldemokratische Partei Deutschlands [Liberal Democratic Party of Germany]
LS	Luftschutz [air defence]
MP	Militärpolizei [Military Police]
Napola	Nationalpolitische Erziehungsanstalt [National political training institute]
NEP	Neue ökonomische Politik [New Economic Policy]
No.	Number
Nr.	Nummer [Number]
NS	Nationalsozialistische(r) [National Socialist]
NSDAP	Nationalsozialistische Deutsche Arbeiterpartei [National Socialist German Workers Party]
NSDDoB	NS Deutscher Dozentenbund [NS German Association of University Teachers]
NSD-Studentenbund	Nationalsozialistischer Deutscher Studentenbund [National Socialist Students' Association]
NSFK	NS Fliegerkorps [NS Flyers' Corps]
NSKK	NS Kraftfahrkorps [NS Motor Corps]
NSKOV	NS Kriegsopferversorgung [NS War Victims' Relief]
NSV	NS Volkswohlfahrt [NS People's Welfare]
OdF	Opfer des Faschismus [Victim of Fascism]
OKW	Oberkommando der Wehrmacht [High Command of the Armed Forces]
OMGUS	Office of Military Government for Germany, United States
op	Operation
OT	Organisation Todt
Pf.	Pfennig
Pibat.SS	Pionierbataillon-SS [SS Pioneer Battalion]
Prof.	Professor
RAD	Reichsarbeitsdienst [Reich Labour Service]
RAF	Royal Air Force
RAM	Reichsaußenministerium [Reich Foreign Ministry]
Rdvfg.	Rundverfügung [circular order]
RGBL	Reichsgesetzblatt [National Register of Published Laws]
RM	Reichsmark
RMdI	Reichsministerium des Innern [Reich Ministry of the Interior]
RNST	Reichsnährstand [Agency representing farmers and other food producers]
RSHA	Reichssicherheitshauptamt [Reich Security Main Office]
SA	Sturmabteilung [Stormtroopers]
SD	Sicherheitsdienst der SS [Security Service of the SS]
SED	Sozialistische Einheitspartei Deutschlands [German Socialist Unity Party]
SiPo	Sicherheitspolizei [Security Police]
SMAD	Sowjetische Militäradministration in Deutschland [Soviet Military Administration in Germany]
Sopade	Sozialdemokratische Partei Deutschlands [German Social Democratic Party]
SPD	Sozialdemokratische Partei Deutschlands [German Social Democratic Party]
SS	Schutzstaffel [lit.: Protection Squadron]
Stalag	Stammlager für Kriegsgefangene [prisoner of war camp]
Str.	Straße
Stuka	Sturzkampfbomber [dive bomber]
T-34	Soviet tank
T4	Tiergartenstraße 4
TN	Technische Nothilfe [Technical Emergency Aid]
u.a.	und andere, unter anderem [et al, among other things]
UdSSR	Union der Sozialistischen Sowjetrepubliken [Union of Socialist Soviet Republics]
UNRRA	United Nations Relief and Rehabilitation Administration
USA	United States of America
USAAF	United States of America Air Force
USFET	United States Forces European Theater
USSR	Union of Socialist Soviet Republics
v.	von
V 1	Vergeltungswaffe 1
V 2	Vergeltungswaffe 2
vH	von Hundert [percent]
VVN	Vereinigung der Verfolgten des Nazi-Regimes [Association of Persons Persecuted by the Nazi Regime]
WFA	Wehrmachtführungsamt [Armed Forces Operations Office]
WFSt	Wehrmachtführungsstab [Armed Forces Operations Staff]
z.b.V.	zur besonderen Verwendung [seconded for special duty]

Sources of Texts

Table pp. 13 f. (Air-raids)
Laurenz Demps, "Die Luftangriffe auf Berlin. Ein dokumentarischer Bericht". Part 2. *Jahrbuch des Märkischen Museums*, Heft VIII, 1982, pp. 21f.

Text 1 Heinz Boberach, ed. *Meldungen aus dem Reich 1938–1945. Die geheimen Lageberichte des Sicherheitsdienstes der SS*, vol. 16 (reprint). (Herrsching, 1984), pp. 6315f.

Text 2 Ursula von Kardorff. *Berliner Aufzeichnungen. Aus den Jahren 1942–1945.* (Munich, 1962), pp. 110f.

Text 3 Theo Findahl. *Letzter Akt – Berlin 1939-1945.* (Hamburg 1946), pp. 68f.

Text 4 Landesarchiv Berlin, Außenstelle Breite Straße, Rep 134, No. 230.

Text 5 Theo Findahl. (see Text 3), pp. 70f.

Text 6 Konrad Warner, Schicksalswende Europas? Ich sprach mit dem deutschen Volk … Ein Tatsachenbericht, Rheinfelden 1944, in: Hans Dieter Schäfer, Berlin im Zweiten Weltkrieg …, (München 1985), p. 150.

Text 7 Albert Speer. *Erinnerungen.* (Frankfurt a.M., 1969), p. 446.

Text 8 Bengt von zur Mühlen, ed. *Der Todeskampf der Reichshauptstadt.* (Kleinmachnow, 1994), pp. 19–22.

Text 9 Klaus Scheel, ed. *Die Befreiung Berlins 1945. Eine Dokumentation.* (Berlin, 1985), p. 130.

Text 10 Landesarchiv Berlin, Zs 588.

Text 11 Helmut Altner. *Totentanz Berlin. Tagebuchaufzeichnungen eines Achtzehnjährigen.* (Offenbach, 1947), p. 85f.

Text 12 Klaus Scheel (see Text 9), p. 154f.

Text 13 Peter Gosztony, ed. *Der Kampf um Berlin 1945 in Augenzeugenberichten.* (Munich, 1975), p. 303f.

Text 14 Percy E. Schramm. *Kriegstagebuch des Oberkommandos der Wehrmacht (Wehrmachtführungsstab) 1940–1945,* vol. 8/II: 1944/45, (reprint). (Herrsching, 1982), p. 1692.

Text 15 Klaus Scheel (see Text 9), pp. 184f.

Text 16 Bundesarchiv/Militärarchiv, RW 44 I/37D.

Text 17 Ursula von Kardorff (see Text 2), pp. 134–38.

Text 18 Theo Findahl (s. Text 3), S. 100.

Text 19 Karl Friedrich Borée. *Frühling 1945. Chronik einer Berliner Familie.* (Darmstadt, 1954), pp. 57–59.

Text 20 Bundesarchiv/Militärarchiv.

Text 21 Bundesarchiv/Militärarchiv.

Text 22 Bundesarchiv, R 58/213.

Text 23 Bundesarchiv/Abt. Potsdam, R 58/3575.

Text 24 Konrad Warner (see Text 6), pp. 148–72.

Text 25 Klaus Scheel (see Text 9), p. 67.

Text 26 Landesarchiv Berlin, Außenstelle Breite Straße, Rep. 146, Nr. 66.

Text 27 Bundesarchiv/Militärarchiv.

Text 28 Konrad Warner (see Text 6), pp. 148–72.

Text 29 Susanne zur Nieden. *Alltag im Ausnahmezustand. Frauentagebücher im zerstörten Deutschland 1943 bis 1945.* (Berlin, 1993), p. 160.

Text 30 *Berlin in Zahlen.* (Berlin, 1949), p. 158.

Text 31 *Leben und Werk von Hermann Kasack. Ein Brevier.* (Frankfurt a. M., 1966), p. 77.

Text 32 Susanne zur Nieden (see Text 29), pp. 178f.

Text 33 Statistisches Amt von Groß-Berlin, ed. *Berliner Statistik,* Heft 1, January 1947, p. 12.

Text 34 Alfred Döblin. *Autobiographien und letzte Aufzeichnungen,* ed. Edgar Pässler. (Olten – Freiburg im Brsg., 1980), p. 407.

Text 35 Isaac Deutscher. *Reportagen aus dem Nachkriegsdeutschland.* (Hamburg, 1980), p. 114.

Text 36 Klaus Scheel (see Text 9), pp. 198f.

Text 37 Stephen Spender. *European Witness.* (London, 1946), p. 235.

Text 38 William L. Shirer. *End of a Berlin Diary 1944–1945.* (New York, 1947), p. 160.

Text 39 Brigitte Bermann Fischer. *Sie schrieben mir. Oder was aus meinem Poesiealbum wurde.* (Zürich, 1978), p. 195f.

Text 40 Alfred Döblin (see Text 34), pp. 401–05.

Text 41 Arnold Zweig. *Werke,* vol. 16/2: *Essays.* (Berlin, 1967), p. 377.

Text 42 Johannes R. Becher. "Deutsches Bekenntnis", *Aufbau,* I (1945).

Text 43 *Berliner Statistik* (see Text 33), p. 31.

Text 44 Walther Schneider. "Wiederaufbau der Berliner städtischen Nahverkehrsmittel", *Berliner Statistik* (see Text 33), p. 194.

Text 45 William L. Shirer (see Text 38), p. 164.

Text 46 Olaf Groehler. "Der strategische Luftkrieg und seine Auswirkungen auf die deutsche Zivilbevölkerung", in: *Luftkriegführung im Zweiten Weltkrieg. Ein internationaler Vergleich,* im Auftrag des Militärgeschichtlichen Forschungsamtes, ed. Horst Boog. (Herford, 1993), p. 332.

Text 47 Gerhard Förster and Olaf Groehler eds. *Der zweite Weltkrieg. Dokumente,* 3rd ed. (Berlin, 1989), pp. 48f.

Text 48 Bundesarchiv/Militärarchiv, Lw 107/22.

Text 49 Karl Klee, ed. *Dokumente zum Unternehmen »Seelöwe«. Die geplante deutsche Landung in England.* (Göttingen, 1959), pp. 298f.

Text 50 Max Domarus, ed. *Hitler. Reden und Proklamationen 1932–1945,* vol. II/1. (Munich, 1965), p. 1580.

Text 51 Bundesarchiv/Militärarchiv, RH 20-6/131.

Text 52 Hans-Adolf Jacobsen, ed. *Generaloberst Halder. Kriegstagebuch,* vol. 3 (22.6.1941–24.9.1942). (Stuttgart, 1964), p. 53.

Text 53 Bundesarchiv/Militärarchiv, RW 4/v. 578.

Text 54 Jerzy Sawicki. *Vor dem polnischen Staatsanwalt.* (Berlin, 1962), p. 113.

Text 55 *Der Prozess gegen die Hauptkriegsverbrecher vor dem Internationalen Militärgerichtshof. Urkunden und anderes Beweismaterial,* vols 5/6, (reprint) (Munich, 1989), p. 711.

Text 56 Wolfgang Ribbe, ed. *Geschichte Berlins,* vol. 2. (Munich, 1987), p. 934.

Text 57 Hans Sahl. *Memoiren eines Moralisten.* (Frankfurt a. M., 1990), p. 214f.

Text 58 Kurt Hiller. "Schutzhäftling 231", Parts VI and VII, *Neue Weltbühne* 1 (1935), p. 19 and 2 (1935), p. 41.

Text 59 *Das Tagebuch der Helga Narthoff. Berlin – New York. Aufzeichnungen 1933–1945,* ed. with an introduction by Wolfgang Benz. (Frankfurt a. M., 1988), p. 38.

Text 60 André François-Poncet. *Als Botschafter in Berlin 1931–1938.* (Mainz, 1947), p. 267.

Text 61 William L. Shirer. *Berlin Diary: The Journal of a Foreign Correspondent 1934–1941.* (London, 1941), p. 109 f.

Text 62 William L. Shirer (see Text 61), p. 335.

Text 63 Ruth Andreas-Friedrich. *Der Schattenmann. Tagebuchaufzeichnungen.* (Frankfurt a. M., 1986), pp. 82f.

Text 64 *Deutschland-Berichte der Sozialdemokratischen Partei Deutschlands (Sopade) im Auftrag des Exilvorstands der Sozialdemokratischen Partei,* ed. Klaus Behnken, vol. 7, (reprint). (Nettelbeck, 1980), p. 24.

Text 65 Ursula von Kardorff. *Berliner Aufzeichnungen 1942–1945.* (Munich, 1976), p. 76.

Text 66 *Meldungen aus dem Reich 1938–1945* (see Text 1), vol. 12, p. 4831.

Text 67 *Meldungen aus dem Reich 1938–1945* (see Text 1), vol. 14, pp. 5445–50.

Text 68 *Gestapo-Berichte über den antifaschistischen Widerstand der KPD 1933–1945,* vol. 3. (Berlin, 1990), p. 19.

Text 69 Albert Speer (see Text 7), p. 128f.

Text 70 *Reichsgesetzblatt (RGBl.),* Part I, 1933, No. 17, p. 83.

Text 71 *Reichsgesetzblatt (RGBl.),* Part I, 1933, No. 24, p. 135.

Text 72 *Reichsgesetzblatt (RGBl.),* Part I, 1933, No. 25, p. 141.

Text 73 *Reichsgesetzblatt (RGBl.),* Part I, 1933, No. 81, p. 479.

Text 74 *Preußische Gesetzessammlung,* 1936, No. 5, p. 21f.

Text 75 *Deutsches Recht,* 6. Jg., Heft 7/8, 15.4.1936.

Text 76 *Meldungen aus dem Reich 1938–1945* (see Text 1), p. 382.

Text 77 *Internationaler Militärgerichtshof, Der Prozeß gegen die Hauptkriegsverbrecher vom 14. November 1945 – 1. Oktober 1946.* (Nuremberg, 1947), vol. XXVI, p. 291ff. (Dokument 778-PS).

Text 78 *Internationaler Militärgerichtshof* (see Text 77), p. 201 (Dokument 654-PS).

Text 79 Arbeitsgruppe der ehemaligen Häftlinge des Konzentrationslagers Auschwitz beim Komitee der Antifaschistischen Widerstandskämpfer in der Deutschen Demokratischen Republik, ed. *I.G. Farben – Auschwitz – Massenmord. Dokumentation zum Auschwitzprozeß.* (n.p., n.d.), p. 19.

Text 80 Kurt Pätzold, ed. *Verfolgung, Vertreibung, Vernichtung. Dokumente des faschistischen Antisemitismus 1933 bis 1942.* (Leipzig, 1987), p. 118.

Text 81 Compiled using: Bundesminister der Justiz, ed. *Im Namen des Deutschen Volkes. Justiz und Nationalsozialismus.* (Cologne, 1989), p. 206.

Text 82 Adolf Hitler. *Mein Kampf.* (Munich, 1940), pp. 739 ff.

Text 83 Vierteljahrshefte für Zeitgeschichte, 3. Jg. (1955), p. 210.

Text 84 Internationaler Militärgerichtshof (see Text 77), vol. XXV, pp. 403 ff. (Dokument-386-PS).

Text 85 Internationaler Militärgerichtshof (see Text 77), vol. XXVI, p. 523 (Dokument 1014-PS).

Text 86 Martin Broszat. *Nationalsozialistische Polenpolitik 1939–1945.* (Stuttgart, 1961), p. 97.

Text 87 *Europa unterm Hakenkreuz. Die faschistische Okkupationspolitik in Polen (1939–1945).* (Berlin, 1989), p. 346 f.

Text 88 Internationaler Militärgerichtshof (see Text 77), Nuremberg 1949, vol. XXXIX, S. 428 (Dokument 172-USSR).

Text 89 Internationaler Militärgerichtshof (see Text 77), Nuremberg 1949, vol. XXXVI, pp. 138 ff. (Dokument 126-EC).

Text 90 Bundesarchiv/Militärarchiv, RH 2/2082.

Text 91 Bundesarchiv/Militärarchiv, RH 22/155.

Text 92 Bundesarchiv, R 58/240.

Text 93 Bundesarchiv, Berlin Document Center, SS-HO 2272.

Text 94 *Europa unterm Hakenkreuz. Die Okkupationspolitik des deutschen Faschismus in Jugoslawien, Griechenland, Albanien, Italien und Ungarn.* (Berlin, 1992), pp. 178 f.

Text 95 *Die Geheimen Tagesberichte der deutschen Wehrmachtsführung im zweiten Weltkrieg,* vol. 9. (Osnabrück, 1987).

Text 96 Internationaler Militärgerichtshof (see Text 77), Nuremberg 1949, vol. XXXVII, p. 572 f. (Dokument 090-L).

Text 97 Zdzislaw Jaroszewsi, ed. *Die Ermordung der Geisteskranken in Polen 1939–1945.* (Warsaw, 1993), p. 97.

Text 98 *Aussonderung und Tod. Die klinische Hinrichtung der Unbrauchbaren.* (Berlin, 1985), p. 97.

Text 99 Bundesarchiv, RD 19/28-15.

Text 100 Bundesarchiv (see Text 99).

Text 101 Compiled using: Danuta Czech. *Kalendarium der Ereignisse im Konzentrationslager Auschwitz-Birkenau 1939–1945.* (Reinbek bei Hamburg, 1989).

Text 102 Bundesarchiv, R 58/871.

Text 103 Rudolf Höss. *Kommandant in Auschwitz. Autobiographische Aufzeichnungen,* ed. Martin

Broszat, 9th ed. (Munich, 1983), pp. 126 f.

Text 104 Politisches Archiv des Auswärtigen Amtes Bonn/Inland II g 177.

Text 105 *Eine Frau in Berlin. Tagebuchaufzeichnungen.* (Geneva, 1959), pp. 204 f.

Text 106 Karla Höcker. *Beschreibungen eines Jahres. Berliner Notizen 1945.* (Berlin, 1984), pp. 83 ff.

Text 107 *Eine Frau in Berlin* (see Text 105), pp. 269 f.

Text 108 Landesarchiv Berlin, LAZ No. 1191.

Text 109 Landesarchiv Berlin, Omgus 5/37-2-11.

Text 110 Collection Andreas Hallen, Berlin.

Text 111 Landesarchiv Berlin, Rep. 9, No. 0010.

Text 112 *Eine Frau in Berlin* (see Text 105), p. 205.

Text 113 Karla Höcker (see Text 106), pp. 45 f.

Text 114 *Sehr selten habe ich geweint. Briefe und Tagebücher aus dem zweiten Weltkrieg von Menschen aus Berlin,* ed. Ingrid Hammer und Susanne zur Nieden (Zürich, 1992), p. 448.

Text 115 Margret Boveri. *Tage des Überlebens.* (Berlin, 1945, Munich, 1985), p. 135 f.

Text 116 Hilde Thurnwald. *Gegenwartsprobleme Berliner Familien. Eine soziologische Untersuchung an 498 Familien.* (Berlin, 1948), pp. 66 f., 116 f.

Text 117 Karla Höcker (see Text 106), p. 111.

Text 118 Landesarchiv Berlin, Rep 101, No.20.

Text 119 *Verordnungsblatt der Stadt Berlin,* No.1, July 1945, pp. 13 f.

Text 120 Landesarchiv Berlin, Zeitgeschichtliche Sammlung No. 2664.

Text 121 Landesarchiv Berlin, Zeitgeschichtliche Sammlung No. 7677.

Text 122 Landesarchiv Berlin, Rep 101, No. 127.

Text 123 Landesarchiv Berlin, Omgus 11/148-1/5.

Text 124 Landesarchiv Berlin, Rep 200, Acc 3453, No. 30, Bl. 1–7.

Text 125 *Berliner Zeitung,* 30 June 1945.

Text 126 Collection Hellmut Bock.

Text 127 Privately owned.

Text 128 *Berlin am Abend,* 17 July 1945.

Text 129 *Berliner Zeitung,* 16 September 1945.

Text 130 Wolfgang Leonhard. *Die Revolution entläßt ihre Kinder.* (Frankfurt a. M., 1961), pp. 313 f.

Text 131 *Der Erste Monat,* Forschungsgruppe für Berliner Nachkriegsgeschichte, im Auftrag des Senators für Volksbildung, Berlin 1953, p. 12.

Text 132 Landesarchiv Berlin, Zeitgeschichtliche Sammlung No. 8500/6.

Text 133 Privately owned.

Text 134 Landesarchiv Berlin, Rep 240, Acc 2407, No. 23.

Text 135 Landesarchiv Berlin, Rep 240, Acc 2407, No. 23.

Text 136 Collection Siegfried Heimann.

Text 137 Wolfgang Schivelbusch. *Vor dem Vorhang. Geist, Kunst, Politik in Berlin 1945–1948.* (Munich, 1995), p. 57.

Text 138 Wolfgang Schivelbusch (see Text 152), pp. 59 f.

Text 139 Inge Deutschkron. *Ich trug den gelben Stern.* (Cologne, 1978), p. 211.

Text 140 Paul Rilla. *Theaterkritiken.* (Berlin, 1978), p. 20.

Text 141 Friedrich Wolf. *Briefwechsel.* (Berlin, 1968), p. 119 f.

Text 142 Brewster S. Chamberlin. *Kultur auf Trümmern. Berliner Berichte der amerikanischen Information Control Section Juli–Dezember 1945.* (Stuttgart, 1979), p. 107 f.

Text 143 Collection Ekhard Haack.

Text 144 *Berliner Zeitung,* 18 September 1945.

Text 145 St.Thomas-Gemeinde, Berlin.

Text 146 Schering AG, Berlin.

Sources of Illustrations

The numbers given refer to the illustrations, not to the pages.

Berlin, Archiv für Zeitgeschichte Hans Gräfer: 163 f.
–, Berlin Museum: 199.
–, BEWAG-Archiv: 204 f.
–, Bildarchiv Preußischer Kulturbesitz: 1, 8 –10, 12, 15–17, 26, 28, 30, 38, 40, 46, 49–51, 53 f., 61, 63 f., 65, 74, 77, 79 f., 82, 84, 88, 90 f., 107, 115, 123, 126, 130 f., 142, 152 f., 155, 157, 161, 176, 178, 187, 191, 196.
–, Bilddokumentation Berliner Verlag: 172, 189 f., 216.
–, Bundesarchiv, Stiftung Archiv der Parteien und Massenorganisationen der DDR: 184–86.
–, Bundesarchiv, Zwischenarchiv Dahlwitz-Hoppegarten: 116.
–, Deutsches Historisches Museum: 2, 143, 173, 177, 182, 195, 198, 201, 206 f., 209, 214.
–, Landesarchiv Berlin: 19, 33, 55, 57, 144, 166 f., 171, 175, 179–81, 215.
–, Landesarchiv Berlin, OMGUS 11/147 - 2/1: 210.
–, Landesbildstelle Berlin: 20 f., 25, 31, 43, 70, 73, 85, 87, 110, 121, 132, 147 f.
–, Museum für Verkehr und Technik: 213.
–, Museum Karlshorst: 97.
–, Privatbesitz: 11.
–, Sammlung Friedrich: 183, 192 f.
–, Sammlung Heimann: 188.
–, Ullstein Bilderdienst: 18, 94, 96, 98, 113, 165, 194, 200.
Dresden, Sächsische Landesbibliothek / Deutsche Fotothek: 81, 211 f.
Freiburg, Bundesarchiv/Militärarchiv: 48.
Hamburg, Keystone Pressedienst: 120, 140.
Koblenz, Bundesarchiv: 3, 6, 23, 27, 32, 52, 56, 60, 62, 68 f., 86, 108 f., 112, 114, 117, 122, 124, 129, 141, 149, 197, 202.
London, Hulton Deutsch Collection: 127, 138 f., 156, 158, 160, 169, 174, 203, 208.
–, Imperial War Museum: 4, 76, 78, 89, 128, 135–37, 162, 168, 170.
Moscow, Central Museum of the Armed Forces: 39.
–, Central Museum of the October Revolution: 118.
–, Yevgeny Khaldeij: 36
–, Novosti Press Agency: 37, 41 f., 44 f., 47.
–, State Historical Museum: 59.
Munich, Bilderdienst Süddeutscher Verlag: 13 f., 29, 34 f., 58, 75, 83, 92, 100–06, 111, 125, 146, 154, 159, cover.
Northhampton, Popperfoto: 93, 95, 99, 145, 150 f.

Publications

Hans Dieter Schäfer. *Berlin im zweiten Weltkrieg. Der Untergang der Reichshauptstadt in Augenzeugenberichten.* (Munich, 1985): 5.

Werner Girbig. *... im Anflug auf die Reichshauptstadt. Die Dokumentation der Bombenangriffe auf Berlin – stellvertretend für alle deutschen Städte.* (Stuttgart, 1973): 7.

Zerstört – Besiegt – Befreit. Der Kampf um Berlin bis zur Kapitulation 1945, ed. Pädagogisches Zentrum Berlin. (Berlin, 1985): 24.

Statistisches Amt von Groß-Berlin, ed. *Berliner Statistik,* Heft 1, January 1947: 67.

Berlin in Zahlen. (Berlin, 1949): 66.

Berlin in Zahlen 1946/47. (Berlin, 1947): 72.

Dokumente deutscher Kriegsschäden, ed. Bundesministerium für Vertriebene, Flüchtlinge und Kriegsgeschädigte. (Bonn, 1962), 2nd ed.: 71.

Europa unterm Hakenkreuz. Die Okkupationspolitik des deutschen Faschismus in Jugoslawien, Griechenland, Albanien, Italien und Ungarn (1941–1945). (Berlin – Heidelberg, 1992): 119.

Gerhard Keiderling. *Die Spaltung Berlins.* (Berlin, 1985): 133 f.

The photographs mentioned above were taken by the following photographers (to the extend that they are known):

Dahlke: 50

Edo Dietrich 154

Fritz Eschen : 78, 200, 211 f.

Arthur Grimm: 9, 15–17, 49

Gerhard Gronefeld, Munich: 143, 173, 177, 182, 195, 198, 201, 206 f., 209

Haine: 102

Herbert Hensky: 87

Hoffmann: 13 f.

Holtfreter: 117

Hanns Hubmann: 53

Yevgeny Khaldeij, Moscow: 37, 62, 178

George Koenig: 203

Erich Krueger: 215

Leonard McCombe: 145

Hilmar Pabel: 54

Pilz: 6

Frederick Ramage: 128, 138–40, 156, 158, 169, 174, 208, 214

Heinrich Sanden: 114

Schwahn: 56, 104, 106

Schwanke 105

Friedrich Seidenstücker: 161

Alexander Ustinov: 142

Carl Weinrother 75 f., 79 f., 82, 91, 131, 153, 155

Ivan Zhagin: 125

Rudolf Zscheile: 146

Index

The numerous National Socialist organisations that are mentioned only in the lists on pp. 143 ff. and p. 147 have not been included in the Index.